UNDERGRADUATE TEXTS IN COMPUTER SCIENCE

Editors
David Gries
Fred B. Schneider

Springer Science+Business Media, LLC

UNDERGRADUATE TEXTS IN COMPUTER SCIENCE

Jon Pearce

Programming and Meta-Programming in Scheme

Springer

Jon Pearce
Department of Mathematics and Computer Science
San Jose University
San Jose, CA 95192-0103
USA

Series Editors:
David Gries
Fred B. Schneider
Department of Computer Science
Cornell University
Upson Hall
Ithaca, NY 14853-7501
USA

Library of Congress Cataloging-in-Publication Data
Pearce, Jon.
   Programming and meta-programming in Scheme / Jon Pearce.
     p. cm. — (Undergraduate texts in computer science)
   Includes bibliographical references and index.
   ISBN 978-1-4612-7243-4   ISBN 978-1-4612-1682-7 (eBook)
   DOI 10.1007/978-1-4612-1682-7
   1. Scheme (Computer program language) I. Title. II. Series
QA76.73.S34P4   1997
005.13'3—dc21   97-28476

Printed on acid-free paper.

Production managed by Steven Pisano; manufacturing supervised by Johanna Tschebull.
Photocomposed pages prepared from the author's Microsoft Word files.

9 8 7 6 5 4 3 2 1

ISBN 978-1-4612-7243-4

To my parents

Preface

The current domination of computing by C and C++ is so complete that publishing a book on Scheme almost seems subversive. My heresy goes beyond language. Informed by the anticorporate intellectual values of my computer gurus, I have come to possess the unpopular notion that ideas are more important than technology, that principles like abstraction and modularity take us further than gigabytes and megahertz. This is really a book about those ideas disguised as a book about Scheme. Scheme was selected partly for historical reasons, but mostly because it allows us to encounter ideas without first mastering memory management, compilers, I/O, and advanced idioms. I want to congratulate my co-conspirators at Springer for their courage in joining me.

For the last five years I have successfully used drafts of this book as a text in a junior-level declarative programming course taught at San Jose State University. The course is modeled after Scheme-based freshman-level courses taught at other universities, hence prerequisites are minimal. Motivated students with basic computer and mathematical literacy will be able to read this book.

By confining lectures to the core sections of each chapter and a few critical appendices, leaving the other appendices and problem sections as homework assignments, I typically manage to cover all but the last chapter in a semester. Occasionally students read and solve problems from the last chapter as special projects. Students who finish the course know Scheme. They have been introduced to important principles, concepts, paradigms, and techniques, and they have a functional perspective they confidently carry into subsequent courses.

Jon Pearce

Contents

Introduction

Soon after the first commercial computers appeared in the early 1950s people began seeing analogies between computers and brains, and they wondered if computers could exhibit human-like intelligent behavior. Could computers be programmed to reason, learn, and plan? Could computers solve problems they weren't explicitly programmed to solve?

Anthony Newel and Herbert Simon attempted to answer this question by studying the techniques people use to solve problems, and then incorporated these techniques into general problem-solving programs. They discovered humans are "symbol pushers." People tend to solve problems by producing and manipulating symbolic expressions representing pieces of solutions. They formalized this finding as the **Physical Symbol System Hypothesis**:

> A physical symbol system (i.e., any device or agent that produces an evolving collection of symbols and expressions) has the necessary and sufficient means for general intelligent action.

Unfortunately, computers are "number crunchers." They solve problems by translating them into massive arithmetic problems, and then grind them down by performing millions of blindingly fast computations. Theoretically, the difference between "number crunching" and "symbol pushing" is more a matter of style than substance, but in practice translating a "symbol-pushing" procedure into a "number-crunching" procedure is difficult, dirty, dull work. Even the appearance of the first high-level (i.e., machine-independent) languages in the late 1950s and early 1960s—FORTRAN, COBOL, Algol60, APL, and BASIC—didn't help much because these languages tended to reflect rather than disguise the "number-crunching" character of the underlying computer.

I.1   LISP

In 1960 John McCarthy introduced a high-level language called LISP. (Actually, LISP is the second-oldest high-level language; FORTRAN predates it.) Unlike FORTRAN, BASIC, and the other languages mentioned earlier, LISP could treat symbols and expressions like ordinary data. This made LISP a natural language for expressing symbol processing, and it quickly gained a loyal following among artificial intelligence researchers. LISP is still the language of choice for most artificial intelligence applications.

I.1.1. LISP Dialects

A language is **stable** if there is widespread agreement among its users about what features are part of the language. Stability is achieved through an official or semi-official description of the language. Unfortunately, major differences between LISP dialects developed soon after it was introduced. Eventually, programs written in one dialect wouldn't run using an interpreter for another. Some of the most popular dialects are shown in Figure I.1. Arrows indicate which dialects influenced others.

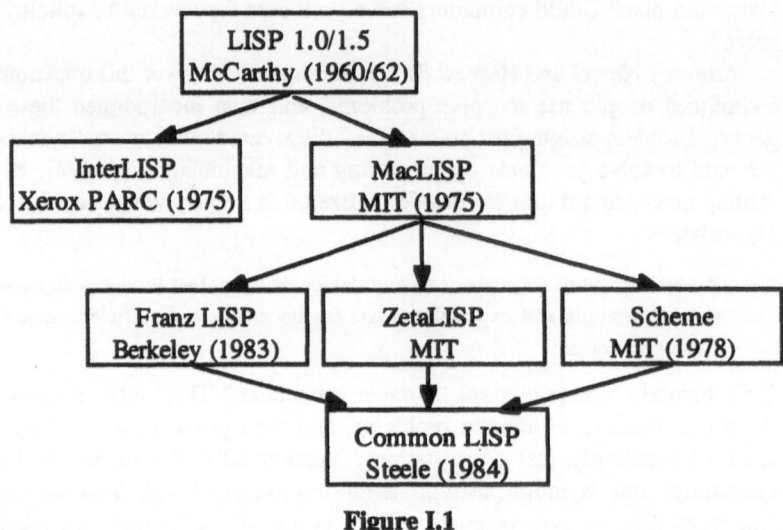

Figure I.1

In 1980 work began on a standard dialect called **Common LISP**. In 1984 Guy Steele described this language in his book, *Common LISP: The Language*. Common LISP is now widely accepted by industry, and an ANSI standard is about to appear.

I.2   Scheme

> I like the Scheme programming language because it is small. It packs a large number of
> ideas into a small number of features.
>
> —Guy Steele, Jr.

The dialect of LISP used in this text is called **Scheme**. Scheme was introduced in 1978 by Guy Steele and Gerald Sussman. Like LISP, Scheme is an interpreted, expression-oriented language. Scheme is a simple language in the sense that there are only a few data and program constructors (about 25). Furthermore, these constructors are uniform in the sense that there are no seemingly unnecessary restrictions on their use.

Normally, expressiveness is sacrificed for simplicity, but Scheme is an exception. Scheme allows programmers to define recursive, polymorphic, over-loaded, and higher-order procedures. All of the major programming paradigms can be expressed in Scheme. Scheme also features macros, continuations, promises, streams, and excellent support for number, string, symbol, and list processing. (Don't worry, all of these things will be defined soon.)

As Scheme became popular, its local dialects began to diverge, and it too became unstable. In 1984 representatives of the major Scheme user communities met and agreed on a standard description of Scheme. Their report has undergone four revisions over the years, popularly known as the *Revised, Revised Revised (Revised²), Revised Revised Revised (Revised³),* and *Revised Revised Revised Revised (Revised⁴) Reports on the Algorithmic Language Scheme.* (Several attempts at a *Revised⁵ Report* have been made.) Readers should refer to this as the most authoritative description of Scheme. The *Revised⁴ Report* served as the basis for the IEEE (P1178) specification of Scheme, which became the ANSI specification of Scheme.

In this text we refer to the version of Scheme described in the *Revised⁴ Report* as **IEEE/ANSI Scheme** and to the features described in the report as essential features. Warning: An implementation of Scheme should include all essential features, but this is often not the case.

I.2.1. Scheme on the Web

There are many commercially available implementations of Scheme, but there are just as many, if not more, free implementations of Scheme available on the Internet. In addition, there are Scheme newsgroups, documentation, FAQs, and tools available on the Internet. The best starting place is the Scheme home page at MIT:

http://www-swiss.ai.mit.edu/scheme-home.html

I.3. Structure of the Text

Eight chapters follow. Each is divided into three sections: core, appendices, and problems. It is assumed that students will read the appendices and solve most of the problems on their own. (Nearly all of the problems require students to write short Scheme procedures.) More essential topics are covered in the core sections. Some skipping around is possible; for example, list and tree recursion aren't covered until Chapter 6, but could be covered immediately after Chapter 3.

The text introduces Scheme in four fragments:

IS	= imperative Scheme	= IEEE/ANSI Scheme
FS	= functional Scheme	= IS minus variables and commands
AS	= application Scheme	= FS minus control and block structures
NS	= necessary Scheme	= AS minus all redundant features

The first two chapters are restricted to applicative Scheme. (Necessary Scheme surfaces from time to time in various problem sections.) The idea is to wean readers away from command sequencing, the principle program-building tool provided by languages like Pascal and C. Readers will be surprised (and challenged) to see how much can be accomplished in this tiny fragment of Scheme.

Except for a few minor lapses, functional Scheme is the language of Chapters 3 through 6. As such, the book could be used as an introduction to functional programming. The pedagogical advantage is that students master the power of functional programming before the picture is complicated by commands and variables. Stores, variables, commands, and hence imperative Scheme, are introduced in Chapter 7.

The last chapter formalizes the semantics of three languages: Alpha (FS minus some features), Beta (IS minus some features), and Lambda (NS) in the form of three interpreters written in Scheme and following the style of semantic prototyping.

I.3.1. Themes

Although the primary goal of this text is to teach students to program in Scheme, several subplots deserve special mention. First is the emphasis on programming paradigms, starting with the functional paradigm, and then building up to the imperative paradigm with side trips into the signal-processing, data-driven, and object-oriented paradigms.

Second is the use of general concepts, models, and terminology from my programming language principles course. Readers should have no trouble adapting the concepts introduced in this text to other programming languages.

Third is the notion of meta-programming. Theoretical computer science, software engineering, and systems programming are all based on a critical idea that separates them from routine data processing: that programs can be treated like ordinary data, and therefore, like ordinary data, they can be derived, analyzed, and modified algorithmically. We appropriate the term **"meta-programming"** to refer to this idea.

"Meta-programming" is derived from the term **"meta-language,"** which is used by philosophers, linguists, and mathematicians to refer to any language used to describe or analyze another language. In this context the language being described or analyzed is referred to as the **object language**. For example, the meta-language used in this book is English, while the object language is Scheme. The **meta** prefix ultimately traces back to Aristotle's term, **metaphysics**, which meant "beyond Physics." Meta-programming can also mean "beyond programming" in the sense that some topics in this book evolve from or into subjects beyond programming, such as logic, cognitive science, physics, mathematics, and linguistics.

Why emphasize meta-programming in a Scheme text? Most programming languages make a sharp distinction between programs and data. **Data** refers to passive, dumb entities like numbers, lists, tables, and text; **programs** are active, intelligent entities that manipulate data. Scheme doesn't have such prejudices, and this makes Scheme an excellent meta-language. Writing meta-procedures that process expressions, procedures, symbols, or other program elements is natural, easy, and fun.

1
Expressions and Values

> "Alright," said Deep Thought, "The Answer to the Great Question... Of Life, the Universe, and Everything... Is... Is... Forty-two."
>
> —Douglas Adams, *The Hitch Hiker's Guide to the Galaxy*

A Scheme interpreter is a primitive version of Deep Thought, the enigmatic supercomputer in Douglas Adams' book. We type a question on a keyboard, the Scheme interpreter displays the answer on a screen, and then asks for another question.

Unlike Deep Thought, a Scheme interpreter won't answer a vague question. Instead, all Scheme questions have the form: "What answer does the following **algorithm**[1] produce ... ?" where algorithms must be stated in the precise language of Scheme expressions. We define this language later in the chapter.

Like Deep Thought, the answers a Scheme interpreter provides are from a carefully defined domain of all possible answers. We call Scheme answers **values**. Because it's always better to know the answers before the questions, we begin with a description of the domain of Scheme values.

1.1. Values

Scheme values can be divided into simple and composite values[2]:

```
VALUE ::= SIMPLE | COMPOSITE
```

Simple values—numbers, characters, Booleans, etc.—can't be decomposed into component values. A **composite value** is several values grouped together. Lists, vectors, pairs, and strings are examples of such groupings:

```
SIMPLE ::= NUMBER | CHAR | BOOLE | SYMBOL | etc.
COMPOSITE ::= STRING | VECTOR | PAIR | LIST
```

---

[1] Algorithm: Any step-by-step problem-solving procedure.

[2] We use EBNF rules to describe domains. This notation is discussed in Appendix 1.1: Defining Domains.

1.1.1. Numbers

All implementations of Scheme provide binary, octal, decimal, and hexadecimal representations of integers. Here are five ways to represent 42 in Scheme:

```
42 = #b101010 = #o52 = #d42 = #x2A
```

Most implementations of Scheme provide **truncations** using decimal and scientific notation. For example:

```
.0333 = 3.33e-2
```

are two Scheme representations of 3.33×10^{-2}. Notice that Scheme's version of scientific notation uses e to represent 10. Don't confuse this with the natural exponent e.

Some implementations of Scheme also provide rationals and complex numbers with real and imaginary parts that can be integers, truncations, or rationals. Here are some samples of legal Scheme representations:

```
2/3    4+6i   3e-2+1.5i    1/2+2/3i etc.
```

All implementations of Scheme identify the domain of numbers with the domain of complex numbers:

```
NUMBER ::= COMPLEX
```

This makes sense mathematically because all other domains of numbers are subsets of the complex numbers. For example, if we ask the Scheme interpreter if 3.0 is a complex number, it will answer "true."

Because 3.0 is equivalent to 3, the Scheme interpreter will answer "true" if we ask if 3.0 is an integer. For the same reason, if we ask if 3 is real, the Scheme interpreter will again answer "true." This is different from languages like C and Pascal, which determine the type of a number by its representation rather than its interpretation.

A Scheme interpreter will also answer that 3.0 is a rational number and an inexact number. It will answer that 3 is a rational number, but when asked if 3 is inexact, it will answer "false." This happens because 3 only represents itself, while 3.0 is used to approximate any real number x such that, $2.95 \leq x < 3.05$.

1.1.2. Characters

The CHAR domain consists of all keyboard characters: upper- and lowercase letters, digits, punctuation marks, symbols, and control characters. Scheme uses the #\ prefix to distinguish characters appearing as themselves and characters appearing in strings, numbers, names, and other contexts. For example, 5 is the number 5, but #\5 is the character 5. Scheme uses special names for nonprinting control characters:

```
#\backspace, #\escape, #\newline, #\page,
#\return, #\rubout, #\space, #\tab
```

Inside the computer each character is represented by an integer between 0 and 127. This number is called the **ASCII code** (American Standard Code for Information Interchange) for the character. For example:

```
ASCII #\A = 65
ASCII #\a = 97
ASCII #\0 = 48
ASCII #\tab = 9
```

1.1.3. Booleans

> Truth is the kind of error without which a certain species of life could not live.
>
> —Friedrich Nietzsche, *The Will to Power*

In his influential book, *Laws of Thought*, the British mathematician George Boole (1815–1864) used algebra to model logical reasoning. He viewed propositions as expressions denoting one of two possible values: true or false. But instead of thinking of true and false in philosophical terms, he conceived of them as arbitrary but distinct members of a truth-value domain, and he interpreted the **connectives** used to combine simple propositions into compound propositions—"and", "or", and "not"—as primitive algebraic operations on this domain.

Today any domain containing distinct members representing true and false, combined with primitive operations corresponding to the connectives, is called a **Boolean algebra**. The circuitry used to build digital computers is based on Boolean algebra. In this context, true and false are identified with high and low voltages, and the connectives are implemented as solid-state switches called **logic gates**. Boolean algebra is also incorporated into every programming language (high-level and machine languages) as a foundation for algorithmic testing and decision making.

In Scheme the BOOLE domain consists of the two truth values: #t for true and #f for false:

```
BOOLE ::= #t | #f
```

Note the difference between the characters #\t and #\f and the Booles #t and #f. In both cases Scheme uses a special prefix to indicate the domain.

1.1.4. Symbols

The SYMBOL domain seems out of place. In the next section we will learn that symbols are names used in programs to denote values. For example, pi is a name denoting the number 3.1416 and true is a name denoting the Boole #t. It's clear that symbols are an essential building block of Scheme programs, but why should symbols be included among the value domains?

Recall Newell and Simon's Physical Symbol System Hypothesis:

> A physical symbol system—i.e. any device or agent that produces an evolving collection of symbols and expressions—has the necessary and sufficient means for general intelligent action.

If we want to model human problem solving, then it appears our programs will be based on symbol and expression manipulation, and this means symbols have to be treated like data.

More so than other languages, Scheme liberally allows the use of punctuation marks and operator symbols in names:

```
SYMBOL ::= PECULIAR | NORMAL
```

Scheme recognizes three "peculiar" symbols:

```
PECULIAR ::= + | - | ...
```

The initial character of a normal symbol can be any letter or special initial character:

```
SPECIAL-INIT ::=
! | $ | % | & | * | / | : | < | = | > | ? | ~ | _ | ^
```

The subsequent characters of a normal symbol include the initial characters, digits, and special subsequent characters:

```
SPECIAL-SUBSEQUENT ::= . | + | -
```

We can (and should) use special symbols to create readable and suggestive names:

```
int->real, cube-root, close?, halt!, a+bi, $profit, %loss
```

Symbols can be any length and are case insensitive. The following symbols are equivalent:

```
cat CAT cAt CaT
```

1.1.5. Procedures

Sometimes an algorithm becomes so practiced we come to view it as a single operation. For example, we seldom think of starting a car as an algorithm:

1. Shift to neutral
2. Adjust the choke
3. Pump the accelerator
4. Hold the clutch down
5. Turn the ignition key
6. Repeat if necessary

Instead it becomes so automatic that we think of it as a single operation:

1. Start the car

A **procedure** is an algorithm encapsulated as a single operation, an algorithm-in-a-box. Procedures provided by Scheme are called primitive procedures. It is also possible for programmers to box their own algorithms.

Unfortunately, procedures don't have standard representations. For now, we denote the procedure named proc by [proc]. For example, [sin], [+], [*], [<], [=] denote the sine, addition, multiplication, less-than, and equality procedures, respectively.

Like symbols, procedures also seem out of place among the Scheme value domains. It seems clear that procedures, like symbols, are important building blocks of Scheme programs, but why do they need to also be treated as data? Remember, Scheme is a meta-programming language. This means we will be interested in writing procedures that manipulate other procedures as ordinary data.

1.1.6. Strings

A **string** is any sequence of characters (including blanks) bracketed by double quotes. Here are some examples:

```
"Hello World"
"A man, a plan, a canal, Panama!"
"42"
```

If a double quote appears in a string as a literal character rather than signaling the end of the string, it must be preceded by a special escape character. The Scheme escape character is the backslash: \. For example, inside the computer the string:

```
"The phrase \"meta programming\" has many meanings."
```

represents the string:

```
The phrase "meta programming" has many meanings.
```

If a backslash appears in a string as a literal character rather than an escape character, it too must be preceded by a backslash escape. For example, the DOS path name:

```
c:\scheme\libs\string.scm
```

must be written in Scheme programs as the string:

```
"c:\\scheme\\libs\\string.scm"
```

The differences between strings, characters, Booles, and symbols can get confusing. For example, the following four values belong to different domains:

```
"t" = the string consisting of the single character t
#\t = the character t
t   = the symbol t
#t  = the Boole true
```

1.1.7. Lists

Any sequence of values can be grouped together into a list:

```
LIST ::= (VALUE ... )
```

Here are some examples of lists:

```
(a e i o u)
(#\a #\e #\i #\o #\u)
("a" "e" "i" "o" "u")
("(1 2 3)")
(3 "3" #\3)
()
(1 (1 2) (1 (1 2)))
```

Notice that a list is bracketed by parenthesis and that blanks, not commas, are used to separate the members of the list. More importantly, the members of a list can belong to different domains. A list can' also be empty. Finally, lists can be nested inside lists. The last example given is a list of three members: the number 1, the two-member list (1 2), and the two-member list (1 (1 2)). How many members does the fourth list: ("(1 2 3)") have?

1.1.8. Vectors

A **vector** is just like a list except it is prefixed by the # symbol:

```
VECTOR ::= #(VALUE ... )
```

For example:

```
#(a e i o u), #(3 "3" #\3), #(), #(1 #(1 2) (1 (1 2)))
```

are all vectors. In the last example the vector consists of three elements: the number 1, the vector #(1 2), and the list (1 (1 2)).

Logically, there is no difference between lists and vectors, but the vector #(1 2 3) and the list (1 2 3) may have different representations in the computer's memory. These differences allow certain operations to be performed more efficiently on one but not the other.

1.1.9. Pairs

Any two Scheme values can be grouped together to form a pair:

```
PAIR ::= (VALUE . VALUE)
```

Here are three examples of pairs:

```
(.1 . .1)
("hello world" . (() . -2-i))
(#\f . #f)
```

There doesn't seem to be much difference between a pair and a two element list. Notationally, the only difference is the dot used to separate the members of the pair. Thus, (1 .2) is the list containing 1 and .2, while (1 . .2) is the pair containing 1 and .2. As with vectors, the difference is in the internal representation.

Note that the following values belong to different domains:

```
(1 . .2) = the pair consisting of 1 and .2
(1 .2)   = the list consisting of 1 and .2
#(1 .2)  = the vector consisting of 1 and .2
```

Sequences versus Sets

How is the list (1 2 3) different from the set {1 2 3}? The main difference is that the members of a sequence (i.e., list, vector, string, or pair) are ordered by their position in the sequence. Therefore the list (3 2 1) is different from the list (1 2 3) while the set {3 2 1} is the same as the set {1 2 3}. This also implies that sequences can have multiple occurrences of the same item, while sets cannot. Thus, the list (1 2 3 1 2 3) is different from the list (1 2 3), while the set {1 2 3 1 2 3} is the same as the set {1 2 3}.

1.1.10. Other Value Domains

Although all implementations of Scheme must provide the domains just described, some implementations provide additional value domains. Later we will encounter two variations of procedures: **continuations** and **promises**, as well as two variations of lists: **ports** and **streams**.

1.2. Expressions

Algorithms are represented in Scheme by expressions. The algorithm described by a Scheme expression normally produces a value. For example, the arithmetic expression 5 * 8 + 2 represents the algorithm, "add 2 to the result of multiplying 5 and 8." The result of performing these operations is 42. The expression 5 * 8 + 2 produces the value 42.

Like values, Scheme expressions can be divided into subdomains:

```
EXPRESSION ::=
    LITERAL | SYMBOL | APPLICATION | STRUCTURE
```

1.2.1. Literals

Almost[3] any Scheme value can be turned into a Scheme expression by placing a single quote in front of it. Such an expression is called a **literal** because the value it produces is gotten by simply removing the quote. For example, '42 is the literal expression that produces the value 42.[4]

```
LITERAL  ::=  'VALUE
```

In most cases programmers can safely leave off the quote without confusing the interpreter. This is because programmers only produce expressions, while interpreters only produce values. Thus, if 42 is typed at the interpreter's prompt, the interpreter understands that the programmer is really asking for the value of '42.

There are a few types of values that require the single quote to avoid ambiguity. These will be discussed soon.

1.2.2. Symbols and the Global Environment

We have already encountered the SYMBOL domain. These are just the names used to denote procedures, constants, and other values. Scheme provides some predefined names, for example, +, *, sin, and < are pre-defined names for [+], [*], [sin], and [<]. Some implementations of Scheme provide nil, pi, true, and false as predefined names for (), 3.1416, #t, and #f, respectively.

An association between a name and a value is called a **binding**. The Scheme interpreter stores predefined bindings in a symbol table called the **Global Environment** (Figure 1.1):

NAME	VALUE
pi	3.1416
nil	()
+	[+]
true	#t
false	#f
etc.	etc.

Figure 1.1

---

[3] Procedures don't have standard representations, hence they can't be used as literals.

[4] We can also express '42 as (quote 42).

1.2.3. Applications

An **application** or **procedure call** is simply a list of one or more expressions:

```
APPLICATION ::= (EXPRESSION EXPRESSION ... )
```

The first expression in an application, called the **operator**, always denotes a procedure, while the remaining expressions, called the **operands**, denote the procedure's inputs.

   A procedure computes a mathematical function, which we can visualize as an abstract input-output device (see Figure 1.2).

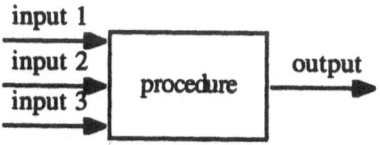

Figure 1.2

Data enters the "device" through input "wires," and a "circuit" (i.e. the algorithm) inside the device computes an output, which eventually emerges through the output "wire."

   For example, the value denoted by the application:

```
(max (+ 2 3) (abs -4) (remainder 12 5))
```

is 5, the output produced by the max procedure given inputs 5, 4, and 2 (see Figure 1.3).

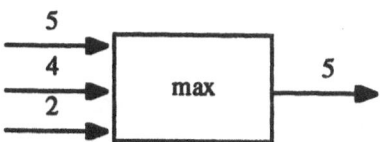

Figure 1.3

The value denoted by the application:

```
(<= (- 5 3) (+ 2 (* 3 3)) 14)
```

is #t, the output produced by the <= procedure given inputs 2, 11, and 14 (see Figure 1.4).

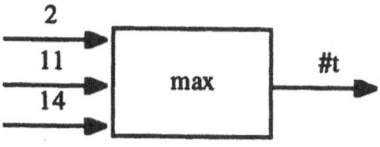

Figure 1.4

Notice that Scheme uses **prefix notation** instead of **infix notation**. In other words, Scheme will not understand the infix expression 2 + 3. Instead, programmers must write the + symbol in front of the operands: (+ 2 3). Although prefix notation normally doesn't require parenthesis, prefix notation in Scheme does. Parenthesis have special meaning in Scheme, namely, they indicate that a procedure is being called. This means Scheme programmers are not free to use parenthesis to make their programs more readable. For example, the expression (+ 2 (3.1e-5)) will cause an error because Scheme will assume the subexpression (3.1e-5) is an attempt to call the nonprocedural value 3.1e-5.

Finally, notice that expressions can be **nested**. In other words, operands and operators may also be applications. In both sample applications shown earlier:

```
(max (+ 2 3) (abs -4) (remainder 12 5))
```

```
(<= (- 5 3) (+ 2 (* 3 3)))
```

the operands (boldface) are themselves applications.

Translating Algebraic Expressions into Scheme

Translating algebraic expressions into equivalent Scheme expressions requires working backwards. For example, in the expression:

$$\frac{\sin(x + 1)}{\cos(x - 1)}$$

division is performed last, so this will be the first operation to appear in the corresponding Scheme expression:

```
(/ NUMERATOR DENOMINATOR)
```

The sin in the numerator is performed after 1 is added to x, so sin appears first in NUMERATOR. Remember, the name sin goes inside the parenthesis with its operand:

```
(/ (sin SUM) DENOMINATOR)
```

SUM is simple; just remember that + comes first:

```
(+ x 1)
```

Following the same procedure for DENOMINATOR and substituting into the original quotient yields:

```
(/ (sin (+ x 1)) (cos (- x 1)))
```

Make sure all the parentheses are balanced.

Let's look at one more example:

$$\sqrt{3^x + 1} \neq y$$

Unfortunately, ANSI/IEEE Scheme doesn't provide an inequality operator. We'll have to combine Scheme's not procedure with Scheme's = procedure:

```
(not (= ROOT y))
```

We consult the list of primitive number procedures in the *Revised⁴ Report* (or Chapter 2) and notice that sqrt is supplied by all implementations of Scheme that supply real numbers. We can replace ROOT with a call to sqrt:

```
(not (= (sqrt SUM) y))
```

Avoid inserting unnecessary parenthesis.
   SUM is simply:

```
(+ EXPONENT 1)
```

Another quick scan of the *Revised⁴ Report* reveals Scheme supplies two possible candidates for computing exponentials: exp and expt. Checking the *Revised⁴ Report* , we discover that (exp x) computes e^x, but (expt x y) computes x^y. Thus, we can formalize EXPONENT as:

```
(expt 3 x)
```

Putting these pieces back into our original expression gives:

```
(not (= (sqrt (+ (expt 3 x) 1) y))
```

Data Flow Structures

Sometimes it is helpful to think of a complicated application as a Scheme representation of an abstract "circuit" called a **data flow structure** or a **data flow diagram**. A data flow structure is built by connecting the input and output "wires" of function "devices." For example, the Scheme expression:

```
(/ (sqrt x) (- (cos x) 1))
```

represents a data flow structure built from four devices: sqrt, cos, –, and /. The input to both sqrt and cos is x. The output of cos, together with 1, are the inputs to –. The output of sqrt and – are the inputs to /. The final diagram is shown in Figure 1.5.

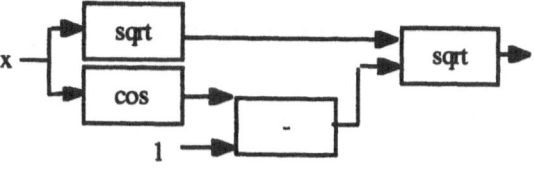

Figure 1.5

No device in a data flow structure produces an output until all its inputs have arrived. Thus, data flows through a data flow structure from left to right. The subtraction procedure (–) can't produce an output until the cos procedure produces its output. Similarly, the division procedure (/) must wait for the outputs of the subtraction procedure and the sqrt procedure before producing its output.

Let's consider another example:

```
(>= (length (cons (car x) (cdr y)) 42)
```

This expression compares 42 to the length of the list obtained from the expression (cons (car *x*) (cdr *y*)) (never mind what this means for now). The corresponding data flow structure is built from five components: >=, length, cons, car, and cdr. The inputs to cons are the outputs of car and cdr. The output of cons is the input to length. The output of length, together with 42, is the input to >= (see Figure 1.6).

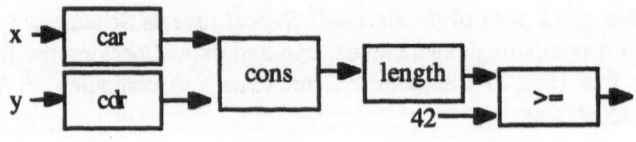

Figure 1.6

1.2.4. Structures

Structures, also called **special forms**, allow programmers to control the flow of evaluation (**control structures**), the visibility of data (**block structures**), and the contents of memory (**assignment structures**):

```
STRUCTURE ::=
    CONTROL | BLOCK | QUASIQUOTE | ASSIGNMENT
```

Structures look like specially formatted applications of the following seventeen special form constructors:

> if cond case and or do let let* letrec lambda set! begin begin0 delay quote
> quasiquote unquote

These will be explained in Chapters 3 through 5.

1.2.5. Literals Revisited

There's a problem with our practice of not quoting literals. Notice that the expression pi could be interpreted as a literal denoting itself—the symbol pi —or as a symbol denoting the number 3.1416. Similarly, the expression (+ 2 3) could be interpreted as a literal denoting a list containing a symbol and two numbers or as an application denoting the number 5. How do we determine the correct interpretation of these expressions?

To resolve this ambiguity, Scheme requires programmers to put a single quote in front of symbols, pairs, vectors, and lists when they are intended as literals. Thus, the expression pi is always interpreted as a symbol denoting 3.1416, while the expression 'pi is the literal denoting itself, the symbol pi. Similarly, the expression (+ 2 3) is always interpreted as the application denoting the number 5, while the expression '(+ 2 3) is the literal denoting itself, a list containing a symbol and two numbers.

It is not necessary to put quotes in front of symbols, lists, and pairs if they occur inside a vector, list, or pair. For example:

```
'#(x (x . x) (x x))
'((a . #\a) (e . #\e) (i . #\i) (o . #\o) (u . #\u))
'((a e i o u) . (#\a #\e #\i #\o #\u))
```

are all acceptable literals despite the fact that the pairs, symbols, and lists appearing inside are not quoted.

1.3. The Scheme Interpreter

Defining the EXPRESSION and VALUE domains is only half the job of specifying a programming language; the other half is describing a processor that can evaluate expressions to produce values. A processor can be a physical device such as the CPU of a computer, or it can be a virtual device such as an interpreter or compiler.

The Scheme interpreter consists of three components: the Global Environment, an expression evaluator, and a control loop. The evaluator actually does the work of interpreting expressions. We will describe the operation of these components in detail in subsequent chapters.

1.3.1. The Expression Evaluator

The evaluator, called **eval**, is a procedure that accepts an expression and an environment—called the current environment, often this is just the Global Environment—as input and outputs the value denoted by the expression. The arrow between eval and the current environment is shown going two ways in Figure 1.7, because sometimes evaluating an expression can produce changes in the current environment.

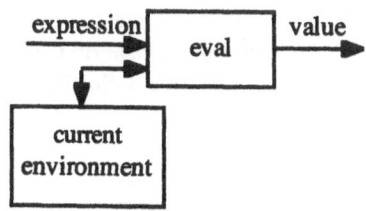

Figure 1.7

If the expression input is a literal, eval returns the expression itself as a value. If the expression input is a symbol, eval searches the current environment input for the corresponding value. If the expression input is a structure, eval invokes a special evaluation algorithm tailored for the particular type of structure. If the expression input is an application, eval employs an algorithm called eager evaluation, described in Chapter 2.

1.3.2. The Control Loop

If the evaluator is the engine of the Scheme interpreter, then the control loop is the driver. The control loop, also called the **read-eval-print loop**, or **REPL**, is a procedure that perpetually waits for a Scheme expression to be typed on the computer's keyboard. When an expression is typed, the control loop reads it, evaluates it using the eval procedure, displays the result, and then waits for the next expression to be typed: (see Figure 1.8)

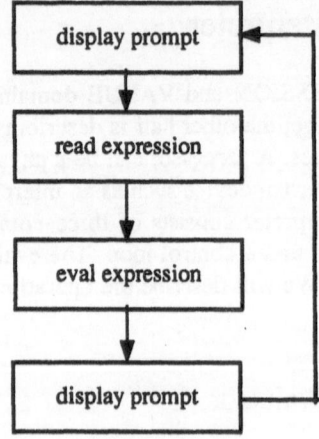

Figure 1.8

1.4.   Definitions

All values computed by the Scheme interpreter are **volatile**. They disappear from the computer's memory the instant they appear on the screen. To save the value produced by an expression it must be named using a **definition**:

```
DEFINITION ::=
   (define SYMBOL EXPRESSION)
```

A definition **declares** an association between SYMBOL and the value produced by EXPRESSION. We call associations between names and values **bindings**:

For example, the definition:

```
(define num1 (* 7 6))
```

declares the binding num1 = 42, between the symbol num1 and 42, the value produced by the expression (* 7 6), and the definition:

```
(define num2 (* 13 3))
```

declares a binding num2 = 39, between the symbol num2 and 39, the value produced by the expression (* 13 3).

Bindings declared by definitions are saved in the Global Environment for future reference. After the preceding definitions the Global Environment shown in Figure 1.1 can be pictured as in Figure 1.9.

NAME	VALUE
pi	3.1416
nil	()
+	[+]
true	#t
false	#f
etc.	etc.
num1	. 42
num2	39

Figure 1.9

The symbols num1 and num2 now denote 42 and 39, respectively. Naturally, we can incorporate num1 and num2 into new Scheme phrases. For example, the expression:

```
(+ num1 num2)
```

now produces 81, and the definition:

```
(define num3 (* num1 num2))
```

now declares a binding between num3 and 1638.

Num1 and num2 will continue to denote 42 and 39 until the session ends or until they are redefined. For example, the definition:

```
(define num2 (+ 9 num2))
```

creates a new binding of num2 to 48, which replaces the old binding in the Global Environment. (But not before 9 is added to 39, the old value of num2, to create the new value.)

Appendices

Appendix 1.1. Defining Domains

> And each law or pattern is itself a pattern of relationships among still other laws, which are themselves just patterns of relationships again.
>
> —Christopher Alexander, *The Timeless Way of Building*

A **domain** is a set of objects that have similar representations and interpretations. If a is an object and A is a domain, then "$a \in A$" means "a is a member of A," and "$a \notin A$" means "a is not a member of A." For example, if EVEN is the domain of all even, non-negative integers—0, 2, 4, 6, etc.—then $42 \in$ EVEN, but $43 \notin$ EVEN.

We can succinctly describe domains using domain equations. A domain equation has the form:

```
DOMAIN ::= PATTERN | PATTERN | etc.
```

where DOMAIN is the name of the domain being defined (domain names will always be in uppercase), "::=" means "consists of," "|" means "or" or "union," and PATTERN is a string describing the format of some members of DOMAIN. These members are called **instances** of PATTERN.

There are several types of patterns. A pattern may be an actual member of the domain being defined. The only instance of a pattern like this is itself. For example, the equations:

```
CREW ::= Picard | Whorf | Spock
STOOGE ::= Larry | Curly | Moe
```

mean:

> An instance of CREW consists of an instance of Picard, Whorf, or Spock.
> An instance of STOOGE consists of an instance of Larry, Curly, or Moe.

In other words, the domain CREW contains three members: Picard, Whorf, and Spock; and the domain STOOGE contains three members: Larry, Curly, and Moe. A mathematician would define these domains using set enumeration notation:

```
CREW = {Picard, Whorf, Spock}
STOOGE = {Larry, Curly, Moe}
```

A pattern may also be the name of another domain. In this case the instances are members of the domain. For example, the equation:

```
HERO ::= CREW | STOOGE
```

means:

> An instance of HERO consists of an instance of the CREW or STOOGE domain.

A mathematician would simply express this as a union:

HERO = CREW ∪ STOOGE

Patterns can also be formed by **concatenating** (i.e., gluing together) patterns. For example, the first pattern on the right side of the equation:

INTRODUCTION ::= CREW meet STOOGE | STOOGE meet CREW

is built by concatenating three patterns: the domain CREW, the word "meet", and the domain STOOGE. The meaning of the equation is:

> An instance of INTRODUCTION consists of an instance of CREW followed by an instance of the word " meet " followed by an instance of STOOGE; or an instance of STOOGE followed by an instance of the word " meet " followed by an instance of CREW.

Here are some sample members of the INTRODUCTION domain:

Moe meet Picard
Whorf meet Moe
Curly meet Picard

However,

Spock meet Whorf

is not a member of the INTRODUCTION domain. (Why?)

A mathematician would probably define the INTRODUCTION domain using unions and set builder notation:

INTRODUCTION = INTRODUCTION1 ∪ INTRODUCTION2

where

INTRODUCTION1 = {c meet s: c ∈ CREW & s ∈ STOOGE}
INTRODUCTION2 = {s meet c: s ∈ STOOGE & c ∈ CREW}

Surrounding a pattern with square brackets indicates instances of the pattern are optional. For example, we can extend our definitions of CREW and STOOGE to allow more formality:

CREW2   ::= [Mr.] CREW
STOOGE2 ::= [Mr.] STOOGE

The members of CREW2 include the members of CREW:

Spock, Picard, Whorf

as well as:

Mr. Spock, Mr. Picard, Mr. Whorf

Alternatively, we could have defined CREW2 as a union of two domains using either a domain equation:

```
CREW2 ::= CREW | Mr. CREW
```

Finally, we can place an **ellipsis** (i.e., "...") behind a pattern. This means the pattern can be repeated zero or more times. The ellipsis is useful for defining domains of arbitrarily long sequences. For example:

```
HEROS ::= (HERO ... )
```

means:

> An instance of HEROS consists of an instance of a left parenthesis followed by zero or more instances of HERO followed by an instance of a right parenthesis.

Without the ellipsis the domain equation for HEROS would be infinitely long:

```
HEROS ::=
   () | (HERO) | (HERO HERO) | (HERO HERO HERO) | etc.
```

Here are some sample instances of the pattern (HERO ...) (i.e., members of the domain HEROS):

```
()
(Picard Curly Spock)
(Larry)
(Moe Moe Moe Moe Moe Moe Moe Moe Moe Moe Moe Moe Moe)
```

The first example shows that an instance of zero repetitions of HERO. The last example shows members of the HEROS domain can contain repeated instances of the HERO domain, and therefore the HEROS domain has an infinite number of members.

   Warning: Domain equations are not part of the Scheme language. Computer scientists use domain equations to define the program domains and—less frequently—the data domains of all programming languages:

```
DATA ::= NUMBER | STRING | etc.
PROGRAM ::= INSTRUCTION ...
```

Computer scientists call the format of domain equations **Extended Backus-Naur Form**, or EBNF for short.[5] Domain theory and formal language theory are two areas of computer science that study domains.

Appendix 1.2. Sessions

A Scheme session begins when the control loop is started from the operating system's prompt. When the Scheme application:

---

[5] In 1960, John Backus, who created FORTRAN, and Peter Naur developed this notation to describe the PROGRAM domain for the Algol60 language.

```
(exit)
```

is typed, the session ends and control is returned to the operating system.

Saving Transcripts

The written dialogue between programmer and interpreter is called a **transcript**. Unless the transcript is saved to a file, it scrolls out of view and into oblivion. Scheme provides a procedure for saving transcripts to files. Assume file is the name of a file:

```
(transcript-on "file")  =
```
   an unspecified value. As a side effect, the standard
   output port is connected to both the monitor and file.

```
(transcript-off)  =
```
   an unspecified value. As a side effect the standard
   output port is disconnected from file.

A file containing a Scheme session is called a **transcript file**.

An Example

Let's study a fragment of a Scheme session. Expressions entered by the user appear next to the interpreter's prompt: >, followed immediately by their values. All computer generated text is shown in boldface:

```
> 100
100
> "Hello world"
"Hello world"
> pi
3.14159265358979
> (cos pi)
-1.0
> (>= 3 5)
#f
> '(+ 2 3 4)
(+ 2 3 4)
> (+ 2 3 4)
9
> +
[+]
>
```

This session shows literals, symbols, and applications being evaluated. Note that placing a quote in front of the list (+ 2 3 4) turns it into a literal that simply denotes itself, a list consisting of a symbol followed by three numbers. The control loop displays the list without the single quote because values don't need quotes, only literal expressions. But when the user types the list (+ 2 3 4) again without the quote, eval interprets it as a procedure application, adds the operand values, and prints the resulting value, 9. Finally, when the user types + without the surrounding parenthesis, eval interprets it as a symbol, searches the Global Environment, and displays the corresponding value, the procedure [+]. (Different implementations of Scheme will use different notations for [+].)

Warning: PC-Scheme identifies the Boole #f and the empty list, ( ). This is inconsistent with ANSI Scheme, which, in most testing contexts, identifies all values with #t except #f.

Appendix 1.3. Numbers

We will encounter the function-structure duality in many forms throughout this text. In the context of numbers, **function** refers to the interpretation of a number, while **structure** refers to the way the number is represented.

Mathematicians interpret real numbers as points on a number line, or more precisely, as distances from points on a number line to a fixed point called the origin. The unit of measurement can be miles, inches, meters, light-years, Angstroms, anything. Positive reals are the points to the right of the origin, negative reals are to the left. While there is only one interpretation of a real number, there are many representations.

Representing Real Numbers

The **decimal representation** of a positive real number is an infinite sequence of digits. For example:

x = 42.142857142857142857...

represents the infinite sum of distances:

$$4 * 10^1 + 2 * 10^0 + 1 * 10^{-1} + 4 * 10^{-2} + 2 * 10^{-3} + \ldots$$

We call 42 the **integer part** of x. The infinite sequence of digits to the right of the decimal point constitutes the **fraction part** of x.

This representation scheme is called decimal because there are ten possible digits that can occur in a sequence, 0 through 9. Why is ten special? Surely this is only an accident of biology or culture. In some places people count between instead of on the tips of their fingers. These people favor **octal representations** based on eight "digits": 0 through 7, and interpret them as sums of powers of eight:

$$\begin{aligned} x &= 52.1111\ldots \\ &= 5 * 8^1 + 2 * 8^0 + 1 * 8^{-1} + 1 * 8^{-2} + 1 * 8^{-3} + \ldots \end{aligned}$$

Programmers often prefer **hexadecimal representations** based on 16 "digits"—0 through 9, A (10), B (11), C (12), D (13), E (14), and F (15)—and interpret them as sums of powers of 16:

$$\begin{aligned} x &= 2A.249249\ldots \\ &= 2 * 16^1 + 10 * 16^0 + 2 * 16^{-1} + 4 * 16^{-2} + \ldots \end{aligned}$$

Computers store, process, and communicate data as voltage levels. To avoid ambiguity only two levels are distinguished: high and low. For this reason computers favor **binary representations** using only two "digits," 0 and 1 (called **bits**), and interpret them as sums of powers of two:

$$x = 101010.001001001\ldots = 1 * 2^5 + 0 * 2^4 + 1 * 2^3 + 0 * 2^2 + 1 * 2^1 + 0 * 2^0 + 0 * 2^{-1} + 0 * 2^{-2} + 1 * 2^{-3} + \ldots$$

The **radix** of a representation scheme is the number of allowable digits. The hexadecimal radix is 16, the octal radix is eight, the decimal radix is ten, and the binary radix is two.

Representing Integers and Rationals

All of the representations of x given so far are infinitely long. We are forced to use an ellipses (...) to indicate that the fraction part continues forever. Computers too have difficulty dealing with infinitely long representations. For this reason three subsets of the reals are of particular interest.

If all of the digits in the fraction part are zeros, we can safely ignore them and just represent the real by its integer part. Such reals are called **integers**.

Another special case occurs when the decimal part is periodic. This means the decimal part consists of a finite sequence of nonrepeating digits followed by an infinitely repeating pattern of digits. It turns out that such reals result from integer divisions and therefore can be finitely represented as a ratio of two integers. We call these numbers **rationals**. Because the fraction part of x in the previous example is periodic (the repeating pattern appears to be 142857, but who knows what "..." really means), x is rational. It results from dividing 295 by 7, hence it can be represented as the ratio:

$$x = 295/7$$

Clearly, integers are rationals. For example $42 = 42/1$.

A **truncation** of a decimal representation, i.e., the result of chopping off all digits in the fraction part beyond some arbitrary point, is also a type of rational number because it is equivalent to the nontruncated number gotten by appending an infinite repeating pattern of zeros. For example:

$$y = 42.142857 = 42.142857000\ldots = 42142857/1000000$$

Approximating Irrational Numbers

It seems rational to call reals that aren't rational **irrational**. Pi, the natural exponent e, and square roots of prime numbers are examples of irrationals. Irrational numbers are so ubiquitous that if we removed all of them from the number line, the length of what remained would be zero!

How does a computer represent an irrational number? Sadly, it doesn't. Instead, irrational numbers must be approximated by truncations. For this reason truncations are sometimes called **inexact numbers**. For example, some computers approximate the irrational number pi by the truncation 3.141592654.

Scientific Notation

An alternative, more compact representation for a truncation is **scientific notation**. Scientific notation can be used to compress long strings of consecutive zeros into an integer exponent of 10. For example, the following decimal representation:

```
z = 0.0000000000123
```

can be compressed into the scientific notation:

```
z = 1.23 * 10^-10
```

Problems

Warning: Many versions of Scheme—including the TI and UG versions of PC-Scheme —are not 100% compliant with the IEEE/ANSI specification. While it is acceptable to use these versions for testing and experimenting, your answers must be based on IEEE/ANSI Scheme.

Problem 1.1.

Assume the following definitions have been made:

```
(define x 10)
(define y 20)
(define z -5)
(define m *)
```

Compute the values denoted by the following Scheme expressions. Use a Scheme interpreter to check your answers. Some expressions contain errors. Explain the nature of these errors, and if possible, suggest corrections. If you are not sure about a procedure, look its definition up in the *Revised⁴* Report.

```
a. (+ x y (m z z))
b. '(+ x y (m z z))
c. "(+ x y (m z z))"
d. #(+ x y (m z z))
e. (x + y + z * z)
f. '#(x y z)
g. (x y z)
```

Problem 1.2.

The type of a number is the lowest level in the hierarchy of number domains to which it belongs. For example, 42 belongs to the INTEGER, RATIONAL, REAL, and

COMPLEX domains, hence its type is INTEGER. Classify the types of the following numbers. Also classify the representations as exact or inexact, and convert them into an equivalent decimal representation:

```
#x2.8e3   #b111+#o32i   #e#d32.0   #b.001   #x#iFFFF
```

Problem 1.3.

Assume the following definitions have been made:

```
(define a 6)
(define b 10)
(define c 30)
```

Because of the leading quote, the literal expression '(+ a b c) denotes the list (+ a b c) instead of the number 46. The quote tells the evaluator to interpret everything that follows it literally.

Scheme has a structure called a **quasiquote**, which is denoted by a back quote: `. Quasiquote is similar to quote. For example, the expression `(+ a b c) also denotes the list (+ a b c). The difference is that the evaluator takes everything following a quasiquote literally unless it is preceded by the unquote operator (which is denoted by a comma). The evaluator evaluates unquoted values appearing inside a quasiquote. Thus, the expression `(+ a ,b c) denotes the list (+ a 10 c).[6]

Compute the values of the following Scheme expressions:

```
`(+ ,a ,b ,c)
`(,a a ,b b ,c c)
`(,"a" ",a" ,'a ',a)
`((a b c) (,a ,b ,c))
```

Problem 1.4.

Indicate to which subdomain of VALUE and EXPRESSION each of the elements listed here belongs to. The choices for EXPRESSION subdomains are LITERAL, SYMBOL, APPLICATION, and NONE. The choices for VALUE subdomains are BOOLE, CHAR, SYMBOL, PROCEDURE, LIST, VECTOR, PAIR, STRING, NONE, or, in the case of numbers, give the domain lowest in the number hierarchy to which the element belongs.

a. "f"	f. #()	k. (1 .2)	p. '+
b. f	g. '()	l. (+ 1 .2)	q. +3.0
c. #\f	h. ()	m. #(+ 1 .2)	r. '3.0
d. 'f	i. (1 . .2)	n. '(+ 1 .2)	s. 3.111
e. #f	j. "(1 . .2)"	o. +	t. .2+0i

---

[6] We can also express `(+ a ,b c) as (quasiquote (+ a (unquote b) c)).

Problem 1.5.

Write Scheme expressions equivalent to the following mathematical expressions. You may use any ANSI Scheme procedures or constants. You may also use the "and" and "or" structures. Hint: Use Scheme's define procedure to give arbitrary definitions to x, y, z, a, and b. Once these symbols have values, you should be able to check your Scheme translations of the following expressions using your Scheme interpreter.

```
a. (sin(x + y)/cos(x - y))²
b. ln(xy + 3)
c. 5.3 x 10⁻¹¹⁹
d. pi
e. e  (i.e. the natural log)
f. tan(x)/(log⁷(x)/y)
g. (x ≤ y) or (x²≠2)
h. ((x/y)/(a/b))/(a/x)
i. -1 < eˣ < 1
j. arcsin(2x)
```

Problem 1.6.

A **natural number** is an unsigned integer. Write a domain equation for naturals:

```
NAT ::= ???
```

Problem 1.7.

Complete the following domain equations for number representation formats. NAT domain is the domain of natural number formats. (A natural number is just an unsigned integer.) UREAL is the domain of unsigned REAL formats. You may introduce supporting domains as you see fit.

```
a. FORMAT ::= REAL | COMPLEX
b. REAL ::= INT | RATIO | DECIMAL | SCIENTIFIC
c. INT ::= [-]NAT
d. NAT ::=
e. DIGIT ::=
f. RATIO ::=
g. DECIMAL ::=
h. SCIENTIFIC ::=
i. COMPLEX ::= REAL+UREALi | REAL-UREALi | REALi
j. UREAL ::=
```

Problem 1.8.

Write the following numbers in as many formats as possible. Classify each number as integer, rational, irrational, real, and/or complex. If a number belongs to several of these domains, list them all. Also, classify each format as exact or inexact:

```
-2.16, 1/20, 100, 1/7, 3.33, 2.5e-3, -2i, -2e10, 1+0i
```

Problem 1.9.

Compute the values of the following Scheme expressions assuming complex and rational numbers are fully implemented:

```
a. (+ 3+2i 4/3 .1)
b. (* 2/7 -i 3.1e2)
c. (expt -4 .5)
d. (exp 100)
e. (/ 2-i 2+i)
f. (* 3e42 .2e-16)
```

Problem 1.10.

Which of the following names are not members of Scheme's SYMBOL domain (as defined earlier). Explain why.

```
i +i ::: <.*.> /++} 3+ +3 + ++ C++ A<==>B&C=3 Hi-Ho!
-Ho! x+y+z x+(y+z) <NUM>::=<INT>|<REAL> c^2 [x] f'
.tax. a/b  Scheme C++ Modula2.1 ___ x... ...x ... #x%
=? ??? a+bi smith@sjsu.edu  smith/project/foo.scm
c:smith\project\foo.scm
```

Problem 1.11.

Why doesn't Scheme allow symbols to begin with ., −, or +?

Problem 1.12.

Investigate what happens when the following strings are typed into your Scheme interpreter:

```
a. "\cat"
b. "\\cat"
c. "\\\cat"
```

Problem 1.13.

Draw data flow diagrams for the following Scheme applications:

```
a. (+ (cos (* 3 x)) (sqrt (/ 1 x)))
b. (+ (+ (+ x y) (+ z z)) (+ x z))
c. (expt (* 3 z) (max x y z))
```

Problem 1.14.

Assume exp is a Scheme expression. Some versions of Scheme allow programmers to call the eval procedure directly:

```
(eval exp)  =
    the value of exp in the Global Environment
```

Assume the following definitions have been made:

```
(define val1 42)
(define val2 'val1)
(define val3 'val2)
(define val4 '(quotient val1 6))
```

Compute the values of the following Scheme expressions:

```
a. (eval val1)
b. (eval val2)
c. (eval val3)
d. (eval (eval val3))
e. (eval '(eval val3))
f. (eval val4)
```

Problem 1.15.

Find the hexadecimal (i.e., base 16) representations of the following numbers:

```
124    215    248.625    1/6
```

2
Procedures

2.1. Defining and Applying Procedures

Although Scheme provides quite a few procedures, there are many more it does not provide. This isn't a problem because programmers can define their own procedures using **lambda expressions**. The format of a lambda expression is:

```
LAMBDA ::= (lambda PARAMETERS BODY)
```

The first input to lambda is simply a list of symbols called **parameters**:

```
PARAMETERS ::= (SYMBOL ...)
```

The body of a lambda expression is a parameterized expression:

```
BODY ::= PARAMETERIZED-EXPRESSION
```

A **parameterized expression** is a Scheme expression that may contain parameters from the parameter list. For example, here's a new procedure that computes $|x - y|$, the distance between two real numbers x and y:

```
(define dist (lambda (x y) (abs (- x y))))
```

The parameters are x and y, and the body is the parameterized expression: (abs $(- x y)$).

Unlike ordinary expressions, a parameterized expression can't be evaluated until the parameters are replaced with appropriate Scheme values called **arguments**. This happens when the procedure appears as the operator in an application. The arguments are the values of the operands.

For example, assume the following definitions have been made:

```
(define num1 30)
(define num2 -14)
```

To evaluate the application:

```
(dist (+ num1 8) num2)
```

the Scheme evaluator (1) evaluates the name, dist, (2) evaluates the operands (+ num1 8) and num2, (3) replaces x and y in the body of dist by the operand values, the arguments

38 and −14. This produces the expression: (abs (− 38 −14)). Finally, (4) since this expression no longer contains parameters, it can be evaluated to produce the ultimate answer, 52:

```
> (dist (+ num1 8) num2)
52
```

Some people feel the format of a definition involving a lambda expression is too complicated. For this reason many Scheme implementations provide an alternative format called a **procedure block**, which drops the lambda operator and combines the procedure name and parameters into a single list called the **header**:

```
PROCEDURE-BLOCK ::= (define HEADER BODY)
HEADER ::= (PROCEDURE-NAME PARAMETER ...)
```

Here is the definition of the distance procedure using a procedure block:

```
(define (dist x y) (abs (- x y)))
```

Although we will use procedure blocks, there are places where it is still necessary to use lambda expressions. Readers should develop the ability to translate quickly between the two forms.

2.1.1. The Environmental Influence

Let's work through another example. Comparing truncated numbers using = or zero? can be dangerous due to rounding errors. Assume the following definitions have been made:

```
(define (square z) (* z z))

(define num (- 1 (+ (square (sin 3)) (square (cos 3)))))
```

A fundamental trigonometric identity tells us num should be 0, but Scheme seems to believe differently:

```
> (zero? num)
#f
> (= num 0)
#f
```

When truncated numbers are combined, rounding errors can accumulate to produce significant errors. For example, the actual value of num is a tiny but positive real number:

```
> num
1.11022e-16
```

In these situations it might be better if we had a procedure that determined if two numbers were close in the sense that the distance between them was less than some small constant, Δ. Unfortunately, Scheme doesn't provide such a procedure, so we'll have to define our own.

A **predicate** is any procedure that returns a Boolean value: #t or #f. Scheme predicates conventionally have names ending with a question mark. For example, the name big? suggests the procedure returns #t if its input is big and #f if it isn't. The only exceptions to this convention are the not predicate and the primitive predicates that compare numbers: =, <, >, <=, and >=. (Older implementations of Scheme allow =?, <?, >?, <=?, and >=? as synonyms for these procedures.)

We want a predicate that determines if two numbers are close; following Scheme's convention, let's name this procedure close? The definition of close? can take advantage of the dist procedure defined earlier:

```
(define (close? a b) (<= (dist a b) delta))
```

Where delta is a constant representing our error tolerance. For now we can set its value to 10^{-20}.

```
(define delta 1e-20)
```

If close? is the inexact analog of =, then the inexact analog of zero? should be called small?:

```
(define (small? z) (close? z 0)) ; i.e., near zero
```

When it encounters the application (small? num), the Scheme evaluator replaces z by the value of num in the parameterized body of small?

```
(close? 1.11022e-16 0)
```

Next, 1.11022e-16 replaces a and 0 replaces b in the parameterized body of close?:

```
(<= (dist 1.11022e-16 0) delta)
```

Before the comparison can be made, 1.11022e-16 replaces x and 0 replaces y in the body of dist:

```
(abs (- 1.11022e-16 0))
```

Because there are no parameters in this expression, it can be fully evaluated. Its value replaces the application of dist in the body of close?:

```
(<= 1.11022e-16 delta)
```

Notice that delta is not a parameter; it is a constant defined in the global environment. Therefore, this expression can be fully evaluated to produce the final answer, #t:

```
> (small? num)
#t
```

If a user inadvertently defines a new constant called delta:

```
(define delta 100)
```

then small? no longer works:

```
> (small? num)
#f
```

The definitions of small?, close?, dist, and delta can be placed in a file called math.scm. The expression:

```
(load "math.scm")
```

can be placed at the top of any file of definitions that need them.

2.1.2. The Modularity Principle and Top-Down Design

Suppose we want to define a procedure called pipe-volume that computes the volumes of pipes closed at both ends by hemispherical caps, as in Figure 2.1.

Figure 2.1

The inputs to the procedure will be the length and radius of the cylinder component of the pipe. We can express the form of the definition using a **stub** (i.e., the header is specified, but the body is undetermined):

```
(define (pipe-volume len rad) ???)
```

How should we begin? A top-down strategy is suggested by the **modularity principle**:

> The body of a procedure should be explicit and purposeful (rather than obscure and arbitrary). This is achieved if we cleanly decompose the procedure into subtasks performed by calls to independent and logically coherent supporting procedures.

The pipe is built out of three pieces: a cylinder and two hemispherical caps. Glued together, the caps form a sphere with the same radius as the cylinder. This suggests we can naturally decompose the procedure into a sum of volumes:

```
; = volume of length len & radius rad capped pipe
(define (pipe-volume len rad)
   (+ (cylinder-volume len rad)
      (sphere-volume rad)))
```

Programs should not be needlessly difficult to understand. To achieve this goal, experienced programmers follow three basic **literacy principles**:

1. There are few restrictions on the names of parameters, procedures, and constants. Therefore names should be chosen to reflect the interpretation of the values they represent.
2. The interpretation of a name can be further elaborated with a comment, but don't restate the obvious. Comments are also welcome inside procedures to explain

tricky algorithms, etc. In Scheme, a comment is placed between a semicolon and the next end-of-line.

3. A program's physical structure should reflect its logical structure. Use indentation to indicate the depths of nested expressions, and use blank lines to separate tasks.

Returning to our procedure, we discover that the supporting procedures, cylinder-volume and pipe-volume are not predefined. We'll have to provide our own definitions. We can consult a geometry book to find the formulas for the volumes of a cylinder and a sphere:

$V_{cylinder}$ = length * area of circular base

V_{sphere} = 4/3 * π * radius^3

Translating the first formula into Scheme gives:

```
; = volume of length len & radius rad cylinder
(define (cylinder-volume len rad)
   (* len (circle-area rad)))
```

The product of 4/3 and π is constant. It would be inefficient to compute this value each time sphere-volume is called, therefore we define it as a global constant:

```
(define four-thirds-pi (* (/ 4 3) pi))
```

Pi is often predefined. If not, it can be defined by:

```
(define pi (acos -1)) ; since (cos pi) = -1
```

Translating the second formula into Scheme gives:

```
; = volume of radius rad sphere
(define (sphere-volume rad)
   (* four-thirds-pi (cube rad)))
```

The area of a radius r circle is πr^2. Translating this into Scheme gives:

```
; = area of radius rad circle
(define (circle-area rad)
   (* pi (square rad)))
```

To finish, we only need to define square and cube:

```
; = z^2
(define (square z) (* z z))
```

```
; = z^3
(define (cube z) (* z z z))
```

Compare these definitions with the following equivalent but inefficient, hard-to-understand, and poorly structured definition:

```
(define (pipe-volume i x) (+
       (* i pi x x) (*. 2
(/ 2 3) x x x)))
```

We can make this definition even harder to understand by decomposing it into incoherent subtasks:

```
(define (pipe-volume a b) (+
       (* (helper1 a b) b)
(* (helper2 b) b b)))
```

Where the helper1 and helper2 procedures compute incoherent mathematical functions that only have meaning in the context of the volume procedure:

```
(define (helper1 u v) (* u pi v))
(define (helper2 l) (* 2 (/ 2 3) l))
```

2.2.   Building Procedures Using Application

In **applicative Scheme** the only tools for building procedures are application and abstraction (i.e.,, lambda expressions). Although we will learn in Chapter 8 that this is all we need, building procedures with such simple tools is like making furniture with a Swiss Army knife: possible, but challenging.

In this chapter we restrict ourselves to applicative Scheme. Our purpose is to wean readers away from statement sequencing, the principle program-building tool provided by languages like Pascal, FORTRAN, and C.[1] In the next chapter we will begin adding to our tool kit.

2.2.1.   Example: Coercions

A **coercion** is a procedure that transforms members of one domain into equivalent members of another domain, where the meaning of **equivalent** is subject to interpretation and debate. By convention, the name of a Scheme coercion usually has the form:

domain->range

Where "domain" indicates the input domain, "->" means to, and "range" indicates the output domain. Scheme provides ten basic coercions:

> number->string, string->number, char->integer, integer->char, list->string, string->list, symbol->string, string->symbol, vector->list, list->vector

In addition, Scheme provides four procedures for coercing real numbers into integers:

---

[1] Applicative C would be C with all functions restricted to a single statement: return
EXPRESSION

floor, ceiling, truncate, round

and procedures that coerce exact numbers into inexact numbers and back again:

exact->inexact, inexact->exact

The best way to remember these coercions is to remember the coercion map in Figure 2.2:

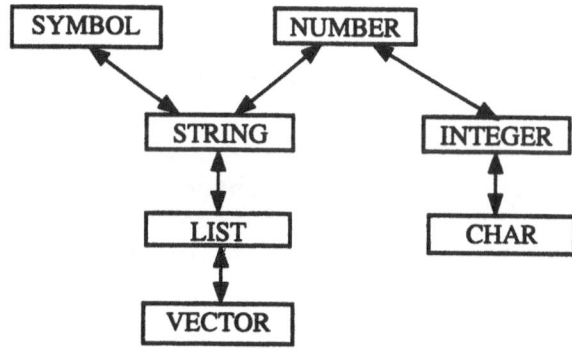

Figure 2.2

Notice that all coercions are reversible, and we don't need a coercion from integers to numbers because integers are already numbers. We can get an idea of what these coercions do from the following transcript:

```
> (string->number "532.678")
532.678
> (number->string 532.678)     ; 10 = default radix
"532.678"
> (number->string 26 2)        ; 2 = optional radix
"11010"
> (string->number "1A" 16)2 ; 16 = optional radix
26
> (string->symbol "cat")3
cat
> (symbol->string 'cat)
"cat"
> (list->string '(#\c #\a #\t))
"cat"
> (string->list "cat")
(#\c #\a #\t)
```

---

[2] In PC-Scheme: (string->number STRING EXACTNESS RADIX) where EXACT ::= 'e | 'i and RADIX ::= 'b | 'd | 'o | 'x and (number->string STRING FORMAT) where FORMAT ::= (INT) | (FIX N) | (FLO N) | SCI N M) | (HEUR).

[3] In PC-Scheme |cat| is returned.

```
> (list->vector '(42 #t "hello"))
#(42 #t "hello")
> (vector->list #(42 #t "hello"))
(42 #t "hello")
> (char->integer #\a)
97                              ; 97 = ASCII code for #\a
> (integer->char 97)
#\a
```

The coercions from reals to integers are subtly different. Assume r is any real number, then:

```
(floor r)      = largest integer ≤ r.
(ceiling r)    = smallest integer ≥ r.
(round r)      = closest integer to r.⁴
(truncate r)   = integer part of r.
```

The differences between these procedures are tricky when r is negative:

```
> (floor -4.5)
-5                          ; = largest int ≤ -4.5
> (truncate -4.5)
-4                          ; = int part of -4.5
> (ceiling -4.5)
-4                          ; = smallest int ≥ -4.5
> (round -4.5)
-4                          ; = closest (even) int to -4.5
```

Here are some sample calls to the coercions between exact and inexact numbers. Unfortunately, these coercions don't always yield the expected result:

```
> (inexact->exact .5)
1/2
> (exact->inexact 1/2)
.5
```

We can define our own coercions by composing these coercions. For example, the following procedures coerce character vectors into symbols and vice-versa:

```
; = symbol made from a vector of chars
(define (vector->symbol char-vector)
   (string->symbol
      (list->string (vector->list char-vector))))

; = char vector made from a symbol
(define (symbol->vector symbol)
```

---

⁴ Returns nearest even integer when argument is halfway between two integers.

```
(list->vector
   (string->list
      (symbol->string symbol)))
```

The data flow structures of these procedures can be viewed as pipelines formed by composed procedures as in Figure 2.3.

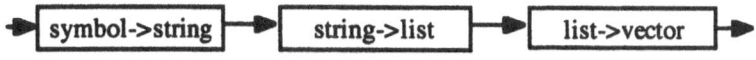

Figure 2.3

Of course it makes sense to define coercions between domains other than the ones provided by Scheme. For example, assume we introduce four new domains:

```
MILE, YARD, FOOT, INCH ::= REAL
```

There are six basic coercions between these domains, these three:

```
; = # yards in m miles
(define (mile->yard m)
   (* 1760 m)) ; 1 mile = 1760 yards

; = # feet in y yards
(define (yard->foot y) (* 3 y))

; = #inches in f feet
(define (foot->inch f) (* 12 f))
```

together with their inverses: inch->foot, foot->yard, and yard->mile. Other coercions can be defined by composing the basic coercions. For example:

```
; = # inches in m miles
(define (mile->inch m)
   (foot->inch (yard->foot (mile->yard m))))
```

2.2.2. Example: Palindromes

Doc note, I dissent. A fast never prevents a fatness. I diet on cod!

A **palindrome** is any string that is the same spelled forward or backward (upper- and lowercase letters aren't distinguished). For example, **Rotator**, **YrekaBakery**, and **Race-Car** are palindromes. How can we define a predicate that detects palindromes?

```
; = #t, if string is a palindrome
(define (palindrome? string) ???)
```

If we had a procedure for reversing strings:

```
; = reverse of string
(define (string-reverse string) ???)
```

we could use it to reverse palindrome?'s input string, then compare the result with the original input string using string-ci=?:

```
; = #t, if string is a palindrome
(define (palindrome? string)
   (string-ci=? string (string-reverse string)))
```

Scheme does provide a procedure for reversing lists:

```
(reverse vals) = list formed by reversing vals
```

For example:

```
> (reverse '(a e i o u))
(u o i e a)
```

Unfortunately, Scheme does not provide procedures for reversing strings and vectors, but these are easily defined using our coercions. For example:

```
; = reverse of string
(define (string-reverse string)
   (list->string (reverse (string->list string))))
```

2.3.   The Abstraction Principle

> Structure is organization in space, while function is organization in time.
>
> —C. Judson Herrick and George Coghill, *Naturalist and Philosopher*

Every organism plays a special role in its environment. We think of this role as the organism's **purpose** or **function**. Biologists explain an organism's function in terms of its internal organization or structure. Of course function does not always follow structure. Evolution, adaptation, learning, differentiation, and mutation are all examples of the environment imposing new roles on an organism or species that may eventually lead to structural changes.

The **structure-function duality** is also important in computer science and programming. For a procedure, we identify structure with body and function with purpose. The structure-function duality also applies to data. For example, the structure of a number is its representation: binary, octal, decimal, hexadecimal, etc. The function of a number is its interpretation: the distance between two points on a number line. (Can environment influence function?)

The **abstraction principle** simply states:

> Structure and function should be independent.

This means people should be able to use a procedure or value without knowing how it is implemented. It also means programmers can change the implementation without worrying about breaking user programs.

One technique for hiding the representation of data in a given domain is to present the user with abstract procedures for manipulating domain members. This collection of procedures is called an **interface**, an **abstract data type**, or an **ADT**. Typically, an ADT consists of **constructors** for building new members of the domain, **selectors** for dissecting existing members of the domain, and predicates for recognizing domain members.

Following the abstraction principle, we will not have much to say about how pairs, lists, vectors, and strings are represented. Instead, we present the constructors and selectors for each domain.

2.3.1. Constructors

A **constructor** is a procedure that builds a composite value from its components. Scheme provides six basic constructors. Assume val and val_i are arbitrary Scheme values and c and c_i are arbitrary Scheme characters:

```
(cons val1 val2)        = (val1 . val2).

(list val1 ... valn)    = (val1 ... valn).

(vector val1 ... valn)  = #(val1 ... valn).

(make-vector n val)
        = length n vector #(val ... val)

(string c1 ... cn)      = "c1...cn"

(make-string n c)       = length n string "c ... c"
```

In addition, some implementations of Scheme provide constructors for complex and rational numbers:

```
(/ n m)    = n/m.

(make-rectangular x y)  = x+yi.

(make-polar x y)        = x*e^iy
```

Where n and m are integers ($m \neq 0$), and x and y are reals. Here are some sample applications:

```
> (cons 't #t)
(t . #t)
> (list #f "f" #\f 'f)
```

```
(#f "f" #\f f)
> (vector #f "f" #\f 'f)
#(#f "f" #\f f)
> (make-vector 10 0)
#(0 0 0 0 0 0 0 0 0 0)
> (string #\I #\B #\M)
"IBM"
> (make-string #\? 10)
"??????????"
> (/ 4 6)
2/3
> (make-rectangular 3 -4)
3-4i
> (make-polar 3 -4)
-1.960930862590836+2.2704074859237844i
```

Why do we need constructors? Why can't we replace every call to a constructor by an equivalent literal? For example, why would we write:

```
(define origin (list 0 0 0))
```

when we could write:

```
(define origin '(0 0 0))
```

Constructors are needed when components aren't known in advance. Compare the following programmer-defined constructors for three-dimensional points represented as lists:

```
(define (make-point1 x y z) '(x y z))
```

```
(define (make-point2 x y z) (list x y z))
```

The second constructor works well:

```
> (make-point2 0 0 0)
(0 0 0)
> (make-point2 1 2 3)
(1 2 3)
```

But the first constructor always returns the same incorrect result:

```
> (make-point1 0 0 0)
(x y z)
> (make-point1 1 2 3)
(x y z)
```

Why did this happen? Remember, the single quote instructs the evaluator to interpret what follows literally. Thus, the evaluator interpreted the body of make-point1 as a list of three symbols: x, y, and z. Each time make-point1 is called, this same list is returned.

The same problem occurs with vectors, strings, and pairs. Assume the following definitions have been made:

```
(define x #\a)
(define y #\b)
(define z #\c)
```

Now compare the following evaluations:

```
> (vector x y z)
#(#\a #\b #\c)
> #(x y z)
#(x y z)
> (string x y z)
"abc"
> "xyz"
"xyz"
> (cons x y)
(#\a . #\b)
> '(x . y)
(x . y)
```

2.3.2. Selectors

A **selector** is a procedure that returns the component of a composite value at a given position. In a sense, constructors and selectors are inverse operations. Scheme provides five basic selectors:

```
(car '(v0 . v1))     = v0
```

```
(cdr '(v0 . v1))     = v1
```

```
(list-ref '(v0 ... vn) k)     = vk
```

```
(vector-ref #(v0 ... vn) k)   = vk
```

```
(string-ref "c0...cn" k)      = ck
```

where v_i is any value, k is any unsigned integer, and c_i is any character. Notice the first item in a list, vector, or string has position 0.

In addition, some implementations of Scheme provide selectors for rational and complex numbers:

```
(numerator n/m)    = n
```

```
(denominator n/m) = m
```

```
(real-part a±bi)  = a

(imag-part a±bi)  = ±b
```

$$(\text{magnitude a±bi}) = \sqrt{a^2 + b^2}$$

```
(angle a±bi)      = atan(±b/a)
```

2.3.3. Lists as Pairs

One violation of the abstraction principle has become a tradition among LISP and Scheme programmers. Assume the following definition has been made:

```
(define vowels '(a e i o u))
```

Inside the computer vowels is identical to the pair:

```
(a . (e i o u))
```

Of course the list (e i o u) is represented as the pair (e . (i o u)), therefore vowels is actually represented as the pair:

```
(a . (e . (i . (o . (u . ()))))))
```

The point is, we can use car and cdr to extract the head and tail of vowels, and cons to add new elements to the beginning of vowels:

```
> (car vowels)
a
> (cdr vowels)
(e i o u)
> (cons 'y vowels)
(y a e i o u)
```

Like all the procedures discussed so far, these are nondestructive. The volatile lists produced by cdr and cons disappeared and vowels remained unchanged:

```
> vowels
(a e i o u)
```

Be sure you understand the different behavior of cdr on lists and pairs. The list (a b) is the same as the pair (a . (b)), not the pair (a . b). Therefore cdr returns (b) when applied to (a b), and b when applied to (a . b):

```
> (cdr '(a b))
(b)
> (cdr '(a . b))
b
```

Scheme provides some popular compositions of car and cdr. Assume *p* is any list or pair, then:

```
(cadr p)    = (car (cdr p))
(cdar p)    = (cdr (car p))
(caar p)    = (car (car p))
(cddr p)    = (cdr (cdr p))
(caadr p)   = (car (cadr p))
(cdddr p)   = (cdr (cddr p))
etc.
```

If your implementation of Scheme doesn't predefine the combination of cars and cdrs you need, just define it yourself:

```
(define (cddadr x) (cdr (cdadr x)))
```

Scheme provides other procedures for searching, appending, and computing lengths of sequences. These are described in detail in Appendix 2.2: Sequences.

2.3.4. Example: Association Lists as Records

An **association list (alist)** is a list of pairs called associations or bindings:

```
ALIST ::= (ASSOCIATION ... )
```

An **association** is a pair of the form:

```
ASSOCIATION ::= (ATTRIBUTE . VALUE)
```

where ATTRIBUTE is any Scheme value that identifies a type of attribute (name, height, marital status, etc.) and VALUE is the value of the attribute (Smith, 6'2", single, etc.)

Association lists are useful for representing records, graphs, and tables. Tables and graphs will be discussed later in the chapter. In this section we consider records.

A **record** (called a struct in C) represents the relevant properties of a person, place, or thing. We can represent a record as a list of associations in which ATTRIBUTE is a symbol that names the attribute. For example, a student record might contain the name, social security number, and grade point average of a student:

```
((name . "Picard") (ssn . 998869999) (gpa . 3.75)))
((name . "Moe") (ssn . 002869999) (gpa . 1.5))
((name . "Spock") (ssn . 905869999) (gpa . 3.9))
```

We can view student records as a new domain of composite values:

```
STUDENT ::=
    ((name . STRING) (ssn . INTEGER) (gpa . REAL))
```

As such, it makes sense to define an ADT (constructors and selectors) for the new domain. The constructor for the student domain expects a name, social security number, and grade point average for input:

```scheme
; = record representing a student
(define (make-student name ssn gpa)
   (list (cons 'name name)
         (cons 'ssn ssn)
         (cons 'gpa gpa)))
```

We can use pair and list selectors to implement student selectors:

```scheme
; = name of student
(define (name student)
  (cdar student))
```

```scheme
; = social security number of student
(define (ssn student)
  (cdadr student))
```

```scheme
; = grade point average of student
(define (gpa student)
  (cdaddr student))
```

Because the computer must perform some bookkeeping work each time a procedure is called, it is more efficient to define these selectors as synonyms for the single procedures they call:

```scheme
(define name cdar)
(define ssn cdadr)
(define gpa cdaddr)
```

Of course, we could have used list-ref to select associations. This might have been a better choice, but it is important to gain experience combining car and cdr.

Here are some sample constructions:

```scheme
(define picard (make-student "Picard" 998869999 3.75))
(define moe (make-student "Moe" 002869999 1.5))
(define spock (make-student "Spock" 905869999 3.9))
```

and some sample evaluations:

```scheme
> (ssn spock)
905869999
> (name moe)
"Moe"
> (gpa picard)
3.75
```

Here are some trivial applications of our selectors and constructor:

```scheme
; = #t if student's gpa < 2.0
(define (probation? student)
   (< (gpa student) 2.0))
```

```
; = result of updating student's gpa to new-gpa
(define (update-gpa student new-gpa)
   (make-student
       (name student) (ssn student) new-gpa))
```

Note that updating the gpa of a student record involves constructing a new record identical to the old record except for the new gpa.

2.4. Polymorphic Procedures

A procedure that expects each of its inputs to be from a specific domain is called **monomorphic**. Attempting to apply a monomorphic procedure to inputs from different domains results in a type error. Except for the constructors, all the procedures we have studied so far have been monomorphic.

The body of a **polymorphic procedure** is completely or partially type-independent. In other words, the algorithm doesn't particularly care about the types of its inputs. Therefore a polymorphic procedure appears to work on inputs from a variety of domains. It's easy for programmers to define polymorphic procedures. Here are a few examples; make sure you understand why they are polymorphic:

```
(define (id val) val)          ; the identity procedure
(define (always-0 val) 0)
(define (first val1 val2) val1)
(define (second val1 val2) val2)
(define (make-pair val) (cons val val))
```

Scheme provides several primitive polymorphic predicates that are discussed later.

2.4.1. Equivalence Predicates

In addition to the five monomorphic equality predicates:

```
=, char=?, char-ci=?, string=?, string-ci=?
```

Scheme provides three polymorphic equality predicates:

```
eq?, equal?, eqv?
```

Comparing arbitrary values is controversial because there are two competing notions of equivalence: physical and structural. Two values are **physically equivalent** if they have the same address in the computer's memory, i.e., if they are literally the same object. Two values are **structurally equivalent** if they have the same mathematical structure, or, at the risk of oversimplifying, if they look the same when printed by the Scheme interpreter. The eq? predicate tests for physical equivalence, while the equal? predicate tests for structural equivalence.

Predicting when two values are physically equivalent is tricky. Two composite values are not physically equivalent if they are created by separate calls to a constructor. For example, assume the following definitions have been made:

```
(define vals1 (list 1 2 3))
(define vals2 (list 1 2 3))
(define vals3 vals2)
```

All three lists are structurally equivalent. In addition, vals2 is physically equivalent to vals3, but vals2 and vals1 are not physically equivalent because they were created by separate calls to the list constructor:

```
> (eq? vals1 vals2)
#f
> (eq? vals2 vals3)
#t
```

Structurally equivalent literal values may or may not be physically equivalent depending on the Scheme implementation:

```
> (eq? '(1 2 3) '(1 2 3))
unspecified
> (eq? 5 5)
unspecified
```

The empty list, #f, and structurally equivalent symbols are the notable exceptions. These are unique objects in all Scheme implementations:

```
> (eq? 'cat 'CAT) ; symbols are case insensitive
#t
> (eq? #f #f)
#t
> (eq? '() '())
#t
```

The eqv? predicate is a hybrid between eq? and equal? For simple values (numbers, Booles, chars, symbols) it tests for structural equivalence, but for composite values (lists, strings, vectors, pairs) it tests for physical equivalence.

2.4.2. The not and null? Predicates

The eq? predicate is normally used for comparing symbols. Because #f and the empty list are unique values, Scheme provides special polymorphic procedures for recognizing them:

```
(not val)   = (eq? val #f)
(null? val) = (eq? val '())
```

Although #f is a unique object in Scheme, in most contexts any value other than #f can be used instead of #t. Let's call any value other than #f *unfalse*. We can design a simple predicate to test for unfalse values:

```
(define (unfalse? val) (not (not val)))
```

2.4.3. Recognition Predicates

Another category of polymorphic predicates are recognizers. A **recognizer** usually has a name like domain? and returns #t if its input belongs to domain, and #f otherwise. There are fifteen primitive recognizers:

> symbol?, number?, Boolean?, char?, pair?, list?, procedure?, vector?, string?, input-port?, output-port?, integer?, real?, complex?, rational?

Recognizing values can get tricky. Make sure you understand the following evaluations:

```
> (pair? '(a e i o u))
#t                              ; nonempty lists are pairs!
> (pair? '())
#f                              ; but not the empty list!
> (real? 1)
#t                              ; all integers are reals
> (integer? 1.0)
#t                              ; representation independence
> (integer? 1.1)
#f
> (procedure? '+)
#f                              ; '+ is a symbol
> (procedure? +)
#t
> (boolean? '())
#f                              ; = #t in PC-Scheme!
```

2.4.4. Example: Searching Association Lists

Tables

Related data can often be organized into a table. For example, the following table represents scores on some recent Star Fleet Academy math tests:

NAME	TEST1	TEST2	TEST3
Picard	92	90	89
Moe	34	37	36
Spock	99	100	99

Each column in the table can be represented by an association list:

```
(define test1
   '(("Picard" . 92) ("Moe" . 34) ("Spock" . 99)))

(define test2
   '(("Picard" . 90) ("Moe" . 37) ("Spock" . 100)))

 (define test3
   '(("Picard" . 89) ("Moe" . 36) ("Spock" . 99)))
```

In this association, ATTRIBUTE is the name of the student and VALUE is the associated test score. The entire table can be represented by an association list of association lists:

```
(define tests
   (list (cons 'test1 test1)
         (cons 'test2 test2)
         (cons 'test3 test3)))
```

In this case ATTRIBUTE is an identifier that names VALUE, the table of test scores.

Scheme provides three procedures for searching association lists:

```
assoc, assq, assv
```

Each expects an association list and a key as input:

```
(ass* key assocs)
   = the left-most member a of assocs with (car a)
   equivalent to key. Depending on *, equivalent means eq?,
   eqv?, or equal?
   = #f, otherwise
```

Assoc uses equal? to compare keys, while assv uses eqv? and assq uses eq? Here are some sample evaluations:

```
> (assoc "Moe" test1)
("Moe" . 34)
> (cdr (assoc "Moe" test2))
37
> (assv 'test2 tests)
(("Picard" . 90) ("Moe" . 37) ("Spock" . 100))
> (assv "Moe" test2)
unspecified
> (cdr (assoc "Spock" (cdr (assq 'test3 tests))))
99
```

The value of (assv "Moe" test2) was unspecified because eqv? was used to compare "Moe" with the "Moe" inside test2. In some versions of Scheme this returns 37, while in other versions #f may be returned.

Graphs

The graph of a procedure proc is the set of points (x, y) in the plane such that $y = $ (proc x). For example, the graph of the square procedure is the parabola:

$$\{(x, y) \mid y = x^2\}$$

An association list can be used to represent the graphs of procedures with only finitely many inputs. For example, suppose we want to implement a procedure that translates digit names to their corresponding numeric value:

```
> (string->digit "one")
1
> (string->digit "three")
3
> (string->digit "nine")
9
```

This procedure only has ten valid inputs: "zero" to "nine." This suggests we could represent its graph as an association list:

```
(define string->digit-graph
  '(("zero" . 0) ("one" . 1) ("two" . 2)
    ("three" . 3) ("four" . 4) ("five" . 5)
    ("six" . 6) ("seven" . 7) ("eight" . 8)
    ("nine" . 9)))
```

We can implement the procedure as a simple search of the graph:

```
; = coercion of string to corresponding digit
(define (string->digit string)
  (cdr (assoc string string->digit-graph)))
```

Could assv have been used in this definition instead of assoc?

2.5. Meta-Procedures

Map and apply are examples of **meta-procedures** because each expects an arbitrary procedure and a list as input:

```
(apply proc vals) = result of applying proc to vals

(map proc vals)
    = list formed by applying proc to each member of vals.
```

In the case of apply, the list is treated as arguments to the procedure parameter:

```
> (apply + '(2 3 4 5))
14
```

```
> (apply lcm '(2 3 4 5))
60
> (apply cons '(x 2))
(x . 2)
> (apply append '((1 2 3) (4 5 6) (7 8 9)))
(1 2 3 4 5 6 7 8 9)
```

Apply is useful when we may not know the procedure or inputs in advance. For example, to compute the average of a list of numbers we divide the sum of the list by its length. But how can we compute the sum of a list of unknown numbers? The solution is to use apply:

```
; = average of numbers in the list nums
(define (average nums)
    (/ (apply + nums) (length nums)))
```

As another example, here's a simple predicate that determines if a list of names is sorted:

```
; = #t if names is sorted
(define (sorted? names) (apply string-ci<=? names))
```

If map's procedure argument expects two or more inputs, then two or more list arguments of equal length must be provided to map[5] :

```
> (map cons '(1 2 3) '(4 5 6))
((1 . 4) (2 . 5) (3 . 6))
> (map + '(1 2 3) '(4 5 6))
(5 7 9)
```

Assume that test scores are recorded as association lists of the form:

```
TEST ::= ((STUDENT . SCORE) ... )
STUDENT ::= STRING
SCORE ::= REAL
```

We can use map with the average procedure defined earlier to compute the average of arbitrary tests:

```
; = average score of test
(define (test-avg test)
    (average (map cdr test)))
```

We can use the map procedure to define two useful predicates. Both expect a predicate pred? and a list vals as input:

```
(all? pred? vals)
    = #t, if (pred? v) for all v in vals
    = #f, otherwise
```

---

[5] *Warning*: This version of map doesn't work in TI PC-Scheme.

```
(some? pred? vals)
  = #t, if (pred? v) for some vals
  = #f, otherwise
```

The all? predicate converts vals into a list of booleans by mapping pred? along vals. #t is returned if #f is not a member of the mapped list:

```
; = #t if for all v in vals (red? v) = #t
(define (all? pred? vals)
   (not (member? #f (map pred? vals))))
```

The some? predicate also converts vals into a list of booleans using map, but returns #t in case #t is a member of the mapped list:

```
; = #t if some (pred? v) = #t for some v in vals
(define (some? pred? vals)
   (member? #t (map pred? vals)))
```

The member? predicate is defined using Scheme's member procedure, which is defined in Appendix 2.2: Sequences:

```
(define (member? val vals)
   (unfalse? (member val vals)))
```

We can use these predicates to implement many other useful predicates. For example, not all lists can be coerced into strings, only lists of characters. Therefore, it might be useful to have a predicate that determines if a list consists of only characters:

```
; = #t if all members of list vals are characters
(define (char-list? vals)
   (all? char? vals))
```

Suppose we need a predicate that returns #t if its input is a string containing a vowel. We can coerce the string into a list, then use some? with the vowel? predicate defined earlier:

```
; = #t if string contains a vowel
(define (contains-vowel? string)
   (some? vowel? (string->list string)))
```

Appendices

Appendix 2.1. Mathematics in Scheme

Arithmetic

All numbers can be combined by addition (+), subtraction (−), multiplication (*), and division (/). The addition and multiplication operators can combine arbitrarily long sequences of numbers:

```
> (+ 1 2 3 4 5 6 7 8 9 10)
55
> (* 1 2 3 4 5 6 7 8 9 10)
3628800
```

Even a single input or no inputs at all are allowed:

```
> (+ 2)   ; implicit second input is 0
2
> (* 2)   ; implicit second input is 1
2
> (+)     ; implicit inputs are both 0
0
> (*)     ; implicit inputs are both 1
1
```

Division and subtraction normally combine pairs of numbers:

```
> (/ 5 3)
5/3
> (/ 5.6 7.9)
.7088607594936708
> (- 3 8.2)
-5.199999999999999
```

With one input division and subtraction compute multiplicative and additive inverses respectively (i.e., $1/z$ and $-z$):

```
> (- 5.2)
-5.2
> (/ 7)
1/7
> (/ 7.0)
.142857142857143
```

Of course, all four operations can combine numbers from any of the number domains:

```
> (+ 2 3/5 4.9 5+6i 3e2)
312.5+6i
> (* 2 3/5 4.9 5+6i 3e2)
8820.+10584.i
> (/ 3/5 4+2i)
3/25-3/50i
> (- 3/5 5+6i)
-22/5-6i
> (- 4-3i)
-4+3i
> (/ 4+2i)
1/5-1/10i
```

Order and Equivalence Predicates

All numbers can be compared using Scheme's = and zero? predicates. Assume z_i and z are numbers:

```
(= z1 ... zn)
    = #t, if z1 = ... = zn
    = #f, otherwise.
```

```
(zero? z)
    = #t, if z = 0
    = #f, otherwise.
```

The following predicates are based on the usual ordering of the real numbers. Assume r_i and r are reals:

```
(< r1 ... rn)
    = #t, if r1 < ... < rn
    = #f, otherwise.
```

```
(<= r1 ... rn)
    = #t, if r1 ≤ ... ≤ rn
    = #f, otherwise.
```

```
(> r1 ... rn)
    = #t, if r1 > ... > rn
    = #f, otherwise.
```

```
(>= r1 ... rn)
    = #t, if r1 ≥ ... ≥ rn
    = #f, otherwise.
```

```
(positive? r)
    = #t, if r > 0
    = #f, otherwise.
```

```
(negative? r)
    = #t, if r < 0
    = #f, otherwise.
```

```
(max r1 ... rn) = largest ri.
```

```
(min r1 ... rn) = smallest ri.
```

```
(abs r) = |r|.
```

Order predicates are restricted to reals because the complex numbers don't have a "usual" order.

Comparing Characters and Strings

An **ordered domain** is any domain that comes equipped with a natural ordering. REAL is not Scheme's only ordered domain. STRING and CHAR also have natural orderings derived from the ASCII codes of characters.

Assume c_i is a character, $c_i <_A c_j$ means that the ASCII code of c_i is less than the ASCII code of c_j, and $c_i =_A c_j$ means the ASCII code of c_i is the same as the ASCII code for c_j. (Note: The order of ASCII codes for letters and digits agrees with the usual alphabetic order.) Scheme provides the following predicates for comparing characters:

```
(char=? c1 ... cn) = #t, if c1 =A ... =A cn
                   = #f, otherwise.

(char<? c1 ... cn) = #t if c1 <A ... <A cn
                   = #f otherwise.

(char>? c1 ... cn) = #t if c1 >A ... >A cn
                   = #f otherwise.

(char<=? c1 ... cn) = #t if c1 ≤A ... ≤A cn
                    = #f otherwise.

(char>=? c1 ... cn) = #t if c1 ≥A ... ≥A cn
                    = #f otherwise.

(char>? c1 ... cn) = #t if c1 >A ... >A cn
                   = #f otherwise.
```

Scheme provides similar predicates for comparing strings. Assume that s_i is a string, $s_i <_s s_j$ means s_i is a prefix of s_j, or if c_i is the first character in s_i that's different from the corresponding character c_j in s_j, then $c_i <_A c_j$. If s_i and s_j are identical, then we write $s_i =_s s_j$.

```
(string=? s1 ... sn) = #t, if s1 =s ... =s sn
                     = #f, otherwise.

(string<? s1 ... sn) = #t if s1 <s ... <s sn
                     = #f otherwise.

(string>? s1 ... sn) = #t if s1 >s ... >s sn
                     = #f otherwise.
```

```
(string<=? s1 ... sn) = #t if s1 ≤s ... ≤s sn
                      = #f otherwise.

(string>=? s1 ... sn) = #t if s1 ≥s ... ≥s sn
                      = #f otherwise.

(string>? s1 ... sn) = #t if s1 >s ... >s sn
                     = #f otherwise.
```

Scheme also provides case-insensitive (ci) versions of these predicates:

```
char-ci=?, char-ci<?, char-ci>?,
char-ci<=?, char-ci>=?
string-ci=?, string-ci<?, string-ci>?,
string-ci<=?, string-ci>=?
```

Here are some sample evaluations:

```
> (string=? "HeLlO" "hElLo")
#f
> (string-ci=? "HeLlO" "hElLo")
#t
> (char-ci<? #\a #\Z)
#t
> (char<? #\a #\Z)
#f
> (char<? #\tab #\# #\2 #\5 #\? #\Z #\a #\rubout)
#t
> (string<? "" " " "a" "aaa" "ab")
#t
```

Divisibility

Of all the number domains, only the integers are not closed under division. For example, 1 and 2 are integers, but 1/2 is not. This makes the question of which integers divide a given integer critical. Scheme provides seven basic procedures for determining various divisibility properties. Assume n, m, n_1, ..., n_k are integers:

```
(quotient n m) = truncation of n/m

(remainder n m)= n - m * (quotient n m)

(modulo n m)   = integer congruent to n modulo m

(gcd n1 ... nk)
   = greatest common divisor of n1 ... nk
```

```
(lcm n1 ... nk)    = least common multiple of n1 ... nk

(odd? n)  = #t, if n is odd
          = #f, otherwise

(even? n) = #t, if n is even
          = #f, otherwise
```

These procedures require further explanation. Number theory (i.e., arithmetic) begins with the long division algorithm every child learns in elementary school, but which can be stated more pretentiously as a theorem:

Theorem (Euclid) *For any two integers* m *and* n, *if* $n \neq 0$, *then there are unique integers* q *and* r *(called the* quotient *and* remainder *of* m *and* n *respectively) such that* $0 \leq |r| < |n|$, r *and* m *have the same sign, and* $m = (n * q) + r$.

Scheme provides the quotient and remainder procedures for computing q and r given m and n as inputs:

```
> (quotient -14 3)
-4
> (remainder -14 3)
-2
```

We can use Scheme's odd? and even? predicates to determine whether an integer is divisible by two, or, more generally, we can use the remainder procedure to determine if any integer divides another:

```
; = #t if m divides n
(define (divides? m n)
   (zero? (remainder m n)))
```

Congruence

If the difference of two integers m and n is divisible by an integer k, we say that m is **congruent** to n modulo k, and we write:

$$m \equiv n \pmod k$$

We could express this as a Scheme procedure:

```
; = #t if m is congruent to n mod k
(define (congruent? m n k)
   (divides? (- m n) k))
```

A basic theorem regarding congruence is:

Theorem *Given any two integers* m *and* k, *there is a unique integer* n *between* 0 *and* n *such that* $m \equiv n \pmod k$.

For example:

```
14  ≡ 2 (mod 3)    ; m = 14, k = 3 & n = 2
-14 ≡ 1 (mod 3)    ; m = -14, k = 3 & n = 1
14  ≡ -1 (mod -3)  ; m = 14, k = -3 & n = -1
```

Scheme provides the modulo procedure for computing n given m and k:

```
> (modulo -14 -3)
-2
> (modulo -14 3)
1
```

The modulo procedure can be useful for implementing modular arithmetic, i.e., arithmetic that "wraps around" when answers get too big:

```
; = m + n mod k
(define (mod+ m n k) (modulo (+ m n) k))

; = m * n mod k
(define (mod* m n k) (modulo (* m n) k))

; = m - n mod k
(define (mod- m n k) (modulo (- m n) k))

; = m/n mod k
(define (mod/ m n k) (modulo (quotient m n) k))
```

For example, suppose we want to add the hours on a military clock (i.e., $0 \le hour \le 23$). We use the "modulo" implementations of +, *, and −:

```
; = time h hours after time t
(define (hours+ t h) (mod+ t h 24))
```

For another example, binary arithmetic is arithmetic restricted to the domain of binary values, called **bits**:

```
BIT ::= 0 | 1
```

Curiously, the bit 1 is its own additive and multiplicative inverse, i.e., $1 + 1 = 0$ and $1 * 1 = 1$. We can implement bit versions of +, *, −, and /:

```
= binary sum of bits b1 and b2
(define (bit+ b1 b2) (mod+ b1 b2 2))
```

Here are some sample evaluations:

```
> (hours+ 9 10)
19
> (hours+ 9 19)
4
```

```
> (hours+ 20 20)
16
> (bit+ 1 1)
0
```

Obviously the modulo and remainder procedures are very similar. In fact:

$$|(\text{remainder } m\ n)| = |(\text{modulo } m\ n)|$$

where (remainder m n) takes the sign of m, while (modulo m n) takes the sign of n.

Common Multiples and Divisors

A common divisor of an integer sequence n_1, n_2, ..., n_k is any positive integer n that divides each number in the sequence, i.e., for each i:

```
> (divides? nᵢ n)
#t
```

The greatest common divisor of n_1, n_2, ..., n_k is the largest of all the common divisors of n_1, n_2, ..., n_k. Scheme provides a procedure for computing greatest common divisors:

```
> (gcd 32 48 -60)
4
> (gcd 20 30 40)
10
```

Two integers are relatively prime if their greatest common divisor is 1. We can implement this definition as a Scheme predicate:

```
; = #t if m & n are relatively prime
(define (rel-prime? m n)
   (= 1 (gcd m n)))
```

A common multiple of an integer sequence n_1, n_2, ..., n_k is any positive integer n that can be divided by each number in the sequence, i.e., for each i:

```
> (divides? n nᵢ)
#t
```

The least common multiple of n_1, n_2, ..., n_k is the least of all the common multiples of n_1, n_2, ..., n_k. Scheme provides a procedure for computing least common multiples:

```
> (lcm 32 48 -60)
480
> (lcm 20 30 40)
120
```

Logs and Exponents

Logarithms and exponents play an important role in growth and decay problems. Scheme provides procedures for computing logs and exponents to the base e, where e is the irrational number approximated by $e = 2.718281828459045$.

```
(exp z)  = e^z.
(log z)  = ln(z).
```

If e isn't a predefined constant, we can define it ourselves as follows:

```
(define e (exp 1))    ; since e^1 = e
```

Some implementations of Scheme provide a procedure for computing exponents to an arbitrary base:

```
(expt a b)  = a^b
```

Unfortunately, there is no corresponding procedure for computing logarithms to an arbitrary base. Instead, we must define our own using the formula:

$$\log_x(y) = \frac{\log_e(y)}{\log_e(x)}$$

Translating this formula into Scheme is simple. We call it logt to remind us of its relationship with expt:

```
; = log y base x
(define (logt x y) (/ (log y) (log x)))
```

Of course exponents and bases can be decimals, ratios, even complex numbers:

```
> (expt 2 3)
8
> (expt 9 1/2)
3.0000000000000004
> (expt 27 (/ 1 3))
2.999999999999996
> (expt 2+3i 1+1i)
-.8636068988831277+1.03688939691477763i
> (expt 25 1/2)
4.99999999999999
> (expt 2 1000)
10715086071862673209484250490600018105614048117055336074437
50388370351051124936122493198378815695858127594672917553146682
51871452856923140435984577574698574803934567774824230985421074
605062371141877954182153046474983581941267 3
```

The last example shows some implementations of Scheme use multiple-precision arithmetic.

Scheme also provides a square root procedure:

```
(sqrt z) = | √z | .
```

Amazingly, this procedure even works on negative numbers:

```
> (sqrt -1)
+i
```

We don't really need a square root procedure. Recall that the nth root of z is $z^{1/n}$. We can use this formula to define a procedure for computing nth roots:

```
; = z^(1/n)
(define (nth-root z n) (expt z (/ n)))
```

Example

Growth and decay problems concern computing the size of a population after n cycles of growth or decay at a given rate. The population can be organisms, radioactive carbon atoms, dollars, or anything else. Computing compounded interest is a classical example.

We can compute the value V of an investment of P dollars invested for n years at an annual interest rate of r compounded annually using the formula:

$$V = P(1 + r)^n$$

Translating this into Scheme is easy using expt:

```
; = value of $p investment at rate r after n periods
(define (value p r n)
   (* p (expt (+ 1 r) n)))
```

Trigonometry

Trigonometric functions are important for modeling harmonic motion (vibration, oscillation, etc.). Scheme provides the usual assortment of trigonometric procedures. All of these procedures assume that angles are measured in radians:

```
(sin r)   = sin(r)
(cos r)   = cos(r)
(tan r)   = tan(r)
```

The atan procedure accepts one or two inputs. Assume z is a complex number and x and y are real numbers:

```
(atan z) = arctan(z)
(atan x y)  = arctan(x+yi)
```

We can easily define csc, sec, and cot procedures:

```
; = csc of z radians
(define (csc z) (/ (sin z)))
```

```
; = cot of z radians
(define (cot z) ???)

; = sec of z radians
(define (sec z) ???)
```

If pi isn't a predefined constant in the implementation of Scheme we are using, we can define it ourselves as follows:

```
(define pi (acos -1))    ; because (cos pi) = -1
```

Appendix 2.2. Sequences

Scheme provides several groups of procedures for analyzing, combining, and dissecting sequences.

Appending Sequences

Appending two sequences means concatenating them into a single sequence. Scheme provides primitive procedures for appending lists and strings, but not vectors (this is left as an exercise). Assume $vals_i$ is a list and str_i is a string:

```
(append vals1 ... valsn)
   = the list formed by concatenating val1 ... valn.

(string-append str1 ... strn)
   = the string formed by concatenating str1 ... strn.
```

Here are some sample calls:

```
> (string-append "Is" tan" "bul")
Istanbul
> (append '(a) '(e) '(i) '(o u))
(a e i o u)
```

Of course we can use cons to add an element to the beginning of a list, but Scheme provides no procedure for adding an element to the end of a list. However, we can implement such a procedure using append:

```
; = result of adding val to end of vals
(define (cons-last val vals)
   (append vals (list val)))
```

Notice that it was necessary to coerce val into a list before applying append. Unlike cons, append expects all of its inputs to be lists.

Computing Lengths of Sequences

Scheme provides procedures for computing lengths of strings, vectors, and lists:

```
(length vals)         = the number of members in vals
(vector-length vec)   = the number of members in vec
(string-length str)   = the number of characters in str
```

where vals is a list, vec is a vector, and str is a string. Here are some sample evaluations:

```
> (string-length "Hello")
5
> (length '((1 2 3) (4 5 6)))
2
> (vector-length #(a e i o u))
5
```

Why doesn't Scheme provide a procedure for computing lengths of pairs?

Extracting Subsequences

The tail of a sequence is the sequence less some of its initial members. For example, the tails of the string "orange" are:

"orange", "range", "ange", "nge", "ge", "e", and "".

The tails of the vector #(a e i o u) are:

#(a e i o u), #(e i o u), #(i o u), #(o u), #(u), and #().

The tails of the list (a e i o u) are:

(a e i o u), (e i o u), (i o u), (o u), (u), and ().

Scheme provides a wide variety of procedures for extracting list tails. We have already seen that the procedures cdr, cddr, cdddr, etc. can be used for this purpose. Some implementations of Scheme also provide a procedure called list-tail that extracts the tail of a list beginning at a given integer position $n \geq 0$:

```
(list-tail vals n)
   = the tail of vals beginning in position n
```

Assume the following definition has been made:

```
(define vowels '(a e i o u))
```

Here are some sample calls to list-tail. Remember, the first item of a list is in position 0:

```
> (list-tail vowels 3)
(o u)
> (list-tail vowels 0)
(a e i o u)
> (list-tail vowels 100)
()
```

Additionally, Scheme provides three procedures for extracting tails beginning at some specific member:

> member, memv, memq

These procedures all work the same way:

```
(mem* val vals)
   = the tail of vals beginning with the left-most member
   equivalent to val. (depending on *, equivalent means eq?,
   eqv?, or equal?)
   = #f, if no match is found.
```

The three procedures differ in the way val is compared to members of vals. Member uses equal?, memv uses eqv?, and memq uses eq? This can lead to some confusion as the next example shows:

```
> (member "Al" '("Rolf" "Al" "Lars"))
("Al" "Lars")
> (memq "Al" '("Rolf" "Al" "Lars"))
unspecified                ;"Al" may not be eqv? to "Al" in
vals
> (member 'Al '(Rolf Al Lars))
(Al Lars)         ; Al is equal? to a list member
> (member "Al" '(Rolf Al Lars))
#f              ; vals is a list of symbols, not strings
> (memq 'Al '(Rolf Al Lars))
(Al Lars)    ; equal? = eqv? for symbols
```

People often mistake the member procedures for predicates. This isn't true, but we can use them to define corresponding predicates. The idea is if val is a member of vals, then (member val vals) returns a nonempty list; otherwise it returns #f. Hence:

```
; = #t if val is in vals
(define (member? val vals)
   (unfalse? (member val vals)))
```

We can use this predicate to define others. For example, assume the following definition is made:

```
(define vowels
   '(#\a #\A #\e #\E #\i #\I #\o #\O #\u #\U))

(define punctuation '(#\. #\, #\; #\: #\! #\? #\-))
```

To determine if a character is a vowel or a punctuation mark, we only need to search the appropriate list:

```
(define (vowel? char)
   (member? char vowels))
```

```
(define (punctuation? char)
   (member? char punctuation))
```

Oddly, Scheme doesn't provide procedures for extracting the tails of vectors. This is not a problem because we can coerce any vector to a list, extract the tail, then coerce the result back to a vector. For example:

```
; = tail of vec beginning at val
(define (vector-member val vec)
   (list->vector (member val (vector->list vec))))

; = tail of vec beginning at position pos
(define (vector-tail vec pos)
   (list->vector (list-tail (vector->list vec) pos)))
```

Substrings

We don't need string-tail because Scheme provides a more powerful procedure for extracting substrings from strings given the start and end position of the desired substring. Assume n and m are natural numbers:

```
(substring string n m) =
   substring of string beginning in position n and ending in
   position m - 1.
```

Here are some sample evaluations:

```
> (substring "Apple" 2 4)
"pl"
> (substring "Apple" 0 3)
"Apl"
```

Notice that the substring begins with the character in the position indicated by the first position input, but ends with the character one position before the second position input. We can use the sublist procedure to define procedures for extracting prefixes and suffixes of strings:

```
; = prefix of string ending at position pos - 1
(define (prefix string pos)
   (substring string 0 pos))

; = suffix of string beginning at position pos
(define (suffix string pos)
   (substring string pos (string-length string)))
```

These procedures can be used to develop predicates that test if one string is a prefix or suffix of another:

```
; = #t if string2 is a prefix of string1
(define (prefix? string1 string2)
   (string=?
      string2
      (prefix string1 (string-length string2))))
```

```
; = #t if string2 is a suffix of string1
(define (suffix? string1 string2)
   (string=?
      string2
      (suffix
         string1
         (- (string-length string1)
            (string-length string2)))))
```

Sublists

Assume vals is a list, and start and end are unsigned integers such that $0 \leq$ start $\leq$ end $<$ (length vals). Then:

```
(sublist vals start end)
   = the sublist beginning at position
   start, and ending at position (end - 1).
```

Unfortunately, Scheme does not provide this procedure. How can we define it? We could try to combine the substring procedure with the coercions between lists and strings:

```
; = sublist between positions start and (end - 1)
(define (sublist vals start end)
   (string->list
      (substring (list->string vals) start end)))
```

This works pretty well when vals is a list of characters:

```
> (sublist '(#\0 #\1 #\2 #\3 #\4 #\5 #\6 #\7) 2 5)
(#\2 #\3 #\4)
```

But, of course, it doesn't work at all if vals contains noncharacters:

```
> (sublist '(0 1 2 3 4 5 6 7) 2 5)
error: bad input to list->string
```

Let's start again using the top down approach. We can use list-tail to chop off the unwanted members between position 0 and position start:

```
(list-tail vals start)
```

How can we lose the members from position end to the last position of the list? This would be easy if we had a procedure that extracted list prefixes. First, let's be clear about what a list prefix is. A **list prefix** should be a list consisting of all but a few of the last members of a list. For example, the prefixes of (a e i o u) are:

```
(a e i o u)
(a e i o)
(a e i)
(a e)
(a)
()
```

The list-prefix procedure can be specified by:

```
(list-prefix vals pos) =
    the prefix of vals from position 0 up to position pos.
```

We can use this to implement sublist. In this case the input to list-prefix will be the tail: (list-tail vals start). We will want to chop off the elements of this list beginning with pos = (end − 1) - start:

```
; = sublist between positions start and (end - 1)
(define (sublist vals start end)
    (list-prefix (list-tail vals start)
                 (- (- end 1) start)))
```

Unfortunately, Scheme does not provide a procedure for extracting list prefixes. Let's write a procedure to do this. The form of our definition will be:

```
; = prefix of vals ending at position pos
(define (list-prefix vals pos) ???) ; stub
```

Our plan is to reverse the result of applying list-tail to the reversed input list:

```
(reverse (list-tail (reverse vals) position2))
```

What should position2 be? How is it related to the position parameter? Observe that an element in position k of a length n list is in position $n - (k + 1)$ of the reversed list. For example, o is in position 3 of vowels, but in position $5 - (3 + 1) = 1$ of (reverse vowels). Therefore, if we wish to retain the first k members of an arbitrary input list vals, we will want to retain the last $n - (k + 1)$ members of (reverse vals), where n is (length vals):

```
; = prefix of vals ending at position pos
(define (list-prefix vals pos)
    (reverse (list-tail (reverse vals)
                        (- (length vals) (+ pos 1)))))
```

Other Applications of list-prefix

We can use our list-prefix procedure to implement many standard list operations. For example, to remove an item in position k of a list, we merely append the prefix of the list up to position k to the tail of the list beginning in position $k + 1$:

```
; = result of removing item at position k from vals
(define (remove vals k)
   (append (list-prefix vals (- k 1))
           (list-tail vals (+ k 1))))
```

How can we insert an item into position pos of a list vals or replace the item in position pos of vals with a new item:

```
; = result of inserting item at position pos in vals
(define (insert vals item pos) ???)


; = result of replacing member at
;   position pos by item in vals
(define (replace vals item pos) ???)
```

Optional Parameters

The **arity** of a procedure is the length of its parameter list. A **0-ary procedures** has arity = 0. Scheme's exit and transcript-off are examples of 0-ary procedures. Unary procedures have arity = 1. Car, cdr, length, abs, and number? are examples of **unary procedures**. Binary procedures have arity = 2. Cons, eq?, remainder, modulo, apply, and list-ref are examples of **binary procedures**. A **3-ary procedure** has arity = 3. Substring is an example of a 3-ary procedure.

Procedures with higher arities are rare. However, there are some procedures that accept any number of inputs. We call these procedures *n*-ary procedures. Lcm, gcd, list, string, vector, +, *, <, and max are examples of *n*-ary procedures.

Scheme provides a mechanism that allows programmers to define *n*-ary procedures. The last parameter of a procedure is an options parameter if it is preceded by a period. (A space must separate the period and the parameter.) If the number of arguments exceeds the number of parameters, then the interpreter gathers the left-over arguments into a list and binds this list to the options parameter. Otherwise, the options parameter is bound to the empty list.

As an example, let's write an n-ary version of the average procedure:

```
; = average of all parameters
(define (avg . nums) (average nums))
```

The avg procedure can be called with any number of inputs:

```
> (avg 3 4 5)
4
> (avg 5 6 7 8 9)
7
```

Let's rewrite the rel-prime? predicate defined earlier as an *n*-ary procedure. Recall, a list of integers is relatively prime if their gcd = 1:

```
; = #t if all parameters are relatively prime
(define (rel-prime? . ints) (= 1 (apply gcd ints)))
```

Here are some sample calls:

```
> (rel-prime? 2 4 6 8 10)
#f
> (rel-prime? 3 5 7 22 13 17)
#t
```

Although Scheme provides "and" and "or" procedures, they are control structures that won't be introduced until the next chapter. In the meantime, we can define our own versions using the some? and all? predicates defined earlier:

```
; = #t if all parameters _ #f
(define (and? . vals) (all? unfalse? vals))
```

```
; = #t if some parameters _ #f
(define (or? . vals) (some? unfalse? vals)))
```

Recall that a value is unfalse if it is different from #f:

```
(define (unfalse? val) (not (not val)))
```

For example, we can use our or? predicate to determine if a number b is between two other numbers a and c:

```
; = #t if b is between a and c
(define (between? a b c)
   (or? (<= a b c) (<= c b a)))
```

As another example, we can combine apply, or?, and reverse to determine if a list of strings is sorted:

```
; = #t if parameters are sorted
(define (sorted? . strings)
   (or? (apply string<? strings)
        (apply string<? (reverse strings))))
```

Here are some sample evaluations:

```
> (sorted? "cat" "cow" "dog" "rat")
#t
> (sorted? "ray" "fish" "bat")
#t
> (sorted? "cat" "cow" "bat" "dog")
#f
```

Appendix 2.3. The Edit-Test-Debug Cycle

When a Scheme session ends, all declared bindings stored in the Global Environment disappear. At the start of the next session the definitions that created these bindings will have to be repeated. This process is simple if the definitions have been saved in a definition file.

A **definition file** (also called a program or source file) is a text file containing Scheme definitions. The definitions in a definition file can be loaded into Scheme either using special editor commands or Scheme's load procedure. Assume defs.scm is the name of a definition file,[6] then:

```
(load "defs.scm") = an unspecified value. As a side effect,
    all definitions in defs.scm are realized.
```

Warning: Definition files and transcript files are different. Do not attempt to load a transcript file.

The **edit-test-debug cycle** describes the structure of a typical Scheme session. It is shown in Figure 2.4.

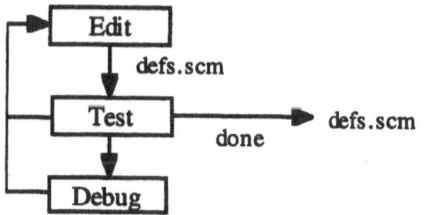

Figure 2.4

During the **edit phase**, programmers use an editor to create and modify definitions in a definition file. At the beginning of the **test phase**, the definition file is loaded into the Scheme interpreter using the load procedure or special editor load commands. The interpreter is used to test each definition loaded. If no problems are revealed, the session ends with a completed definition file, or the programmer returns to the edit phase to write more definitions. If testing reveals a bug, the **debug phase** is entered. Most implementations of Scheme provide special programs called **debuggers** to help locate bugs. The editor, interpreter, and debugger, together with a few other software tools, are collectively called the **programming environment**.

The number of times a programmer loops through the cycle depends on the size of the program being developed. The time it takes to loop through one cycle can range from a few seconds to a few weeks and can depend on the programming environment being used.

---

[6] The part after "." is called the file's extension and usually indicates the type of the file. We use the *scm* extension (others simply use *s*) to indicate that a file is a Scheme program file.

Many versions of Scheme allow programmers to switch between the interpreter, an editor, and a debugger without terminating the session.

Problems

Solutions to the following problems are to be given in applicative Scheme; do not use procedures or special forms discussed in subsequent chapters. You may use the definitions given in this chapter and solutions to other problems in this chapter. (You will have to include these definitions in your definition file so that you can test your definitions.) You may also define any supporting procedures you need. You are *not* required to validate inputs, i.e., assume all inputs are valid. (Input validation begins in Chapter 3.) Be sure to test all your definitions.

Problem 2.1.

Assume the following definitions have been made:

```
(define x 100)
(define y 200)
(define z 300)
(define dog "dog")
(define graph
    '(("one" . 1) ("two" . 2) ("three" . 3)))
```

Evaluate the following expressions. If they contain errors, explain them. If their values are unspecified in Essential Scheme, indicate this with a question mark. Use your Scheme interpreter to check your work, but be careful; your interpreter may not be 100% compliant with Essential Scheme.

Problem 2.1.1

```
a. (eq? "hello" "hello")
b. (assoc "one" graph)
c. (member "one" graph)
d. (real? 'x)
e. (eq? 'hello 'hello)
f. (assq "one" graph)
g. (real? x)
h. (eqv? 5 (+ 2 3))
```

Problem 2.1.2

```
a. (pair? '(1 2 3 4 5))              f. (eq? dog "dog")
b. (eq? dog (string #\d #\o #\g))    g. (eq? 5 5)
c. (char-ci=? #\c 'c)                h. (eq? 'dog 'dog)
d. (+ 2 3 (display (+ 4 1)))
e. (reverse (vector->list #(2 3 4)))
```

Problem 2.1.3

```
a. (reverse (vector->list #(2 3 4)))
b. (member 'i '(a e i o u))
c. (member #\i '(a e i o u))
d. (memq 2 '(1 2 3 4 5))
e. (string=? dog 'dog)
f. (string=? dog (string #\d #\o #\g))
```

Problem 2.1.4

```
a. (map car '((a . b) (c . d) (e . f)))
b. (apply cons '((1 . 2) (2 . 3)))
c. (+ (truncate -4.2)
      (floor -4.2)
      (gcd 4 12 22)
      (lcm 3 4 6))
d. (eq? (string #\h #\e #\l #\l #\o)
        (string #\h #\e #\l #\l #\o))
e. (+ (list-ref (list x y z) 0) (list-ref '(x y z) 1))
```

Problem 2.2.

If Scheme did not provide the string constructor, how could you implement it?

Problem 2.3.

Assume *r* is any real number. Implement the following procedure:

```
(sign r)
    = 1, if r > 0
    = -1, if r < 0
    = unspecified, otherwise
```

Hint: Use the abs procedure.

Problem 2.4.

If Scheme did not provide modulo, how could you define it? (Hint: You may want to use the sign procedure developed herein, and the remainder procedure.

Problem 2.5.

Write a procedure that expects the rate r of return on an investment compounded annually and returns the length of time required for the investment to double. Do not use the "Rule of 72."

Problem 2.6.

If Scheme did not provide expt, how could you define it?

Problem 2.7.

If Scheme did not provide tan, how could you define it?

Problem 2.8.

The sum of a geometric series of the form $ar^0 + ar^1 + ar^2 + ... + ar^n$ is given by the formula $S = a(1 - r^{n+1})/(1 - r)$. Implement this as a Scheme procedure.

Problem 2.9.

If n is any unsigned integer, then $1 + 2 + ... + n =$ the nth triangle number $= n(n + 1)/2$. Implement this as a Scheme procedure.

Problem 2.10.

As a particle moves faster, its mass increases according to the Lorenz formula:

$$m = \frac{m_{rest}}{\sqrt{1 - v^2/c^2}}$$

where $v =$ the velocity of the particle, $c =$ the speed of light, and $m_{rest} =$ the rest mass of the particle. Implement this as a Scheme procedure.

Problem 2.11.

Define the following coercions by composing existing coercions:

```
vector->string, string->vector
```

Problem 2.12.

Recall the formula for transforming degrees to radians:

$$\theta_{deg} = \theta_{rad} \frac{180}{\pi}$$

Use this formula to define the coercions:

```
degree->radian, radian->degree
```

Problem 2.13.

Implement versions of all the trigonometric procedures that assume angles are measured in degrees instead of radians:

```
(define (degree-sin z) ???)
```

Problem 2.14.

Define the following coercions. Don't hesitate to compose your own coercions to form new coercions:

```
a. kbyte->byte, byte->kbyte    ; 1 kilobyte = 2^10 bytes
b. byte->mbyte, mbyte->byte    ; 1 megabyte = 2^20 bytes
c. byte->gbyte, gbyte->byte    ; 1 gigabyte = 2^30 bytes
d. byte->tbyte, tbyte->byte    ; 1 terabyte = 2^40 bytes
e. kbyte->gbyte, gbyte->kbyte
```

Problem 2.15.

Of course the coercion char->integer does not map digits like #\8 to their corresponding numerical values. Write a Scheme procedure that does:

```
> (char->digit #\8)
8
> (char->digit #\0)
0
```

Your procedure should work on computers that encode characters using ASCII codes or IBM's EBCDIC codes.

Problem 2.16.

There are two ways to use vectors to represent a 3×3 matrix like:

$$M = \begin{pmatrix} 3 & 2 & 4 \\ 1 & 0 & 12 \\ 7 & -1 & 5 \end{pmatrix}$$

Row major form represents M as a vector consisting of three points that represent the first, second, and third rows of M:

```
#(#(3 2 4) #(1 0 12) #(7 -1 5))
```

Column major form represents M as a vector consisting of three points that represent the first, second, and third columns of M:

```
#(#(3 1 2) #(2 0 -1) #(4 12 5))
```

In the following exercises we will assume matrices are represented using row major form. We will also use the notation M_{ij} to indicate the row i column j entry of M. For example:

$$M_{23} = 12$$

Assume A, B, and C are 3×3 matrices and P is a point, implement the following procedures:

```
(entry A i j) = Aij
```

```
(mat+ A B) = C, where Cij = Aij + Bij
```

```
(mat* A P) = #(a1 a2 a3), where ai = dot product of row i of
    A with P
```

Problem 2.17.

Generalize mat* in the previous exercise so that it multiplies $n \times n$ matrices with $n \times 1$ points.

Problem 2.18.

Write an n-ary procedure that appends arbitrarily many vectors:

```
(define (vector-append . vecs) ???) ; stub
```

Problem 2.19.

If the graph of a procedure is represented by an association list of the form:

GRAPH ::= (($INPUT_1$. $OUTPUT_1$) ...)

then its inverse is represented by the same association list, but with each pair reversed:

(($OUTPUT_1$. $INPUT_1$) ...)

Implement a reversing procedure that expects an arbitrary alist as input and returns the inverse alist as a value:

```
> (graph-reverse '((a . 1) (b . 2) (c . 3)))
((1 . a) (2 . b) (3 . c))
```

Problem 2.20.

Assume Scheme did not provide truncate. How could you define it?

Problem 2.21.

Implement a procedure that extracts the last element of a list:

```
> (last '(a e i o u))
u
```

Problem 2.22.

Assume Scheme didn't have a string-ref procedure. How could you implement one?

Problem 2.23.

How could you implement quotient if Scheme did not provide it?

Problem 2.24.

How could you define char<? if Scheme did not provide it?

3
Evaluation Control and Recursion

3.1. Evaluation Control

In the last chapter we described the four-step evaluation procedure used by Scheme to evaluate procedure applications:

1. Evaluate operator.
2. Evaluate operands to produce arguments.
3. Replace parameters by arguments in the body.
4. Evaluate body.

This procedure is called **Eager evaluation.** The name derives from the fact that the evaluator is so eager to know the values of the operands, it evaluates them in the second step, even if their values are not needed when the body of the procedure is evaluated in the fourth step.

Eager Evaluation may be compared to **lazy evaluation,** a procedure not normally used by Scheme interpreters:

1. Evaluate operator.
2. Replace parameters in body by unevaluated operands.
3. Evaluate body.

The name derives from the fact that the evaluator postpones evaluation of the operands until they are needed in step 3.[1] With luck, the values may never be needed. For example, consider the following definition:

```
(define (always-0 val) 0)
```

Let's trace the eager evaluation of (always-0 (exp 100000)):

1. The name always-0 is evaluated.
2. The operand (exp 100000) is evaluated. (This may take a while.)
3. The argument e^{100000} replaces the parameter, val, in the body of always-0. (This is not much of a challenge considering val doesn't even appear in the body of always-0.)

---

[1] Lazy evaluation is covered in detail in Chapter 8.

4. The body is evaluated. Again, not much of a challenge because the body is the literal, 0.

Using lazy evaluation the needless evaluation of (exp 100000) is avoided:

1. The name always-0 is evaluated.
2. The unevaluated operand (exp 100000) replaces the parameter val in the body of always-0. Because val doesn't appear in the body of always-0, this produces the literal, 0.
3. The literal 0 is evaluated, producing the value, 0. Because the operand didn't appear in the body, (exp 100000) was never computed.

Although Scheme uses eager evaluation to evaluate procedure applications, there are situations where we would like to avoid eager evaluation. Fortunately, the eager evaluation method is not used on all expressions. Scheme evaluates certain expressions using other methods. These expressions are called **control structures** because they allow programmers to control the flow of evaluation.

3.2. Short Circuit Evaluation

The form of an and-structure is:

```
AND ::= (and EXPRESSION ... )
```

An or-structure has the form:

```
OR ::= (or EXPRESSION ... )
```

Superficially and-structures and or-structures seem like ordinary procedure applications, but they are control structures. Instead of using the eager method to evaluate them, Scheme uses a method called **short circuit evaluation**:

> Evaluate operands from left to right until the final result is known. The remaining operands are left unevaluated.

More specifically, assume $OPERAND_0$, ... , $OPERAND_n$ are arbitrary Scheme expressions. To evaluate the expression:

```
(and OPERAND0 OPERAND1 ... OPERANDn)
```

the Scheme evaluator begins evaluating the operands from left to right. The value of the first operand equal to #f is returned (i.e., #f is returned), and the remaining operands are left unevaluated. Otherwise, the evaluator returns the value of the last operand. If there are no operands, #t is returned.

To evaluate the expression:

```
(or OPERAND0 OPERAND1 ... OPERANDn)
```

the Scheme evaluator begins evaluating the operands from left to right. The value of the first operand that does *not* evaluate to #f is returned, and the remaining operands are left unevaluated. Otherwise, the evaluator returns #f. If there are no operands, #f is returned.

Here are some sample evaluations:

```
> (and 0 #\a "hello" (< 3 2) (/ 0))
#f
> (or (char? 3) #f (< 3 2) 42 (/ 0))
42
> (+ (and 1 2 3) (or 4 5 6))
7
```

In the first example the first four operands were evaluated, but when the evaluator discovered the value of the fourth operand was #f, it immediately returned this value without evaluating the fifth operand. We know this is true because if the evaluator had attempted to evaluate the fifth operand, we would have seen a divide-by-0 error message printed on the screen.

In the second case the first four operands were evaluated, but when the evaluator discovered the value of the fourth operand was not #f, it immediately returned this value without evaluating the fifth operand. We know this is true because if the evaluator had evaluated the fifth operand, again we would have seen a "divide by 0" error message printed on the screen.

(*Warning*: Officially, the value #f is unique, but PC-Scheme identifies #f with the empty list: ( ).)

What is the advantage of short circuit evaluation? We can use it as a method of input validation for predicates. For example, the following polymorphic predicate determines if *b* is between *a* and *c*, if *a*, *b*, and *c* belong to the same ordinal domain (i.e., strings, reals, or characters); otherwise #f is returned:

```
; = #t if ordinal b is between ordinals a and c
(define (between? a b c)
   (or (and (real? a)
            (real? b)
            (real? c)
            (or (< a b c) (< c b a)))
       (and (char? a)
            (char? b)
            (char? c)
            (or (char<? a b c) (char<? c b a)))
       (and (string? a)
            (string? b)
            (string? c)
            (or (string<? a b c) (string<? c b a)))))
```

Notice, if *b* is not a real, then the and-structure:

```
(and (real? a)
     (real? b)
     (real? c)
     (or (< a b c) (< c b a)))
```

returns #f immediately after (real? b) is evaluated, skipping the call to <, which would have resulted in a type error.

A point can be defined as a vector consisting of three reals:

```
POINT ::= #(REAL REAL REAL)
```

We can develop a polymorphic predicate that tests if arbitrary values are points:

```
(define (point? val)
   (and (vector? val)
        (= 3 (vector-length val))
        (real? (vector-ref val 0))
        (real? (vector-ref val 1))
        (real? (vector-ref val 2))))
```

If val isn't a vector, then because of short circuit evaluation the and-structure returns #f immediately after evaluating (vector? val), before calling vector-length would have resulted in a type error. If the input is a vector of length less than 3, then the and-structure returns #f immediately after evaluating (= 3 (vector-length val)), before calling vector-ref would have resulted in an index-out-of-range error.

3.3. Conditional Evaluation

Conditional evaluation is closely related to short circuit evaluation. Certain operands in a conditional expression are designated as conditions or guards. Depending on their values other operands may or may not be evaluated. Scheme provides three control structures that use some form of conditional evaluation: the if-structure, cond-structure, and case-structure.

3.3.1. The if-structure

The form of an if-structure is simple:

```
IF ::= (if CONDITION CONSEQUENT [ALTERNATIVE])
```

where CONDITION, CONSEQUENT, and ALTERNATIVE are arbitrary Scheme expressions. (Recall, [ALTERNATIVE] indicates this operand is optional.) Let's trace the steps taken to evaluate this type of expression:

1. The evaluator evaluates CONDITION.

2a. If the value of CONDITION is *not* #f, then the evaluator evaluates CONSEQUENT, and this value is taken as the value of the entire expression. In this case ALTERNATIVE is never evaluated.

2b. If the value of CONDITION is #f, then the evaluator evaluates ALTERNATIVE, and this value is taken as the value of the entire expression. In this case CONSEQUENT is never evaluated. If there is no ALTERNATIVE, then the value of the expression is unspecified.

The usefulness of the if-structure can best be understood in the context of an example. Assume taxes are computed using a two-rate system. People pay 20% on the first $50,000 earned in a year, and 30% on every dollar earned over $50,000. Assume the following constants are declared:

```
; $50,000 = maximum medium income:
(define   max-medium 50000)
```

```
; 30% = rate for > max-medium incomes:
(define max-rate .3)
```

```
; 20% = rate for <= max-medium incomes
(define medium-rate .2)
```

We want to define a tax-computing procedure that expects as input an income and returns as output the tax owed. The form of the tax procedure is:

```
; = tax owed on income dollars
(define (tax income) ??? )
```

How will our procedure decide which rate to use? Obviously the parameter will have to be compared to the max-medium income constant:

```
(> income max-medium)
```

If this condition is true, then the tax procedure must return:

```
(+ max-medium-tax (* max-rate (- income max-medium)))
```

where max-medium-tax is the tax paid on the maximum medium income:

```
; = tax paid on max-medium income
(define max-medium-tax (* max-medium medium-rate))
```

Otherwise it returns:

```
(* income medium-rate)
```

This is a perfect place to use an if-structure. Here's the complete declaration of our tax procedure:

```
; = tax owed on income dollars
(define (tax income)
```

```
(if (> income max-medium)
    (+ max-medium-tax
       (* max-rate (- income max-medium)))
    (* income medium-rate)))
```

Notice how if-structures are indented. Remember, the physical structure of a procedure should reflect its logical structure.

Nesting if-structures

Let's make the tax problem more complicated by introducing a four-level tax system. People pay no tax on the first $5000 they earn, 10% on every dollar earned between $5000 and $20,000, 20% on dollars earned between $20,000 and $50,000, and 30% on every dollar earned over $50,000. Assume the following additional constants are defined:

```
; $20,000 = maximum low income
(define max-low 20000)

; $5000 = maximum non-taxable income
(define max-min 5000)

; 10% = rate paid on max-min < $ <= max-low
(define low-rate .1)
```

Next, we pre-compute the tax paid on $20,000 and $50,000:

```
; = tax on max-low income
(define max-low-tax (* low-rate (- max-low max-min)))

; = tax on max-medium income
(define max-medium-tax
   (+ max-low-tax
      (* medium-rate (- max-medium max-low))))
```

Unfortunately, the if-structure only offers a choice between two candidates: CONSEQUENT and ALTERNATIVE. However, because if-structures are ordinary expressions, then either CONSEQUENT or ALTERNATIVE can be if-structures. In other words, we can have multiple alternatives by nesting if-structures:

```
; = tax owed on income dollars
(define (tax income)
   (if (> income max-medium)
       (+ max-medium-tax
          (* max-rate (- income max-medium)))
       (if (> income max-low)
           (+ max-low-tax
              (* medium-rate (- income max-low)))
           (if (> income max-min)
```

```
(* low-rate (- income max-min))
0)))))
```

(Notice how the pattern of indentation makes it easier to read the procedure.)

The condition in the second if-structure only compares income to the low constant. It may seem like the appropriate test should have been

```
(and (> income max-low) (< income max-medium))
```

but because this is the alternative of the outer if-structure, it is only evaluated if the first condition, (> income max-medium), has already failed. There is no reason to perform this comparison a second time.

3.3.2. The cond-structure

The form of a cond-structure is:

```
COND ::= (cond CLAUSE ... )
```

Each CLAUSE has the form:

```
CLAUSE ::= (CONDITION EXPRESSION ... )
```

where CONDITION is any Scheme expression or the reserved word *else*:

```
CONDITION ::= EXPRESSION | else
```

Let's trace the steps taken by the evaluator when evaluating a cond-structure. The clauses are evaluated from left to right:

1. If all the CLAUSEs have been tested, the value of the cond-structure is unspecified. Otherwise, pick the next untested CLAUSE.
2. Evaluate the CONDITION of the selected CLAUSE.
3a. If the value of the CONDITION is not #f, then each remaining EXPRESSION in the selected CLAUSE is evaluated. The value of the cond-structure will be the value of the last EXPRESSION in the CLAUSE. The remaining clauses will be left unevaluated.
3b. If the value of the CONDITION is #f, then consider the CLAUSE tested and return to step 1.

The reserved word *else* is identified with #t. Normally *else* is used as the condition of the last clause to insure that at least one clause will be evaluated.

Here is a version of the tax-computing procedure that uses the cond-structure:

```
; = tax owed on income dollars
(define (tax income)
    (cond ((> income max-medium)
            (+ max-medium-tax
                (* max-rate (- income max-medium))))
        ((> income max-low)
```

```
            (+ max-low-tax
               (* medium-rate (- income max-low))))
        ((> income min)
           (* low-rate (- income max-min)))
        (else 0)))
```

(Note the pattern of indentation conventionally used with cond-structures.)

3.3.3. Input Validation

Conditional evaluation gives us the opportunity to validate inputs. If invalid inputs are detected, we can use the error procedure defined in Appendix 3.3: Defensive Programming to display an error message and gracefully terminate the procedure. Here's a final version of the tax procedure with input validation:

```
; = tax owed on income dollars
(define (tax income)
   (cond ((not (real? income))
             (error "bad input" tax income))
         ((> income max-medium)
            (+ max-medium-tax
               (* max-rate (- income max-medium))))
         ((> income max-low)
            (+ max-low-tax
               (* medium-rate (- income max-low))))
         ((> income min)
            (* low-rate (- income max-min)))
         ((>= income 0) 0)
         (else (error "negative income" tax income))))
```

3.3.4. The case-structure

The form of a case-structure is:

CASE ::= (case KEY CLAUSE ...)

where KEY is an arbitrary Scheme expression, and each CLAUSE has the form:

CLAUSE ::= (GUARD EXPRESSION ...)

GUARD is either a list or the reserved word *else*:

GUARD ::= LIST | else

Let's trace the steps taken by the evaluator when evaluating a case-structure. The clauses are evaluated from left to right:

1. Evaluate KEY.
2. If all the CLAUSEs have been tested, then the value of the case-structure is unspecified. Otherwise, select the next untested CLAUSE.
3a. If the guard of the selected clause is *else*, or if it is a list containing a value equal (in the eqv? sense) to the value of KEY, then the remaining EXPRESSIONs in the CLAUSE are evaluated. The value of the last one is the value of the case-structure. The remaining clauses are left unevaluated.
3b. Otherwise consider the CLAUSE tested and return to step 2.

Cond-structures are used when the number of situations that select a clause is large or infinite. Case-structures are useful when the number is small. For example, consider the following domain of expressions:

```
EXP ::= (OPERATOR REAL ... )
```

Various operator synonyms can be used in an EXP-expression:

```
OPERATOR ::= + | add | sum | * | mult | / |
             div | - | sub | < | less
```

The EXP evaluator uses a case-structure to determine the appropriate operation to apply to the operands:

```
; = value denoted by exp
(define (evaluate exp)
   (case (car exp)
      ((+ add sum) (apply + (cdr exp)))
      ((* mult) (apply * (cdr exp)))
      ((/ div) (apply / (cdr exp)))
      ((- sub) (apply - (cdr exp)))
      ((< less) (apply < (cdr exp)))
      (else (error "unrecognized operator"
                   evaluate
                   (car exp))))))
```

Here are some sample calls to the evaluate procedure:

```
> (evaluate '(add 2 3 4 5))
14
> (evaluate '(sum 2 2 2))
6
> (evaluate '(less -1 -2 -3))
#f
> (evaluate '(< -3 -2 -1 0))
#t
```

Notice the input expression to evaluate must be quoted to prevent the eager evaluation mechanisms from evaluating the expression prematurely:

```
> (evaluate (+ 2 3))
Error!
   gripe:         bad input
   source:        car
   irritant(s):   5
```

Make sure you understand what went wrong in this example.

3.4. Recursion

When we use the top-down method, we define a procedure in terms of supporting procedures, some of which may be undefined. Next, the undefined supporting procedures are defined in terms of their supporting procedures. This process continues until there are no more undefined procedures.

Sometimes beginners find it unsettling to define a procedure in terms of supporting procedures that haven't yet been defined. It's like borrowing money to make money. It takes a leap of faith to believe that the supporting procedures can and will eventually be defined according to specification. If this makes you feel uncomfortable, then recursion will make you nauseous. Recursion takes the top-down method one step further by allowing procedures to be defined in terms of themselves! A procedure defined in terms of itself is called a **recursive procedure**. In other words, a recursive procedure is one of its own supporting procedures!

Recursive procedures are appropriate for solving recursive problems. A **recursive problem** is a problem that naturally decomposes into subproblems that are smaller versions of the original problem. A recursive procedure that solves such a problem calls itself to solve the smaller subproblems, then combines these results into the final result.

3.4.1. Example: Triangle Numbers

The nth triangle number is the number of blocks required to make a staircase n steps high. For example, zero blocks are needed to construct a staircase with no steps. Only one block is needed to build a staircase with a single step. To build a two-step staircase requires three blocks, as in Figure 3.1.

Figure 3.1

A three-step staircase requires six blocks (see Figure 3.2).

Figure 3.2

Therefore one, three, and six are the first, second, and third triangle numbers, respectively. (Mathematicians call these **triangle numbers** because staircases are roughly shaped like right triangles.)

How can we write a procedure which, given input *n*, returns the *n*th triangle number:

```
; = n-th triangle number
(define (triangle n) ???)
```

Here are some sample applications of triangle:

```
> (triangle 0)
0
> (triangle 1)
1
> (triangle 2)
3
> (triangle 3)
6
```

Counting the number of blocks in an *n*-step staircase is a recursive problem: saw off the *n* blocks in the right-most column of the staircase, this leaves a staircase with *n* − 1 steps. Because this is a smaller staircase, we can use the triangle procedure to count the number of blocks in it. To finish, we just add to this result the *n* blocks we sawed off initially. We can express this in Scheme by:

```
(triangle n)   = (+ n (triangle (- n 1)))
```

Does this expression work when *n* = 0? In this case our Scheme expression becomes:

```
(triangle 0)   = (+ 0 (triangle -1))
```

Clearly it doesn't make sense to talk about a staircase with a negative number of steps. Anyway, we already know (triangle 0) is supposed to be 0, therefore, we will use our recursive expression when *n* > 0, and simply return 0 when *n* = 0. We can use an if-structure to select the desired expression:

```
; = n-th triangle number
(define (triangle n)
   (if (zero? n)
       0
       (+ n (triangle (- n 1)))))
```

Does this really work? How can a procedure call itself without spinning off into an infinite loop? Oddly, this does work because conditional evaluation of the if-structure guarantees (triangle − 1) won't be evaluated when *n* = 0. (Why?)

3.4.2. Tracing

The Scheme evaluator procedure, eval, is itself a recursive procedure. It evaluates expressions by recursively evaluating smaller subexpressions, then combines these results into a final answer. For example:

```
(+ (* 3 4) (- 2 5))   ; original eval input expression
(+ 12 (- 2 5))        ; eval evaluates (* 3 4)
(+ 12 -3)             ; eval evaluates (- 2 5)
9                     ; eval sums results
```

Each expression in this sequence can be viewed as a reduction or simplification of the expression preceding it. The last expression is a value, which cannot be further reduced. A sequence of expressions, each the result of reducing the previous, is called a **computation**.

We can use this idea to better understand how recursive procedures work. A **trace** is a computation in which only applications of *interesting* procedures are shown. Of course the definition of interesting is subjective, and different definitions will produce different traces. By wisely choosing interesting procedures, we can construct traces that are not too long, yet give insight into why a procedure does or does not work.

Let's construct a trace of an application of the triangle procedure, for example, (triangle 4). We select + and triangle as our interesting procedures. The first step in the trace is:

```
(triangle 4)
 (+ 4 (triangle 3))
```

Notice we didn't show the evaluation of (− 4 1) because − was not selected as an interesting procedure. Before the evaluator can complete the addition to 4, it must evaluate (triangle 3):

```
(triangle 4)
 (+ 4 (triangle 3))
 (+ 4 (+ 3 (triangle 2)))
```

In fact, each recursive call must be evaluated before any addition can be performed:

```
(triangle 4)
 (+ 4 (triangle 3))
 (+ 4 (+ 3 (triangle 2)))
 (+ 4 (+ 3 (+ 2 (triangle 1))))
 (+ 4 (+ 3 (+ 2 (+ 1 (triangle 0)))))
 (+ 4 (+ 3 (+ 2 (+ 1 0))))
```

Now the additions are performed from right to left:

```
(triangle 4)
 (+ 4 (triangle 3))
 (+ 4 (+ 3 (triangle 2)))
```

```
(+ 4 (+ 3 (+ 2 (triangle 1))))
(+ 4 (+ 3 (+ 2 (+ 1 (triangle 0)))))
(+ 4 (+ 3 (+ 2 (+ 1 0))))
(+ 4 (+ 3 (+ 2 1)))
(+ 4 (+ 3 3))
(+ 4 6)
10
```

This is the trace of (triangle 4). It shows how the final result is computed. It also can reveal alternate ways of computing the result. For example, notice the *nth* triangle number is obtained by adding the numbers from 1 to *n*:

```
(triangle n)     = (+ 1 2 ... n)
```

3.4.3. More on Input Validation

Notice that our triangle procedure failed to validate its input, *n*. We could have easily included input validation as a third alternative using either a cond-structure or nested if-structures:

```
(define (triangle n)
   (if (natural? n)
        (if (zero? n)
             0
             (+ n (triangle (- n 1))))
        (error "bad input" triangle n)))
```

where natural? is a polymorphic predicate that tests for unsigned integers:

```
(define (natural? val)
   (and (integer? val) (<= 0 val)))
```

Let's include this predicate among our interesting procedures and retrace (triangle 4):

```
(triangle 4)
 (natural? 4)
 (+ 4 (triangle 3))
 (natural? 3)
 (+ 4 (+ 3 (triangle 2)))
 (natural? 2)
 (+ 4 (+ 3 (+ 2 (triangle 1))))
 (natural? 1)
 (+ 4 (+ 3 (+ 2 (+ 1 (triangle 0)))))
 (natural? 0)
 (+ 4 (+ 3 (+ 2 (+ 1 0))))
 (+ 4 (+ 3 (+ 2 1)))
 (+ 4 (+ 3 3))
```

```
(+  4  6)
10
```

It seems inefficient to ask if 3, 2, 1, and 0 are natural numbers after we have verified that 4 is a natural. For this reason, it is often better to design a special "wrapper" procedure that validates inputs, then calls a recursive procedure that doesn't validate inputs. Using this technique, the triangle procedure becomes a wrapper for unsafe-triangle:

```
(define (triangle n)
    (if (natural? n)
        (unsafe-triangle n)
        (error "bad input" triangle n)))
```

The old triangle procedure becomes the unsafe-triangle procedure:

```
(define (unsafe-triangle n)
    (if (zero? n)
        0
        (+ n (unsafe-triangle (- n 1))))))
```

3.4.4. Mathematical Induction

> *That the sun will not rise tomorrow* is no less intelligible a proposition, and implies no more contradiction than the affirmation, *that it will rise.*
>
> —David Hume, *An Enquiry Concerning Human Understanding*

A scientist verifies a theory by conducting experiments. Confidence in the theory grows as the number of confirming experiments increases. For example, a chemist might verify that gold is inert by dropping samples of gold into beakers containing various strong acids, then observing that the samples aren't dissolved. The more types of acid that fail to dissolve gold, the stronger his conviction that gold is inert. This method of gaining knowledge is called the **Principle of Induction.**

In 1739 the philosopher and skeptic David Hume showed that the Principle of Induction could not be justified by either reason or experience, the two branches of his famous epistemological fork. Any proof that gold is inert would have to rely on other scientific principles, which themselves were justified by induction. Tomorrow we could discover an acid so strong that it dissolves even gold. Of course such a discovery would overturn the entire atomic theory, but the history of science is littered with discarded theories.

Programmers can also get caught on Hume's fork. A procedure, proc, that operates on natural numbers is correct if for every *n*, (proc *n*) returns the specified value. How can we show a procedure is correct? A programmer can trace a few applications of proc. The more successful traces performed, the greater our confidence that proc is correct. Unfortunately, Hume's skepticism applies here, too. Our traces are nothing more than experiments. Tomorrow we could find an input so virulent it sends proc spiraling down some previously undiscovered path of error.

Fortunately, natural numbers are governed by laws that allow us to make mathematically valid inductions. We can conclude that proc is correct if we can confirm (proc 0) returns the specified value, and if we can prove that for any $n > 0$, (proc n) returns the specified value assuming (proc m) returns the specified value for all $m < n$. This form of induction is called **mathematical induction**. More formally, if proc has a natural number parameter, then

Assumptions:
1. (proc 0) returns the specified value.
2. If (proc m) returns the specified value for all $0 \le m < n$, then (proc n) returns the specified value.

Conclusion:
For all n, (proc n) returns the specified value.

Assumption 1 is called the **base case assumption** and assumption 2 is called the **successor case assumption**. At first glance it doesn't appear that the conclusion of mathematical induction is different from the successor case assumption. But notice that the conclusion is an absolute statement: (proc n) returns the specified value for *all* n, while the Successor Case Assumption is a conditional statement: for all n, (proc n) returns the specified value, *if* (proc m) returns the specified value for all $0 \le m < n$. It's quite a bit easier to justify a conditional statement because we get to assume (proc m) returns the specified value for all $0 \le m < n$.

Our proof of Mathematical Induction is based on the fact that every nonempty set of natural numbers has a smallest member. Assume proc is not correct. This means proc returns some incorrect values. Let n be the smallest number for which (proc n) returns an incorrect value. Clearly $n > 0$, because we are assuming (proc 0) returns the specified value. But because n is the smallest value that causes (proc n) to return an incorrect result, this means (proc m) must return a specified value for all $m < n$. Hence (proc n) must return a specified value by our successor case assumption. This contradicts our assumption that proc is not correct.

We can use mathematical induction to prove that the triangle procedure is correct. We only need to show the base and successor case assumptions are satisfied:

Base Case:
(triangle 0) returns 0, the number of blocks needed to build a 0-step staircase.

Successor Case:
Pick an arbitrary $n > 0$, and assume (triangle m) returns the specified value for all $0 \le m < n$. In particular, this means (triangle $(- n\ 1)$) returns the number of blocks needed to build an $(n-1)$-step staircase. We can construct an n-step staircase from this $n-1$ step staircase by attaching a column of n blocks to it. Thus, the number of blocks in an n step staircase is:

```
(+ n (triangle (- n 1)))
```

but this is the definition of (triangle n), hence (triangle n) returns the specified value.

3.5.   Thinking Recursively

Although mathematical induction is a tool for building correctness proofs, it can also be used as a tool for building recursive algorithms. Assume we want to define a procedure called proc that expects a natural number as input (there may be other inputs, too). We can build a recursive algorithm for proc by answering two questions:

Base Case:
What is (proc 0)?

Successor Case:
How can we use (proc m) for $0 \leq m < n$ to compute (proc n)?

In many situations the second question can be restricted to $m = n - 1$:

Successor Case: How can we use (proc $(- n\ 1)$) to compute (proc n)?

Often we can answer the second question by working out a few examples: (proc 1) = ?, (proc 2) = ?, (proc 3) = ?, and then generalizing.

Assume (proc 0) returns val. Assume (proc n) returns the value denoted by exp, where exp is an expression involving applications of the form (proc $(- n\ 1)$). The implementation of proc is:

```
(define (proc n) (if (zero? n) val exp))
```

Of course, in some cases we might control proc with a cond- or case-structure.

3.5.1.   Example: make-list

Scheme provides six constructors:

```
cons, list, vector, make-vector, string, make-string
```

Recall that make-vector expects a length n and a value v as input, and it returns the length n vector #(v ... v). Make-string works in a similar way. It's curious that Scheme does not provide a similar procedure for making lists. Let's try to implement one:

```
; = length n list (val ... val)
(define (make-list n val) ???)
```

Of course we could implement make-list by calling make-vector and coercing the result to a list, but recall our definition of necessary Scheme:

```
necessary Scheme = Scheme - redundant features
```

Strings and vectors are redundant features. We have already seen that all primitive vector and string procedures can be implemented by coercing their inputs to lists, applying the corresponding list procedure, and then coercing the result back to a string or vector. Lists are also redundant because they are simply nested pairs. Therefore it should be possible to implement all primitive list procedures in terms of the primitive pair procedures: car, cdr, and cons, but recursion will be required.

As an exercise in parsimony, let's search for a different solution to this problem. Because n is always a natural number, we could try to find a recursive procedure. We ask two questions:

> (make-list 0 val) = ?
>
> How can we use (make-list (− n 1) val) to compute (make-list n val)?

We can answer these question by computing some initial values, searching for a pattern, and then generalizing:

```
(make-list 0 val) = ()

(make-list 1 val)
   = (val)
   = (cons val (make-list 0 val))

(make-list 2 val)
   = (val val)
   = (cons val (make-list 1 val))

(make-list 3 val)
   = (val val val)
   = (cons val (make-list 2 val))
```

A pattern seems to be emerging, for n > 0:

```
(make-list n val) = (cons val (make-list (- n 1) val))
```

We use this pattern as the basis of our implementation:

```
; = length n list: (val ... val)
(define (make-list n val)
   (if (zero? n)
       '()
       (cons val (make-list (- n 1) val))))
```

We can understand how this procedure works by tracing through a few sample computations. We take make-list and cons to be our interesting procedures:

```
(make-list 3 0)
 (cons 0 (make-list 2 0))
 (cons 0 (cons 0 (make-list 1 0)))
 (cons 0 (cons 0 (cons 0 (make-list 0 0))))
 (cons 0 (cons 0 (cons 0 ())))
 (cons 0 (cons 0 (0)))
 (cons 0 (0 0))
 (0 0 0)
```

3.5.2. Example: nat-expt

Assume Scheme provided neither the exp nor expt procedures. It's easy to implement exp in terms of expt:

```
(define (exp z) (expt e z))     ; = e^z
```

where *e* is approximated by:

```
(define e 2.71828182845905)
```

How could we implement expt? This depends on the type of the exponent:

```
; = b^z where b & z are any numbers
(define (expt b z)
   (cond ((natural? z) (nat-expt b z))
         ((integer? z) (int-expt b z))
         ((rational? z) (rat-expt b z))
         ((real? z) (real-expt b z))
         ((complex? z) (complex-expt b z))))
```

(Is the order of clauses in this definition important?) Most of the variants of expt can be defined in terms of the nat-expt. For example:

```
; = b^i where i is an integer & b is any number
(define (int-expt b i)
   (if (>= i 0)
       (nat-expt b i)
       (/ (nat-expt b (- i))))))
```

Nat-expt can be defined using recursion. We ask:

  (nat-expt *b* 0) = ?

How can we use (nat-expt *b* (− *n* 1)) to compute (nat-expt *b* *n*)? To answer these questions, we work through a few initial cases and generalize:

```
(nat-expt b 0) = b^0 = 1
(nat-expt b 1) = b^1 = b = b * b^0
(nat-expt b 2) = b^2 = b * b^1
(nat-expt b 3) = b^3 = b * b^2
```

The pattern seems clear:

```
(nat-expt b n) =  (* b (nat-expt b (- n 1)))
```

The final version of our procedure is:

```
; = b^n where n is a natural and b is any number
(define (nat-expt b n)
   (if (zero? n)
       1
       (* b (nat-expt b (- n 1)))))
```

Let's trace a computation of nat-expt:

```
(nat-expt 2 3)
 (* 2 (nat-expt 2 2))
 (* 2 (* 2 (nat-expt 2 1)))
 (* 2 (* 2 (* 2 (nat-expt 2 0))))
 (* 2 (* 2 (* 2 1)))
 (* 2 (* 2 2))
 (* 2 4)
 8
```

3.5.3. Example: evaluate

This example shows that a recursive procedure can call itself indirectly by passing itself to a meta-procedure. Let's increase the complexity of the domain of expressions defined earlier by allowing nested expressions. In other words, let's make EXP into a recursive domain:

```
EXP ::= NUMBER | (OPERATOR EXP ... )
```

Various operator synonyms can be used in an EXP-expression:

```
OPERATOR ::= + | add | sum | * | mult |
             / | div | - | sub | < | less | etc.
```

The EXP evaluator uses an if-structure to determine if its EXP input is a number (i.e., a literal) or an application. If it is a number, then there is no work to be done, just return the number. If the EXP input is an application, a case-structure is used to determine the appropriate operation to apply to the actual parameters. The arguments are gotten by recursively applying evaluate to each operand. Because we don't know the number of operands in advance, we will have to use the map and apply meta-procedures:

```
; = value denoted by exp
(define (evaluate exp)
   (if (number? exp)
       exp                    ; exp denotes itself!
       (case (car exp)
         ((+ add sum)
            (apply + (map evaluate (cdr exp))))
         ((* mult)
            (apply * (map evaluate (cdr exp))))
         ((/ div)
            (apply / (map evaluate (cdr exp))))
         ((- sub)
            (apply - (map evaluate (cdr exp))))
         ((< less)
            (apply < (map evaluate (cdr exp))))
```

```
(else
    (error "unrecognized operator"
            evaluate
            (car exp)))))))
```

Because operands can be expressions, we can nest expressions:

```
> (evaluate '(add (sub 6 1) (mult 2 7) (add 3 6)))
28
> (evaluate '(less (sum 6 7) (+ 1.2 (div 9 2))))
#f
```

Appendices

Appendix 3.1. Sequential Evaluation

Earlier we saw that a sequence of expressions can follow the condition or guard in the clause of a cond- or case-structure:

```
CLAUSE ::= (CONDITION EXPRESSION ... )
```

(Recall the ellipsis "..." indicates zero or more repetitions of EXPRESSION.) When such a clause is evaluated, each expression following the condition is evaluated, but the value of the clause is the value of the last expression in the sequence; the values of the preceding expressions are thrown away!

There are several other contexts where Scheme allows expression sequences to appear. For example, the body of a procedure block can be a sequence of expressions:

```
PROCEDURE-BLOCK ::=
    (define (NAME PARAM ...) EXPRESSION ... )
```

The same evaluation rule is used here. When the procedure is called, each expression in the body is evaluated, but the value returned by the procedure is the value of the last expression in the sequence. For example, consider the following definition:

```
(define (always-0) 3 2 1 0)
```

The body of this procedure consists of the literals 3, 2, 1, 0. When the procedure is called, the Scheme evaluator evaluates each expression, but only returns the 0:

```
> (define result (always-0))
unspecified
> result
0
```

Even in contexts where expression sequences are not allowed, such as the consequent or alternative of an if-structure, Scheme allows programmers to group sequences of expressions into a single expression using sequence-structures:

```
SEQUENCE ::= (BEGIN EXPRESSION ... )
```

where BEGIN is either begin or begin0:

```
BEGIN ::= begin | begin0
```

Sequence-structures are evaluated by evaluating each EXPRESSION from left to right. The value of the begin-structure is the value of its last expression, the value of a begin0-structure is the value of its first expression. All other expressions are evaluated, but the values they produce are ignored.

```
> (+ (begin 2 3 4) (begin0 5 6 7))   ; = (+ 4 5)
9
```

Be careful! The value of an expression in a sequence is not passed to the next expression. For example, assume the following definition has been made:

```
(define x 10)
```

What is the value of the expression:

```
> (begin (+ x 1) x)
?
```

It looks as though (+ x 1) increments x, and therefore the value of the last x should now be 11. In fact, the value of (+ x 1), 11, is discarded as soon as it is computed. The value of the last x in the sequence, hence the value of the sequence, is 10. (Pascal and C programmers almost always get this wrong!)

The values of all but one expression in a sequence are thrown away, so what use are they? The answer is none, unless evaluating the expression does more than produce a value. Scheme output procedures are perfect examples of this phenomenon.

Appendix 3.2. Input and Output in Scheme

Input and Output Ports

Normally, Scheme procedures receive their inputs from other procedures and send their output to other procedures (see Figure 3.3).

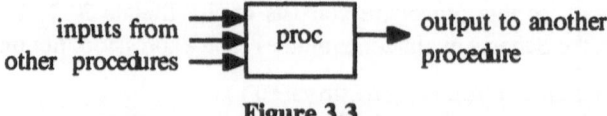

Figure 3.3

Additionally, Scheme procedures can read inputs from input ports and write outputs to output ports. An **input port** is a standard interface to all types of input devices: keyboards, sensors, joysticks, mice, etc. An **output port** is a standard interface to all types of output devices: monitors, printers, modems, controllers, etc. (see Figure 3.4).

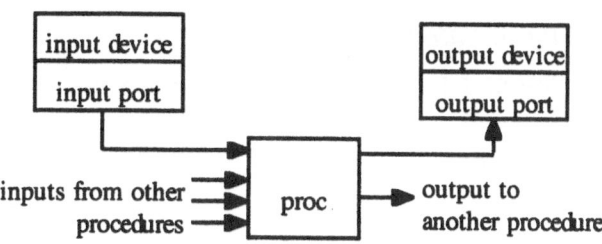

Figure 3.4

Scheme provides two predefined ports called the current-input-port and the current-output-port. We can discover what devices these ports are connected to by calling the procedures current-input-port and current-output-port:

```
> (current-input-port)
#[input-port stdin]
> (current-output-port)
#[output-port stdout]
```

Stdin stands for "standard input device" and stdout stands for "standard output device." The standard input device is the keyboard, and the standard output device is the monitor (i.e., the computer screen).

Reading from the Keyboard

Scheme provides the following procedures for reading data from the current input port:

```
(read)      = the next value typed.
(read-char) = the next character typed.
```

Both of these procedures cause the program to pause until a return character is typed.

Be careful, read and read-char receive their inputs directly from the standard input port and return this value through the usual procedure output channel (see Figure 3.5).

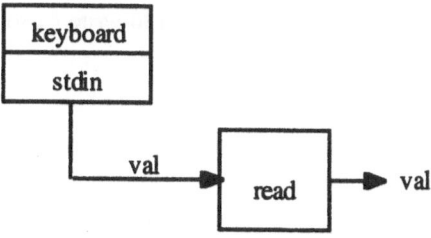

Figure 3.5

Writing to the Monitor

Scheme provides the following procedures for writing data to the current output port:

```
(write val) =
    an unspecified value. As a side effect, writes val on the
    monitor.

(display val) =
    an unspecified value. As a side effect, displays val on
    the monitor.

(write-char char) =
    an unspecified value. As a side effect, writes char on
    the monitor.

(newline)    = (write-char #\newline)
```

What's the difference between displaying and writing a value? There is no difference, unless the value is a character or string. When a character is written, its #\ prefix is also written. When a character is displayed, the #\ prefix is dropped. When a string is written, its surrounding double quotes are also written, and escape characters inside the string are dropped. When a string is displayed, its surrounding double quotes are dropped and escape characters inside the string are displayed as though they were ordinary characters.

Be careful, output procedures send their interesting values to the output port but send a boring unspecified value through the normal procedure return channel (see Figure 3.6).

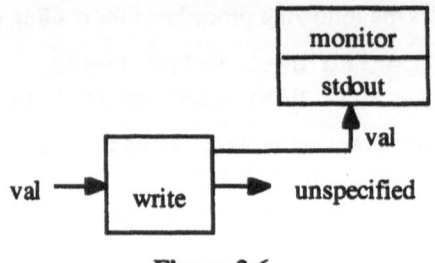

Figure 3.6

For example, the following call may seem to write 42 to the monitor and assign 42 to result:

```
> (define result (write (* 6 7)))
42
unspecified
```

But when we examine result we discover it contains an unspecified value instead of 42. Make sure you understand why:

```
> result
unspecified
```

Interactive Procedures

We can now give examples of how expression sequences can be useful. An interactive procedure reads its inputs from the keyboard and writes or displays its output to the monitor. Here's an interactive version of the cube procedure that uses sequences to display a sequence of messages to the user:

```
(define (cube n)
   (display n)
   (display " cubed = ")
   (display (* n n n))
   (newline))
```

Here are some sample evaluations:

```
> (cube 3)
3 cubed = 27
unspecified
> (cube 4)
4 cubed = 64
unspecified
```

Why is an unspecified value displayed after each call to cube?

Versatility

Granted, the interactive cube procedure just defined is more user friendly than the cube procedure defined in Chapter 2, but only a small percentage of procedures are called by humans. Most procedures are called by other procedures and return their values to other procedures. Our interactive cube procedure would be useless to other procedures because it does not return a predictable output. For example, the following procedure fails to compute the volume of a sphere if it uses the interactive cube procedure just defined:

```
(define (sphere-volume radius)
   (* 4/3 pi (cube radius)))
```

We can see why if we try to capture the output with a definition:

```
> (define result (cube 3))
3 cubed = 27
unspecified
> result
unspecified
```

Make sure you understand these evaluations. The first unspecified was the unspecified value returned by the definition. The cube of 3 was correctly computed and apparently bound to result, but when we examine the value of result we discover its value is unspecified instead of 27. The reason is that the last expression in the body of cube is a call to newline. Because newline returns an unspecified value, cube also returns an unspecified value. Our interactive cube procedure does not satisfy the **versatility goal**:

> If possible, procedures should be reusable in several places within the same program and possibly in other programs as well.

Unwanted Side Effects

We could attempt to have the best of both worlds by defining a special display procedure that returns the value it displays:

```
(define (display&return val)
   (display val)
   (newline)
   val)
```

We can use display&return to redefine cube as follows:

```
(define (cube z)
   (display z)
   (display " cubed = ")
   (display&return (* z z z)))
```

Now cube displays its result on the computer screen *and* returns its result to any calling procedures, as shown in Figure 3.7.

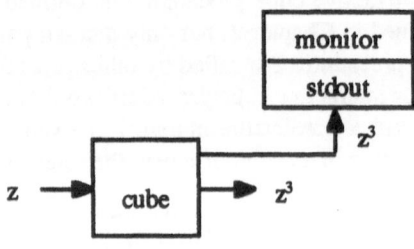

Figure 3.7

To see why this might not be a good idea, imagine the following scenario:

> Your cube procedure is part of a large CAD/CAM (computer aided design and manufacturing) system with a GUI (graphical user interface). All interactions with the user are through windows, menus, and icons. This sounds nice, but customers complain that when they rotate or scale their part models in the graphics window, thousands of little messages saying things like "3 cubed = 27" fill the screen.

Evaluating some expressions changes the state of the computer. This is called a **side effect** or **derived result**. Scheme's output procedures are perfect examples. They return unspecified values, but write values to output ports as a side effect.

Unintended or unneeded side effects usually take the form of environmental pollution: screen garbage, tainted globals, damaged files, etc. Although the definition of cube is very versatile, in the context of a larger application, like the CAD/CAM system, its cheery little messages become annoying screen pollution.

The for-each Meta-Procedure and writeln

As a final example, assume we want to display the values in a list without the surrounding parenthesis. Because the display procedure includes the parenthesis, we will have to write our own procedure for the job.

Fortunately, Scheme provides a meta-procedure we can use. Assume proc is any unary procedure —i.e., a procedure that expects a single input —and assume vals is a list of values. Then:

```
(for-each proc vals) =
    an unspecified value. As a side effect, proc is applied
    to each member of vals.
```

What happens to the values produced by the calls to proc? Unfortunately, they are discarded. If the values were important, then the map procedure should be used instead. However, if proc is an output procedure, then the outputs produced by applying it to the members of vals will be visible. For example:

```
·> (for-each display '(1 2 3))
123>
```

This is almost what we want: the values in the input list are displayed, but the surrounding parenthesis are not. Regrettably, the values are displayed without separating spaces. We can remedy this by using for-each with a modified version of display. Note that the body of our procedure is a sequence:

```
(define (display+ val)
    (display val)
    (display #\space))
```

Here's a sample call:

```
> (for-each display+ '(1 2 3))
1 2 3>
```

We can abstract this into a procedure:

```
(define (display-vals vals)
    (for-each display+ vals))
```

Here's a sample call:

```
> (display-vals '(1 2 3))
1 2 3>
```

Because display-vals doesn't print surrounding parenthesis, it would be nice to have a version that didn't require programmers to type the parenthesis that surround the input. We can use the optional parameter feature to define an *n*-ary procedure that displays any number of inputs followed by a newline:

```
(define (writeln . vals)
   (display-vals vals)
   (newline))
```

Here is a sample call:

```
> (writeln 4 " cubed = " (* 4 4 4))
4 cubed = 64
```

Appendix 3.3. Defensive Programming

Until now we have assumed that users will always call our procedures with valid inputs. This is a dangerous assumption. Procedures written by experienced programmers always validate all inputs before computing a result.

Validating inputs can be done using a conditional:

```
(define (dist x y)
   (if (and (real? x) (real? y))
       (abs (- x y))
       ???))
```

But what happens when a procedure discovers one or more of its inputs are invalid? What replaces ??? in the definition of dist? There are four choices:

1. The procedure attempts to repair the error.
2. The procedure displays an error message, then terminates gracefully.
3. The procedure sets a flag somewhere and hopes the user periodically checks the flag.
4. The procedure ignores the error.

Commercial software always chooses the first option. Nothing annoys or frightens a customer more than seeing hours of work replaced by an obscure error message.

Software under development uses the second option. A programmer wants to know about his errors right away. This is the technique we will use.

The third technique is familiar to assembly language programmers, who must constantly check overflow flags to determine if the last arithmetic operation produced the correct result.

The fourth technique is just lazy programming. The programmer lets the interpreter, operating system, or hardware deal with the error. At best, this produces very obscure error messages. At worst, it crashes the computer.

Using sequential evaluation and the printing procedures discussed earlier, we could design a special procedure for displaying error messages and terminating gracefully [2, 3] :

```
(define (error gripe location . irritants)
    (writeln "Error!")
    (writeln #\tab "gripe:" #\tab gripe)
    (writeln #\tab "location:" #\tab location)
    (if (not (null? irritants))
        (begin
           (writeln #\tab #\space
                    "irritant(s):"
                    #\tab #\space)
           (display-vals irritants)))
    (newline)
    (return error-token))
```

For now, the return procedure is merely the identity procedure, and the error-token is just a special symbol:

```
(define (return val) val)   ; for now
(define error-token 'error)
```

We can even predefine common gripes:

```
(define input-err "Illegal input(s)")
(define range-err "Input(s) out of range")
```

Continuations

> The future is what you make it, so make it a good one.
>
> —Doc Brown from *Back to the Future, III*

The escape procedure does a nice job of informing the user what went wrong, but what about terminating gracefully? The error message is useful to the human programmer, but what about the procedure that called dist and is now waiting for a numeric answer?

```
(define (dist x y)
    (if (and (real? x) (real? y))
        (abs (- x y))
        (error input-err dist x y)))
```

For example, recall the dist, small?, and close? procedures defined at the beginning of the Chapter 2:

---

[2] Some implementations of Scheme provide an error procedure.

[3] An alternative strategy that avoids I/O and sequencing is outlined in the last problem.

```
(define (small? z) (close? z 0)) ; i.e., near zero
(define (close? x y) (<= (dist x y) delta))
```

Assume a user calls small? with an invalid input:

```
> (small? "100")   ; strings are invalid here
```

In this case (close? "100" 0) is called, which calls (dist "100" 0), which calls (error ...), which calls (return error-token):

```
(small? "100")
(close? "100" 0)
(dist "100" 0)
(error input-err dist "100" 0)
(return error-token)
```

At this point close? is waiting for an answer from dist, small? is waiting for an answer from close?, and the user is waiting for an answer from small? Of course return merely returns the error-token, i.e., the symbol 'error. This is returned to error, which passes it to dist, which passes it to close?. Unfortunately, there's not much close? can do with a symbol, unless close? checks for the error-token and passes it on to small?. Of course small? is hoping for a Boolean value from close?, so it too must check for the error-token and pass it on to the user. A lot of work is being done just to propagate an error token (Figure 3.8).

Figure 3.8

It would be better if return could simply abandon the long chain of calling procedures, and return control directly to the user (Figure 3.9).

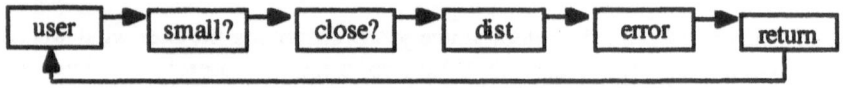

Figure 3.9

Amazingly, this is possible. The Scheme evaluator builds a unary procedure representing the future of the current computation.[4] This procedure is called a **continuation**. For example, at the moment return is called, the continuation is:

```
(lambda (hole) (<= (abs (- hole 0)) delta))
```

where the parameter, hole, represents the value that will be provided by return. The surprise is that programmers can capture continuations. To do this we must first write a procedure that expects the current continuation as an input:

---

[4] This might be a representation of the control stack in some languages.

```
(define (receiver cont) ???)
```

To get Scheme to pass the current continuation to receiver, we place the expression:

```
(call-with-current-continuation receiver)
```

at the point where the continuation is of interest to us.

Continuations can be called like ordinary procedures, but they abandon the context in which they are called and return control instead to the point where they were captured.

What if we capture a continuation at some point where the future looked bright and "redefined" return to be this continuation. A procedure can be redefined using set!, a Scheme assignment command:

```
; change return into a continuation
(define (receiver cont) (set! return cont))
```

Briefly, (set! NAME EXPRESSION) is used to redefine NAME to the value of EXPRESSION. This isn't quite accurate. The full story is the topic of Chapter 7. Assignment commands like set! don't belong in functional Scheme. Readers should refrain from using assignment commands until they are properly introduced in Chapter 7.

What continuation should we redefine return to be? Let's capture the continuation near the interpreter's prompt, just before an informative message is printed:

```
> (begin
    (call-with-current-continuation receiver)
    (writeln "returning to top level ...")
    #f)
#f
```

At the point of capture, the continuation is:

```
(lambda (hole)
   (begin
      hole
      (writeln "returning to top level ...")
      #f))
```

Calling small? with an invalid input will eventually call error, which will print the error message, then call return. Because return has been redefined to be the continuation, it abandons the long chain of calling procedures and returns control to the point immediately before the message is printed. This causes the captured continuation to resume as though it had been frozen in suspended animation and then suddenly thawed out:

```
> (small? "100")
Error!
   gripe:        Illegal input(s)
   source:       #[procedure: dist]
   irritant(s):  "100" 0
```

```
returning to top level ...
#f
>
```

Appendix 3.4. Debugging

> Hacking is like building a scale-model cathedral out of toothpicks, except that if one toothpick is out of place the whole cathedral disappears. And then you have to feel around for the invisible cathedral, trying to figure out which toothpick is wrong. Debuggers make it a little easier, but not much, because a truly screwed-up cutting-edge program is entirely capable of screwing up the debugger as well, so that then you're feeling around for the missing toothpick with a stroke-crippled claw-hand.
>
> But, ah, the dark dream beauty of the hacker grind against the hidden wall that only you can see, the wall that only you wail at, you the programmer, with the brand new tools that you made up as you went along, your special new toothpick lathes and jigs and your real-time scrimshaw shaver, you alone in the dark with your wonderful tools.
>
> —Rudy Rucker, *The Hacker and the Ants*

> When you have eliminated the impossible, whatever remains, however improbable, must be the truth.
>
> —Holmes, Spock, Data

Novice programmers often get caught up in the discipline of coding and neglect the less glamorous aspects of programming: testing and debugging. More experienced programmers know that testing and debugging are integral parts of programming and can be as exacting and demanding as writing code.

Debugging is an art. The idea is to systematically eliminate all potential causes of the bug. The key to systematic debugging is to know the general types and causes of errors. There are three categories: syntax errors, run-time errors, and logic errors.

Syntax Errors

Each time a definition is loaded from the editor into the Scheme interpreter a procedure called a **parser** checks to make sure parentheses are balanced, structures have the expected format, and there are no misplaced definitions. If not, an error message is generated and the load fails.

Syntax errors are fairly easy to fix by visual inspection. Reload definitions one at a time. When the offending definition turns up, count parentheses, double check the formats of structures, and reload.

Run-Time Errors

Run-time errors occur during testing, after the procedure has successfully loaded. Run-time errors are caught either by the evaluator or by error checks installed by the programmer.

Run-time errors caught by the evaluator are a nightmare because sometimes the program is able to limp along a little before it crashes, creating the impression that the error occurred beyond the point it actually occurred. In this case the error messages produced by the evaluator are cryptic and the offending code is often hard to locate. The most common run-time errors are scope errors, type errors, and range errors.

A **scope error** is caused when a symbol is referenced out of scope. The most typical example is calling a procedure or referencing a constant you simply forgot to define.

A **type error** is caused when the number or types of parameters don't match the number or types of arguments. Compiled languages like Pascal and C++ use **static type checking**, which means type errors are caught before the procedure runs. Unfortunately, Scheme uses **dynamic type checking**, which means type errors are only discovered when the procedure is called. For example, the following definition is allowed to load by the Scheme parser:

```
(define (test num) (+ num "42"))
```

But any call produces a run-time type error:

```
> (test 10)
error: non-numeric input to +: "42"
```

Imagine how frustrating it would be to see this message generated by a flight control program seconds before your new satellite plummets into the ocean. With static type checking this message appears and the problem is corrected when the flight control program is first compiled, months before the satellite is launched.

Another kind of type error results when the evaluator attempts to apply a nonprocedure to a list of operands:

```
> ("+" 3 4)
error: procedure expected
```

Range errors occur when a parameter conforms to the expected type of the argument, but is too big or too small:

```
(/ 42 0)
(string-ref "cat" -1)
(list-ref '(1 2 3) 100)
```

A fourth source of run-time errors is the operating system. These errors normally occur when the procedure is performing file I/O, for example, when a procedure attempts to write to a nonexistent file.

Run-time errors must be located before they can be fixed. The Scheme debugger can help locate a run-time error. PC-Scheme also provides trace and untrace procedures. Assume proc is the name of a procedure:

```
(trace proc)   = unspecified value. As a side effect, adds
    proc to the list of procedures to be traced
```

```
(untrace proc) = unspecified value. As a side effect,
    removes proc from the list of procedures to be traced.
```

A low-tech but reliable method is to plant diagnostic messages in the program. This will be discussed shortly.

Logic Errors

Logic errors don't produce error messages. The procedure runs, but the output, if any, is simply wrong. Unfortunately, this type of error usually lies in the logic of the procedure's algorithm.

There are a few less drastic types of logic errors. Sometimes a logic error can be the result of a precision error, such as the example given at the beginning of Chapter 2.

Another common logic error results in the dreaded infinite loop. **Infinite loops** are caused by nonterminating recursions or iterations:

```
(define (undefined) (undefined)) ; loops forever!
```

Sometimes this results in a "stack overflow" message from the evaluator, but in the case of iterations, the interpreter's prompt simply fails to reappear and the keyboard goes dead. Try using the **Break** key to stop the runaway computation.

Diagnostics

We can use the fact that expression sequences are allowed in clauses and procedure bodies to insert diagnostic messages for the purpose of tracking run-time errors. We use the writeln procedure to display our diagnostic messages. For example, here's another version of our tax procedure that includes diagnostics:

```
; = tax owed on income dollars
(define (tax income)
   (writeln "entering tax ... ")
   (cond ((not (real? income))
            (error input-err tax income))
         ((> income max-medium)
            (writeln "income > max-medium")
            (+ max-medium-tax
               (* max-rate (- income max-medium))))
         ((> income max-low)
            (writeln "income > max-low")
            (+ max-low-tax
               (* medium-rate (- income max-low))))
         ((> income min)
            (writeln "income > min")
```

```
          (* low-rate (- income max-min)))
     ((>= income 0) 0)
     (else
          (error "negative income" tax income))))
```

Inserting diagnostic messages allows us to automatically trace the flow of evaluation:

```
> (tax 8000)
entering tax...
income > min
300
```

Suppose we want to insert diagnostic messages into our first tax-computing procedure, the one based on the if-expression. We can use the begin-procedure to group the consequent and alternative with the appropriate diagnostic messages as follows:

```
; = tax on income dollars
(define (tax income)
   (writeln "entering tax procedure")
   (if (> income max-medium)
        (begin (writeln "income > max-medium")
               (+ max-medium-tax
                  (* max-rate (- income max-medium))))
        (begin (writeln "<= max-medium")
               (* income medium-rate))))
```

It is important to realize that reversing the order of the writeln expression and the multiplication in either the cond clauses or the begin expressions causes the tax procedure to return an unspecified value instead of the desired tax. (Why? What if begin0 is used instead?)

Problems

Solutions to the following problems are to be given in functional Scheme; do not use procedures or special forms discussed in subsequent chapters. Do not use any of the I/O procedures discussed in this chapter except to print error or diagnostic messages or unless you are specifically directed by the problem to use them. You may use the definitions given in this or previous chapters as well as solutions to other problems in this or previous chapters. (Although you will have to include these definitions in your definition file so you can test your definitions.) You may also define any supporting procedures you need. You are required to validate inputs.

Problem 3.1.

Assume the following definitions have been made:

```
(define x 100)
(define y 200)
(define z 300)
```

Evaluate the following expressions. If they contain errors, explain them. If their values are unspecified in IEEE/ANSI Scheme, indicate this with a question mark. Use your Scheme interpreter to check your work, but be careful, your interpreter may not be 100% compliant with IEEE/ANSI Scheme.

```
a. (* (or 3 4 5 6) (and 3 4 5 6))
b. (* (and 3 4 5 6) (begin0 3 4 5 6))
c. (* (if 0 3 5) (begin 3 4 5 6))
d. ((lambda (x) (* x x)) x)
e. ((lambda (f) (f x)) number?)
f. ((lambda (f) (f x)) (lambda (x) (+ x x)))
g. (case x ((x) 12) ((y) 32) ((z) 19) (else 0))
```

Problem 3.2.

The eager evaluation procedure outlined at the beginning of Chapter 2 didn't make clear if operands were evaluated from left to right or right to left. How can you use the output procedures described herein to figure out in which direction your Scheme interpreter evaluates parameters?

Problem 3.3.

As a punishment for rowdy behavior, Friedrich Gauss' first grade teacher commanded him to spend the rest of the day calculating the sum of all integers from 1 to 100. A moment later Gauss had the answer, 5050. When asked how he got the solution so fast, Gauss pointed out that the sum could be gotten as follows:

$$(1 + 100) + (2 + 99) + (3 + 98) + \ldots + (50 + 51) = 101 * 50$$

Use this idea to come up with an elementary (i.e., nonrecursive) implementation of the triangle procedure.

Problem 3.4.

The nth pyramid number is the number of blocks required to build a four-sided pyramid n blocks high. For example:

```
(pyramid 0) = 0
(pyramid 1) = 1
(pyramid 2) = 5
(pyramid 3) = 14
```

Implement pyramid using a recursive algorithm. Can you find an elementary implementation?

Problem 3.5.

Mathematicians use the notation $n!$ to denote n factorial, the product of all integers from 1 to n. By convention, $0! = 1$. Implement this as a Scheme procedure:

```
; = (* 1 2 ... n)
(define (fact n) ???)
```

Problem 3.6.

Implement the following procedure twice:

```
(choose n m)    = 0, if n < m

(choose n m)    = 1, if m = 0 or m = n

(choose n m)    =
   number of ways to choose m items from n items,
```

$$= 0, \text{ if } n < m$$

$$= 1, \text{ if } m = 0 \text{ or } m = n.$$

The first implementation should be based on the following observation:

There are two ways to choose m items from n. Pick one item not to be chosen, then choose m items from the remaining n - 1 items:

```
(choose (- n 1) m)
```

Or pick one item to be chosen, and pick m - 1 items from the remaining n - 1 items:

```
(choose (- n 1) (- m 1))
```

The second algorithm is based on the following formula:

$$\text{choose}(n,m) = \frac{n!}{m!(n-m)!}$$

Problem 3.7.

Define a procedure called witnesses, which expects a predicate, pred, and a natural number n as parameters, and which returns a list of all natural numbers $m \leq n$ such that (pred m) is true. For example:

```
> (witnesses even? 10)
(10 8 6 4 2 0)
> (witnesses prime? 10)
(7 5 3 2)
```

Problem 3.8.

Define a procedure called divisors that expects two positive integer inputs n and m, and returns a list of all positive integers below n that divide m. (Recall, k divides m if (remainder m k) = 0.)

```
> (divisors 30 10)
(10 6 5 3 2 1)
> (divisors 8 10)
(8 4 2 1)
```

Problem 3.9.

A positive integer n is prime if $2 \leq n$, and the only divisors of n are 1 and itself. Use the divisors procedure in the last problem to define a prime? predicate.

Problem 3.10.

The Fibonacci sequence is:

```
0 1 1 2 3 5 8 13 21 34 etc.
```

The Fibonacci numbers are interesting because they are ubiquitous in nature. Implement a recursive version of a procedure that calculates Fibonacci numbers:

```
(fib 0)  = 0
(fib 1)  = 1
(fib 2)  = 1
(fib 3)  = 2
etc.
```

Problem 3.11.

The harmonic series is $\sum_{k=1}^{\infty} \frac{1}{k}$. Write a recursive Scheme procedure that computes the partial sums of this series, i.e.,

$$(\text{harmonic-sum } n) = \sum_{k=1}^{n} \frac{1}{k}$$

Problem 3.12.

Recall from Calculus that the fixed point of the derivative procedure is $f(x) = e^x$. The exact value of e is given by the series:

$$e = \sum_{k=0}^{\infty} \frac{1}{k!}$$

Write a recursive Scheme procedure that approximate e to any accuracy by computing partial sums of this series.

Problem 3.13.

Write a recursive Scheme procedure called sum that expects an unsigned integer input n and returns the following partial sum:

$$\text{sum(n)} = \sum_{i=1}^{n} \frac{(-1)^i}{2i}$$

Problem 3.14.

Assume Scheme did not supply * but did supply +. Of course * is an overloaded procedure, but most variants can be defined in terms of nat*, which multiplies two natural numbers. Find a recursive implementation of nat* that doesn't use *.

Problem 3.15.

Assume Scheme did not supply +, but did supply add1 and sub1:

```
(add1 z) = z + 1
(sub1 z) = z - 1
```

(If your version of Scheme doesn't provide add1 and sub1 you'll have to define them using +.) Of course + is an overloaded procedure, but most variants can be defined in terms of nat+, which adds two natural numbers. Find a recursive implementation of nat+ that doesn't use +.

Problem 3.16.

Assume Scheme did not provide gcd. The gcd of n and m is the gcd of m and (remainder n m). Use this fact to implement gcd. Also implement remainder.

Problem 3.17.

Write a meta-procedure called compose that accepts an unsigned integer n and a unary numeric procedure f as input. The compose procedure composes f with itself n times, then applies the resulting procedure to 1:

```
(f (f ... (f 1) ... ))  ; n times
```

Examples:

```
> (compose 4 add1)
5           ; = (add1 (add1 (add1 (add1 1))))
> (compose 3 square)
1           ; = (square (square (square 1)))
> (compose 0 foo)
1           ; = base case
```

Problem 3.18.

Assume m and n are natural numbers. Find a recursive implementation of:

```
(m-to-n m n)
   = (m ... n) if m < n
   = () otherwise
```

Problem 3.19.

Assume n is a natural number. Implement a procedure called nest, which generates a nest of n lists:

```
(nest 0) = ()
(nest 1) = (())
(nest 2) = ((()))
etc.
```

Problem 3.20.

Assume Scheme did not provide list-ref or length. How could you implement these using recursion?

Problem 3.21.

Assume vals is a list and n is a natural number. Find a recursive implementation of the following procedure:

```
(rem-n-th vals n) =
    vals with the item in position n removed
```

Problem 3.22.

Find recursive implementations of the list-tail and list-prefix procedures. (List-prefix was defined in Chapter 2.)

Problem 3.23.

Assume vals is a list and n is a natural number. Find a recursive implementation of the following procedure:

```
(put-n-th vals val n)    =
    vals with val inserted in position n.
```

Problem 3.24.

A leap year is any unsigned integer divisible by 400, or divisible by 4, but not 100. For example, 1700, 1800, 1900, 1901, 1902, and 1903 were not leap years, but 1600 and 1904 were leap years. Without using conditionals (if, cond, or case) and assuming val is any Scheme value, implement the following polymorphic procedure:

```
(leap? val)
    = #t, if val is a leap year
    = #f, otherwise
```

Problem 3.25.

A CVC syllable is a length-three string consisting of a consonant followed by a vowel, followed by a consonant. Implement a procedure that tests for CVCs.

Problem 3.26.

Pig Latin is an artificial language derived from English by the following rules:

If an English word begins with a consonant, then the equivalent Pig Latin word is obtained by moving the consonant to the end of the word and adding "ay." For example:

```
plane    -> lanepay
```

If an English word begins with a vowel, then the corresponding Pig Latin word is obtained by adding an "ay" to the end of the word. For example:

```
apple   -> appleay
```

Implement a procedure that translates strings into their Pig Latin translations. Your procedure should validate its input making sure it's a string consisting of upper- and lower-case letters only. Do not attempt to validate that the string is actually in the English dictionary.

```
(define (latinize string) ???)
```

Problem 3.27.

Consider the following definition:

```
(define (if. condition consequent alternative)
   (if condition consequent alternative))
```

How does if. differ from if? (Apart from the fact that alternative is optional for if, but not for if.) Give an example of a situation where replacing if by if. causes a procedure to fail.

Problem 3.28.

You download a LISP interpreter from an FTP site. Unfortunately, there is no documentation and no source code. You know the interpreter accepts Scheme syntax, but you are unsure if the interpreter uses eager or delayed evaluation. What experiment could you perform to find out?

Problem 3.29.

You download a Scheme interpreter from an FTP site. Unfortunately, there is no source code or documentation. Furthermore, rumor has it that this particular version doesn't support short circuit evaluation. How can you figure out if this is true?

Problem 3.30.

You download a LISP interpreter from an FTP site. Unfortunately, there is no source code or documentation. Furthermore, rumor has it that this particular version uses static type checking. How can you figure out if this is true?

Problem 3.31.

Using the quadratic rule, write a procedure that computes the largest real solution of a quadratic equation:

$$ax^2 + bx + c = 0$$

Your procedure will be passed the coefficients as inputs:

```
(define (max-root a b c) ???)
```

Warning: The largest real root isn't always the one obtained by adding the discriminant. If the quadratic has no real roots, you should generate an error message.

Problem 3.32.

Necessary Scheme (NS) is Scheme with all redundant features removed:

```
NS = Scheme - redundant features
```

Surprisingly, most of the primitive domains, primitive procedures, and structures provided by IEEE/ANSI Scheme are redundant. The following problems will show that most structures are redundant because they can be rewritten using if-structures and lambda-structures:

Problem 3.32.1.

Rewrite the following case-structure as a cond-structure:

```
(case k ((a b c) x) ((d e f) y) ((g h i) z) (else 0))
```

Problem 3.32.2.

Rewrite the following cond-structure using if-structures. You may also want to use sequential structures (i.e., begin, begin0):

```
(cond
    (a1 a2 a3) (b1 b2 b3) (c1 c2 c3) (else d1 d2 d3))
```

Problem 3.32.3.

Rewrite the following expressions using if-structures:

```
a. (and a b c d e)
b. (or a b c d e)
c. (not a)
d. (and (or a b (not c)) (and (not (or b c)) d))
```

Problem 3.32.4.

Assume Scheme did not provide the control structures begin and begin0. Assume Scheme always evaluates operands from left to right. How could you implement begin and begin0 as Scheme procedures:

```
(define (begin0 . vals) ???)
(define (begin . vals) ???)
```

Problem 3.33.

An alternative approach to error handling that avoids I/O and sequential evaluation is to design the error procedure to create an **error descriptor** from its inputs, then return this descriptor through the return procedure described in Appendix 3.3: Defensive Programming.

```
(define (error gripe source . irritants)
   (return
      (make-error-descriptor gripe source errors)))
```

An error descriptor is an association list of the form:

```
ERROR-DESCRIPTOR ::=
   (("gripe" . GRIPE)
   ("source" . SOURCE)
   [("irritant(s):" VALUE ...)])
```

Implement make-error-descriptor. Also, you'll probably want to redefine return as the continuation formed at the point where a debugger is being called:

```
> (debug (call-with-current-continuation receiver))
unspecified
```

For now, debug could simply be the identity procedure. How could you include the continuation at the point of error in the descriptor?

4
Data Control

The theme of this chapter is controlling access to procedures and data by either hiding them or hiding information about how they are represented. In both cases access is restricted to certain privileged procedures. This may sound like censorship, but inviting procedures written by others to access one's own data and procedures invites potential misuse and unwanted alterations. We can formalize our theme as the **information hiding principle**:

Information should only be made available on a need-to-know basis.

4.1. Procedure Blocks

Many implementations of Scheme allow programmers to nest definitions inside procedure blocks:

```
PROCEDURE-BLOCK ::=
    (define HEADER DEFINITION ... EXPRESSION ...)
```

where

```
DEFINITION ::=
    (define NAME EXPRESSION) | PROCEDURE-BLOCK
```

Nested definitions are also called **local definitions**, while non-nested definitions are called **global definitions**. Names introduced by global definitions are called **globals**. Names introduced by local definitions are called **locals** relative to the procedure in which they are defined, while names used but not defined inside a procedure are called **nonlocals**.

For example, in the following procedure block:

```
; = volume of a length len, radius rad cylinder
(define (cylinder-volume rad len)
    (define pi (acos -1))    ; = 3.1416...
    ; = area of a radius r circle
    (define (base-area r) (* pi (square r)))
    ; body of circle-volume
    (* len (base-area rad)))
```

pi and base-area are local, while acos and * are nonlocal relative to cylinder-volume, and rad and len are parameters. In fact, *, acos, and cylinder-volume are globals. Relative to base-area, pi, *, and square are nonlocals, and *r* is a parameter.

The **scope** of a procedure or constant is the region of the program where it can be used. A global has **global scope**. It can be used anywhere in the program. Like a parameter, the scope of a local is limited to the procedure block that contains its definition. This is called **local scope**.

4.1.1. The Nesting Instinct

Why and when to nest? A corollary of the information hiding principle is the **locality principle**:

> Scopes should be as small as possible.

Limiting the scopes of procedures and data improves reliability, understandability, and efficiency.

Improving Understandability

Sometimes the body of a procedure definition gets too complicated for humans to read easily. For example, the max-avg procedure expects as input an association list containing lists of scores on three exams:

```
((exam1 . (score ...))
   (exam2 . (score ...))
      (exam3 . (score ...)))
```

and returns the maximum average score:

```
(define (max-avg exams)
   (max (/ (apply + (cdar exams))
           (length (cdar exams)))
        (/ (apply + (cdadr exams))
           (length (cdadr exams)))
        (/ (apply + (cdaddr exams))
           (length (cdaddr exams)))))
```

We can make this procedure easier to read if we give suggestive names to the intermediate results:

```
(define (max-avg exams)
   (define exam1 (cdar exams))
   (define exam2 (cdadr exams))
   (define exam3 (cdaddr exams))
   (define avg1 (/ (apply + exam1) (length exam1)))
   (define avg2 (/ (apply + exam2) (length exam2)))
```

```
(define avg3 (/ (apply + exam3) (length exam3)))
(max avg1 avg2 avg3))
```

Improving Reliability

Limiting the scopes of procedures and data improves reliability because there are fewer opportunities for them to be redefined, altered, or misused. Recall the definition of the close? predicate given at the beginning of Chapter 2:

```
; = (|x - y| <= delta)
(define (close? x y)
   (<= (dist x y) delta))
```

The body of the close? predicate contains two parameters, x and y, and three globals: <=, the dist procedure defined in Chapter 2 (= |x - y|), and the constant, delta (= 10^{-20}).

It is appropriate to make dist a global procedure. Nesting it inside a procedure block would make it unavailable to any other procedure that need to compute the distance between two real numbers. On the other hand, it is inappropriate to make delta a global constant. If an unwary user inadvertently redefines delta:

```
(define delta 100)
```

the close? predicate will no longer work properly. Nesting the definition of delta inside close? means it can't be redefined inadvertently:

```
(define (close? x y)
   (define delta 1e-20)
   (<= (dist x y) delta))
```

Even if a global delta is defined:

```
(define delta 100)
```

it will have no effect on the behavior of close?. Although the occurrence of delta in the body of close? is in the scope of both the global and local delta, we will soon see that the eager evaluation algorithm automatically chooses locals over nonlocals, and therefore uses the local delta.

As another example, recall the definition of the triangle procedure given in the last chapter:

```
; = (+ n ... 0)
(define (triangle n)
   (if (natural? n)
       (unsafe-triangle n)
       (error "bad input" triangle n)))
```

where unsafe-triangle was a global recursive procedure that, for efficiency reasons, didn't perform input validation. We hope the "unsafe" prefix will discourage people from using unsafe-triangle, but this is no guarantee. However, nesting the definition of un-safe-triangle inside the definition of triangle makes this impossible:

```
(define (triangle n)

    ; local definition
    (define (unsafe-triangle n)
        (if (zero? n)
            0
            (+ n (unsafe-triangle (- n 1)))))

    ; body of triangle
    (if (natural? n)
        (unsafe-triangle n)
        (error "bad input" triangle n)))
```

(Don't be confused by the fact that triangle and unsafe-triangle both have a parameter called *n*. The situation is no different than when unsafe-triangle was a global procedure. Remember, there are almost no restrictions on parameter names.)

Improving Efficiency

Sometimes a lengthy computation based on a procedure's parameters can be performed once, then defined as a local constant, where it can be referenced multiple times inside the procedure without recomputing it. The following variance procedure is an example of this application of definition nesting.

How do we describe the distribution of a list of test scores? The two principle features of a distribution —center and spread —can be quantified by the mean and standard deviation, respectively.

The **mean** is simply the average:

```
(define (mean scores)
    (if (distribution? scores)
        (/ (apply + scores) (length scores))
        (error "bad input" mean scores)))
```

where distribution? is a polymorphic predicate that returns true if its input is a nonempty list of real numbers. We use the all? predicate defined in Chapter 2:

```
(define (distribution? val)
    (and (list? val)
         (all? real? val)
         (not (null? val))))
```

The **standard deviation** is the positive square root of the variance:

```
(define (std-dev scores)
    (if (distribution? scores)
```

```
(sqrt (variance scores))
(error "bad input" std-dev scores)))
```

Basically, the variance of a list of scores is the average deviation, where the deviation of a score x is its signed distance to the mean, μ:

```
deviation of x = x - μ
```

But by the definition of mean, the average deviation is always 0, therefore we modify the definition of variance slightly, and take it to be the average squared deviation. Assume scores $= (x_1 \, x_2 \dots x_N)$, then:

$$variance = \frac{\sum_{i=1}^{N}(x_i - \mu)^2}{N}$$

How do we translate this expression into a Scheme procedure:

```
; = variance of a list of scores
(define (variance scores) ???)
```

Assume deviations $= (x_1 - \mu \; x_2 - \mu \dots x_N - \mu)$. Given the square procedure, we can use the map procedure to convert deviations into a list of squared deviations. The variance is simply the mean of this list:

```
(mean (map square deviations)) ; = variance
```

We could use the map procedure again to translate a list of scores into a list of deviations:

```
(define deviations (map deviation scores))
```

With only a single list argument, map's procedure argument must be unary:

```
; = score - mean
(define (deviation score) ???)    ; 1 input only
```

Given the list of scores as a nonlocal, the deviation procedure could simply compute the mean internally:

```
(define (deviation score)
   (- score (mean scores)))
```

Nesting the definition of deviation inside the definition of variance insures that scores will be available as a nonlocal:

```
(define (variance scores)
   (define (deviation score)
      (- score (mean scores)))
   (define deviations (map deviation scores))
   (mean (map square deviations)))
```

Although this works, it is terribly inefficient. Assume the length of the list of scores is N. Inside the map procedure, the deviation procedure will be called N times. But each time the deviation procedure is called, it calls (mean scores), which requires $N-1$ additions and always produces the same result, μ. Hence, these same $N-1$ additions will be performed N times, for a total of $N^2 - N$ additions.

By computing the mean once and making it a local constant relative to variance, it can be available to deviation as a nonlocal:

```
(define (variance scores)
    (define mu (mean scores))
    (define (deviation score) (- score mu))
    (define deviations (map deviation scores))
    (mean (map square deviations)))
```

This reduces the number of sums from $N^2 - N$ to $N - 1$, a great improvement if N is large.

Finally, notice that we can save ourselves an additional traversal of scores (N steps) by combining square and deviation:

```
(define (variance scores)
    (define mu (mean scores))
    (define (deviation^2 score) (square (- score mu)))
    (mean (map deviation^2 scores)))
```

4.2. The Environment Model of Eager Evaluation

The eager and lazy evaluation algorithms outlined at the beginning of Chapter 3 are called **substitution models** because in the third step of eager evaluation (the second step of lazy evaluation) arguments (operands) substitute or replace the parameters in the procedure's body. Now that procedures can also have local definitions, we need a more elaborate explanation of eager evaluation[1] called the **environment model**.

4.2.1. Bindings

A **binding** is an association between a name and a value. Definitions create bindings and store them in tables called **environments**. The process of creating a binding from a definition is called **resolution**. For example, resolving the definition:

```
(define (cube z) (* z z z))
```

creates a binding between the name, cube, and the procedure (lambda (z) (* z z z)) and then stores this binding in the global environment.

The **extent** or **lifetime** of a binding is the period of time the binding exists. If a binding exists until the end of a Scheme session, it has **global extent**, otherwise it has **local extent**.

---

[1] The environment model of lazy evaluation is presented in Chapter 8.

The **scope** of a binding is the region of the program where the binding is visible. If a binding is visible throughout the entire program, it has **global scope**, otherwise it has **local scope**.

A **global binding** is a binding created by resolving a global definition. Unless a global binding is explicitly replaced, it has global extent and scope. For example, as long as we don't redefine cube, the binding between cube and (lambda (z) (* z z z)) will have global scope and extent. However, if we change our minds and redefine cube:

```
; = a 3D box with height = width = depth = s
(define (cube s) (make-box s s s))
```

then a binding between cube and (lambda (s) (make-box *s s s*)) replaces the binding between cube and (lambda (z) (* z z z)).

Local bindings are bindings created by local definitions. We know that the scope of a local binding is limited to the procedure in which it is defined. In other words, local bindings have local scope. Usually a local binding also has local extent; as soon as the procedure terminates, the binding disappears. Later we will learn how to create bindings with local scope but global extent.

Obviously local bindings can't be stored in the global environment; otherwise they would have global scope. The solution is to adjust the eager evaluation algorithm so it creates a temporary extension of the global environment, adds the bindings created by resolving any local definitions to the extension, then evaluates the body of the procedure relative to this temporary environment.

In fact, instead of replacing parameters by arguments in the procedure's body as required by the substitution model of eager evaluation, we can simply add bindings between parameters and arguments (called **parameter bindings**) to the temporary environment along with the **declared bindings**, then evaluate the parameterized body of the procedure relative to the temporary environment. Here's the environment model of eager evaluation:

1. Evaluate the operator.
2. Produce arguments by evaluating the operands.
3. Resolve all local definitions.
4. Extend the calling environment by adding declared and parameter bindings.
5. Evaluate the parameterized body of the procedure relative to the extended environment.
6. Restore the original calling environment.

4.2.2. Environments

We need to understand the structure of an environment in order to understand how it is extended and restored. An **environment** can be viewed as a list of frames:

```
ENVIRONMENT ::= (FRAME ...)
```

A **frame** is a table of bindings. For example, Figure 4.1 shows a frame containing the bindings $x = 1$, $y = 2$, and $z = 3$.

NAME	VALUE
x	1
y	2
z	3

Figure 4.1

To be more definite, we can model a binding as a pair and a frame as an association list. Thus, we can model the frame in Figure 4.1 as the association list $((x . 1) (y . 2) (z . 3))$.

We will complete the formalization of eager evaluation in the last chapter. For now, let's represent an environment using **environment diagrams**. For example, recall the small? predicate defined in Chapter 2:

```
(define (small? z) (close? z 0)) ; i.e., z near 0
```

Let's assume the close? predicate is the one defined earlier, containing the local definition of delta. Assume also that a global definition of delta has been made:

```
(define delta 100)
```

Thus, the global environment contains bindings for delta, small?, close?, dist, etc. When the application (small? 100) is evaluated, a new frame containing the parameter binding $z = 100$ extends the current (i.e., global) environment. The body of small:

```
(close? z 0)
```

is evaluated relative to this extended environment.

This creates a new frame containing the parameter bindings $x = 100$, $y = 0$, and the declared binding delta $= 10^{-20}$. This frame is added to the calling environment, and the body of close?:

```
(<= (dist x y) delta)
```

is evaluated relative to this environment. This stage of evaluation can be represented with the environment diagram shown in Figure 4.2. We can now begin to see why the global binding delta $= 100$ does not effect the behavior of close?. When the evaluator encounters delta in the expression (<= (dist x y) delta), it searches the first frame in the environment before it searches the last frame, and therefore it finds the binding delta $= 10^{-20}$ before it finds the binding delta $= 100$.

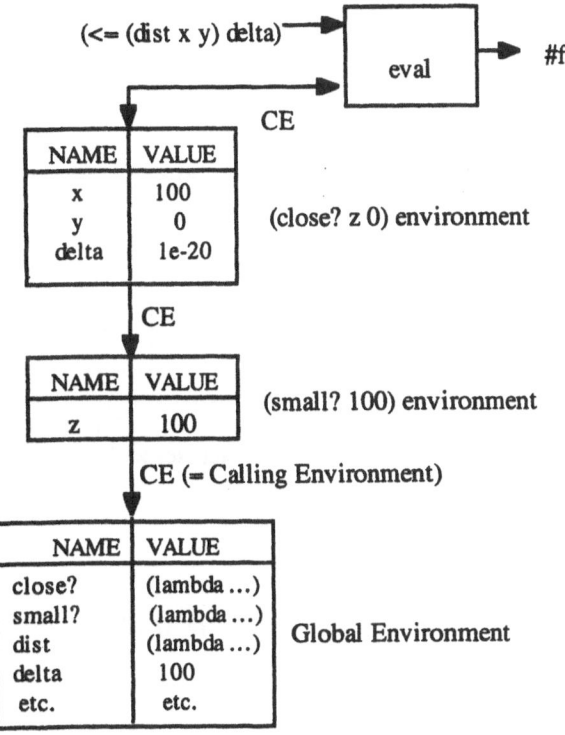

Figure 4.2

4.2.3. Static Versus Dynamic Scope Rules

When eval encounters a name inside an expression, it searches the environment for the corresponding value. To complete our description of eager evaluation, we must give a full account of how this search is performed.

As we saw in the last example, eval begins by searching the first frame in its environment. If the name is a parameter or a local, then eval will find the corresponding value in this frame, and the search will end.

What happens if the name is nonlocal? Clearly a binding won't be found in the first frame. It would seem reasonable for eval to next search the second frame in the environment. If this search fails, the third frame could be searched, and so on until the global environment is finally searched. If searching the global environment fails, an undefined symbol error could be raised.

To get a clearer picture of this search procedure, let's replace the close? predicate in the last example with the close? predicate defined earlier. Recall that this procedure compared (dist x y) to a global constant delta:

```
(define (close? x y)
   (<= (dist x y) delta))

(define delta 1e-20)
```

As long as delta isn't redefined, close? should work properly. Figure 4.3 shows an environment diagram representing the evaluation of (<= (dist *x y*) delta).

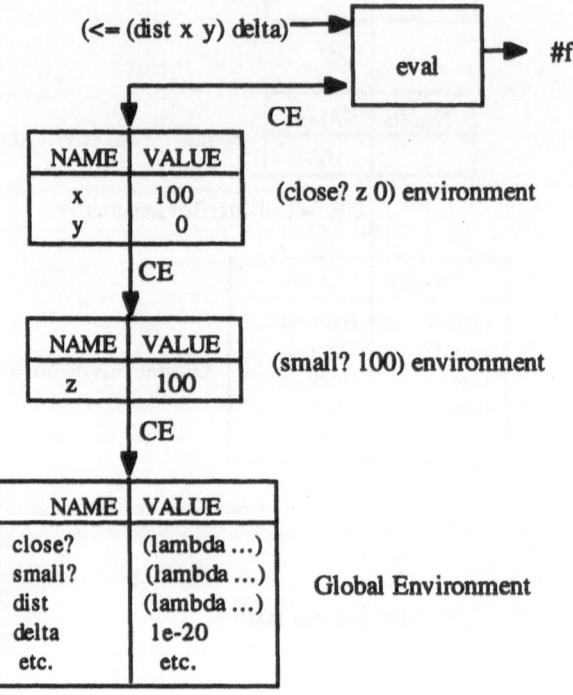

Figure 4.3

When eval encounters the nonlocal delta, the search of the first frame will fail. The search of the second frame will also fail. Eventually, the global environment will be searched, where the binding delta $= 10^{-20}$ will be discovered.

It seems like the search strategy outlined here works well, but consider the following scenario: Suppose close?, dist, and delta are included in a commercial library of mathematical procedures. Although the documentation for the library explains what the dist and close? procedures do, descriptions of how they work are omitted to prevent someone from duplicating the code and reselling it. For the same reason, compiled rather than source code is shipped to customers. (Yes, Scheme can be compiled!)

A library customer decides to use the close? predicate to implement small?. Because there are no restrictions on parameter names and because she couldn't know about the constant delta, she decides to call small?'s parameter delta. (Hey, it's a free country!)

```
(define (small? delta) (close? delta 0))
```

Next, she tests her new procedure:

```
> (small? 100)
#t
> (small? 1000)
#t
> (small? 10000000000000)
#t
```

Confused, frightened, and enraged, she calls the support number and reports that the library's close? procedure has a bug. What went wrong?

Neither close? nor small? has a bug. (Although it may take our software engineers some weeks to come to this conclusion.) The problem is in our environment search strategy. At the point (<= (dist x y) delta) is evaluated, the environment diagram looks exactly like the diagram in Figure 4.3, except the binding delta = 100 replaces the binding z = 100 in the middle frame. Unfortunately, our simple search strategy will encounter this binding before the delta = 10^{-20} binding in the global environment. Thus, the body of close? is equivalent to (<= 100 100), which, of course, is true.

Searching the calling environment (CE) for the values of nonlocals is called the **dynamic scope rule**. Because of problems like the one just described, this rule is rarely used. It's unreasonable to expect procedures to work in any environment other than the environment in which they were defined. An alternative search strategy would be to search the **defining environment** (DE) for values of nonlocals. This is called the **static scope rule**.

In the preceeding example, the defining environment for close? —i.e., the environment that contains the close? procedure —is the global environment. If we search this environment for the value of delta, we skip over the delta = 100 binding in the middle frame and arrive at the correct delta = 10^{-20} binding.

How do we remember the defining environment of a procedure? This information will have to be included with the procedure's parameters and body when the procedure is defined. A procedure, together with its defining environment, is called a **closure**. We can picture a closure as a three-compartment box floating in the computer's memory. The first compartment contains the procedure's parameter list, the second compartment contains the body, and the third compartment contains a pointer to the procedure's defining environment, as in Figure 4.4.

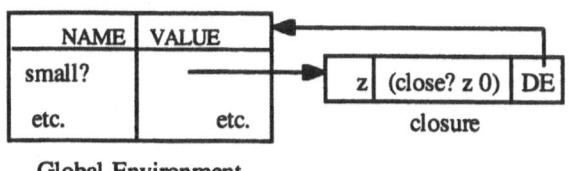

Global Environment

Figure 4.4

4.3.   Abstract Data Types

> Case's virus had bored a window through the library's command ice. He punched him-
> self through and found an infinite blue space ranged with color-coded spheres strung
> on a tight grid of pale blue neon. In the nonspace of the matrix, the interior of a given
> data construct possessed unlimited subjective dimension; a child's toy calculator would
> have presented limitless gulfs of nothingness hung with a few basic commands... He
> began to glide through the spheres as if he were on invisible tracks.
>
> —William Gibson, *Neuromancer*

Unfortunately programmers can't explicitly define new domains in Scheme. Instead, new
domains must be defined implicitly through their constructors and selectors. A domain
defined this way is called an **abstract data type**, or **ADT** for short.

4.3.1.   Example : The CARD ADT

Pairs are useful when two pieces of data need to be grouped together. For example, a
playing card has two attributes, suit and rank. If we represent suits and ranks using symbols, we can represent a card as a pair of symbols:

```
SUIT ::= spade | heart | diamond | club
RANK ::= ace | two | three | ... | jack | queen | king
CARD ::= (RANK . SUIT)
```

Here are some examples of cards:

```
(define card1 '(ace . heart))
(define card2 '(king . club))
(define card3 '(three . spade))
```

Our card constructor could merely cons together its suit and rank inputs:

```
(define (make-card rank suit) (cons rank suit))
```

We can add input validation to our constructor by first defining lists of all suits and
ranks:

```
(define ranks
  '(ace two three four five six seven eight nine ten
    jack queen king))

(define suits '(spade club diamond heart))
```

The improved constructor uses the member? predicate defined in Chapter 2 to determine
if its inputs belong to these lists:

```
(define (make-card rank suit)
   (if (and (member? rank ranks) (member? suit suits))
       (cons rank suit)
       (error "bad input(s)" make-card rank suit)))
```

We also define selectors for extracting rank and suit. These procedures are nothing more than wrappers (as in the fancy paper used to wrap a gift) for car and cdr:

```
(define (rank card) (car card))
(define (suit card) (cdr card))
```

This seems inefficient because the only purpose of rank and suit is to call car and cdr. We can achieve the same effect by explicitly defining rank and suit to be pseudonyms of car and cdr:

```
(define rank car)
(define suit cdr)
```

We can complete the disguise by defining constants representing the suits and ranks:

```
(define spade 'spade)
(define heart 'heart)
(define diamond 'diamond)
(define club 'club)

(define ace 'ace)
(define two 'two)
etc.
(define queen 'queen)
(define king 'king)
```

Assume the following definitions have been made:

```
(define card1 (make-card ace spade))
(define card2 (make-card jack diamond))
```

Here are some sample calls to our selectors:

```
> (suit card1)
spade
> (rank card2)
jack
```

Because suits and ranks are symbols, we can use the efficient eq? predicate to build predicates like the following ones:

```
(define (spade? card)
   (eq? spade (suit card)))

(define (ace? card)
   (eq? ace (rank card)))
```

Here are some sample evaluations:

```
> (spade? card1)
#t
> (ace? card2)
#f
```

Using the CARD ADT

The make-suit procedure constructs arbitrary suits of cards represented as lists:

```
; = list of all cards of input suit
(define (make-suit suit) ???)
```

Its algorithm makes use of the map procedure. The idea is to map the make-card constructor onto the list of ranks defined earlier:

```
(map make-card ranks)        ; this fails!
```

Unfortunately, make-card expects two inputs, but we are only supplying a single list of inputs to map. What's needed is a variant of make-card that expects a single input, rank, and makes a card of a fixed suit determined by a nonlocal:

```
; = (rank . suit)
(define (make-card-of-suit rank)
   (make-card rank suit))     ; suit is nonlocal
```

Because the nonlocal suit is determined by the make-suit parameter, this variant of make-card will have to be defined inside the make-suit procedure:

```
; = list of all cards of suit input
(define (make-suit suit)

   ; local, hence in the scope of suit
   (define (make-card-of-suit rank)
     (make-card rank suit))

   (map make-card-of-suit ranks))
```

We use this procedure as follows:

```
(define spades (make-suit spade))
(define hearts (make-suit heart))
(define diamonds (make-suit diamond))
(define clubs (make-suit club))
```

A deck of cards is gotten by appending the suits:

```
(define deck (append spades hearts clubs diamonds))
```

Some implementations of Scheme provide a random number generator. Assume *n* is an unsigned integer:

```
(random n) =
    a pseudo random integer m such that 0 ≤ m < n
```

We can combine this with length and list-ref to write a procedure that picks a random card from a list of cards:

```
; = a random card selected from the list cards
(define (pick-a-card cards)
    (list-ref cards (random (length cards))))
```

Here are some sample calls:

```
> (pick-a-card deck)
(three . club)
> (pick-a-card deck)
(jack . diamond)
> (pick-a-card hearts)
(eight . heart)
```

4.3.2. Information Hiding and Data Abstraction

Why bother introducing constructors and selectors? Wouldn't it be simpler and more efficient to use cons instead of make-card, car instead of rank, and cdr instead of suit?

Imagine the following scenario: A customer develops a bridge-playing program using version 1 of a library purchased from us containing the CARD ADT and some basic procedures for manipulating cards. Knowing that cards are represented as pairs, the customer freely uses car and cdr to compute the rank and suit of cards and cons to create cards. In version 2 of our library we decide for efficiency reasons to represent suits and ranks as strings and cards as vectors such as: #("spade" "ace"). Unfortunately, the customer will not be able to use (i.e., buy) version 2 of our library without replacing all occurrences of car, cdr, and cons in the bridge-playing program. Furthermore, these occurrences may be so ubiquitous that changing them would be nearly impossible.

Perhaps now would be a good time to recall the abstraction Principle from Chapter 2:

Structure and function should be independent.

In the case of the CARD ADT, structure refers to the way cards are represented as pairs of symbols, while function refers to the interface procedures available for manipulating cards: make-card, suit, and rank. The abstraction principle is related to the information hiding principle, because keeping structure and function independent in effect hides the representation from users.

If the customer in our scenario only uses the intended selectors and constructors, then the bridge-playing program can use version 2 of the library without any changes.

4.3.3. Example: The POINT ADT

Mathematicians use vectors to represent points in three-dimensional space:

```
POINT ::= #(REAL REAL REAL)
```

For example, the point #(2 5 3) represents the point with x-coordinate = 2, y-coordinate = 5, and z-coordinate = 3.

We begin by introducing a polymorphic predicate to determine if values are points:

```
(define (point? val)
   (and (vector? val)
        (= (vector-length val) 3)
        (and (real? (vector-ref val 0))
             (real? (vector-ref val 1))
             (real? (vector-ref val 2)))
```

We can use vector-ref to define procedures for extracting the x, y, and z coordinates of a point:

```
(define (xc point)
   (if (point? point)
       (vector-ref point 0)
       (error "bad input" xc point)))
```

The yc and zc selectors are left as copying exercises:

```
(define (yc point) ???)
(define (zc point) ???)
```

We could define a constructor as a pseudonym for vector:

```
(define make-point vector)
```

Instead, we add some input validation:

```
(define (make-point xc yc zc)
   (if (and (real? xc) (real? yc) (real? zc))
       (vector xc yc zc)
       (error "bad input(s)" make-point xc yc zc)))
```

Basic arithmetic procedures can be extended to points. For example, the x-coordinate of the sum of two points P_1 and P_2 is the sum of the x-coordinate of P_1 and the x-coordinate of P_2. The y- and z-coordinates of the sum of P_1 and P_2 are defined analogously. This leads to the following Scheme procedure:

```
(define (point+ point1 point2)
   (if (and (point? p1) (point? p2))
          (make-point
             (+ (xc point1) (xc point2))
             (+ (yc point1) (yc point2))
```

```
          (+ (zc point1) (zc point2)))
    (error "bad input(s)" point+ point1 point2)))
```

The *x*-coordinate of the (scalar) product of point P and number *n* is *n* times the *x*-coordinate of P. The *y*- and *z*-coordinates of the product are defined analogously. In Scheme this can be formalized as:

```
(define (scalar* num point)
   (if (and (real? num) (point? point))
       (make-point
          (* num (xc point))
          (* num (yc point))
          (* num (zc point)))
       (error "bad input(s)" scalar* num point)))
```

We can combine point+ and scalar* to define point subtraction:

```
(define (point- point1 point2)
   (point+ point1 (scalar* -1 point2)))
```

The (dot) product of two points P_1 and P_2 is a number gotten by adding the products of the *x*-, *y*-, and *z*-coordinates of P_1 and P_2:

```
(define (point* point1 point2)
   (if (and (point? point1) (point? point2))
       (+ (* (xc point1) (xc point2))
          (* (yc point1) (yc point2))
          (* (zc point1) (zc point2)))
       (error "bad input(s)" point* point1 point2)))
```

The distance between two points P_1 and P_2 is the square root of the difference between P_1 and P_2:

```
(define (point-dist point1 point2)
   (sqrt (point* (point- point1 point2)
                 (point- point1 point2))))
```

4.4. Overloading

When several algorithms share the same name, we say the name is **overloaded**. For example, the name + actually denotes four different addition algorithms: integer addition, rational addition, floating-point addition, and complex addition. These algorithms are called **variants** of the + procedure. Scheme determines which variant to invoke by examining the types of the actual parameters:

```
> (+ 2 3)          ; integer addition variant invoked
5
```

```
> (+ 2/3 5/3)      ; rational addition variant invoked
7/3
> (+ 2.3 5.2)      ; floating point addition variant invoked
5.5
> (+ 2+3i 1+4i)    ; complex addition variant invoked
3+7i
```

Of course =, /, *, −, and < are also overloaded procedures. What other primitive procedures are overloaded? What variant of + is invoked when Scheme adds numbers of mixed types:

```
> (+ 3 1/2 3.4)
7.1
```

Overloading makes a procedure more versatile because it can be used in several contexts. Designing procedures so that they accept a wide variety of inputs can be stated as the **completeness principle**:

> Procedures should return outputs for the largest possible number of inputs.

We can define overloaded procedures using type recognizers and conditional structures. For example, let's define an overloaded version of the reverse procedure. Our procedure will reverse lists, strings, vectors, or pairs. If the input is a scalar, we can generate an error message or leave the value unchanged. We choose the latter course of action:

```
; = reverse of string, vector, list, or pair input
(define (val-reverse val)
   (cond ((list? val) (reverse val))
         ((string? val)
            (list->string
               (reverse (string->list val))))
         ((vector? val)
            (list->vector
               (reverse (vector->list val))))
         ((pair? val) (cons (cdr val) (car val)))
         (else val)))
```

Do you think the order of clauses is important in this definition? Why? Why isn't input validation necessary in this procedure? Here are some sample evaluations:

```
> (val-reverse #(a e i o u))
#(u o i e a)
> (val-reverse "hello world")
"dlrow olleh"
> (val-reverse '(a e i o u))
(u o i e a)
> (val-reverse '(1 . 2))
(2 . 1)
```

```
> (val-reverse 'hello)
hello
```

An **ordinal** is any member of a domain that can be naturally ordered. In Scheme reals, characters, and strings have natural orderings:

```
ORDINAL ::= REAL | STRING | CHAR
```

We can define an overloaded version of < as follows:

```
; = #t if val1 < val2, val1 & val2 any ordinals
(define (ord<? val1 val2)
   (cond
      ((and (real? val1) (real? val2))
         (< val1 val2))
      ((and (string? val1) (string? val2))
         (string<? val1 val2))
      ((and (char? val1) (char? val2))
         (char<? val1 val2))
      (else (error "bad input(s)" ord<? val1 val2))))
```

In this case we generate an error message when we fail to recognize val1 or val2 because there seems to be no reasonable alternative. Why did we restrict val1 and val2 to be reals instead of arbitrary numbers? How could an *n*-ary version of ord<? be implemented?

4.5.   Domains as Data

A **type expression** is a phrase that denotes a domain. Languages like Pascal and C provide type expressions such as real, float, char, and int. Unfortunately, Scheme does not provide type expressions. We can remedy this situation by introducing our own:

```
(define number-type 'number)
(define char-type 'char)
(define boole-type 'boole)
(define port-type 'port)
(define string-type 'string)
(define procedure-type 'procedure)
(define vector-type 'vector)
(define list-type 'list)
(define pair-type 'pair)
(define symbol-type 'symbol)
(define value-type 'value)      ; the universal type
```

We can use Scheme's polymorphic classification predicates to build a polymorphic procedure that computes types:

```scheme
(define (get-type val)
   (cond ((symbol? val) symbol-type)
         ((number? val) number-type)
         ((string? val) string-type)
         ((procedure? val) procedure-type)
         ((vector? val) vector-type)
         ((char? val) char-type)
         ((boolean? val) boole-type)
         ((list? val) list-type)
         ((pair? val) pair-type)
         (else value-type)))
```

Here's an example of our get-type procedure in action:

```scheme
> (get-type '(a e i o u))
list
> (get-type "+")
string
> (get-type +)
procedure
> (get-type '+)
symbol
```

4.5.1. Programmer-Defined Types

The get-type procedure works because Scheme uses **dynamic type checking**, which implies that Scheme must attach type information —called a **type tag** —to every Scheme value. The type tag is used by the recognizers: number?, pair?, string?, etc.

We can use the same idea. When we define an ADT, we can define our constructors so they attach type tags to the values they construct. First we need to develop some machinery for attaching and removing type tags. In a sense, we are introducing type tags as an abstract data type on their own. A programmer-defined type tag will be a pair of the form:

```
TYPE-TAG ::= (type . TEXP)
```

where TEXP is a Scheme value representing a type expression. Here's our type tag constructor:

```scheme
(define (make-type-tag texp) (cons 'type texp))
```

Tagging type tags with the symbol `type allows us to distinguish between ordinary pairs and type tagged values:

```scheme
; = #t if val is type tagged
(define (typed? val)
   (and (pair? val)
```

```
      (pair? (car val))
      (eq? (caar val) 'type)))
```

The following procedures allow programmers to attach and remove types from values:

```
; = ((type . texp) . untyped-val)
(define (put-type texp untyped-val)
   (if (typed? val)
       (cons (make-type-tag texp)
              (rem-type untyped-val)) ; switch
       (cons (make-type-tag texp) untyped-val)))

; = val, where typed-val = ((type . texp) . val)
(define (rem-type typed-val)
   (if (typed? typed-val)
       (cdr typed-val)
       typed-val))    ; no type to remove
```

We can extend the get-type procedure defined earlier to extract the types of programmer-tagged values:

```
; = type of user or system typed val
(define (type val)
   (if (typed? val)
       (cdar val) ; = texp of ((type . texp) . xxx)
       (get-type val))
```

To implement type checking it will be important to determine when two types are equivalent:

```
(define (type=? texp1 texp2)
   (equal? texp1 texp2)) ; structural type equivalence
```

4.5.2. Example: Complex Numbers

Assume complex numbers aren't represented in Scheme. Instead, we can introduce them as an ADT. A complex number can be pictured as a point z in the complex plane (Figure 4.5).

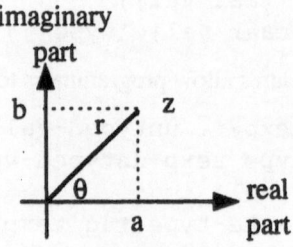

Figure 4.5

We can represent z in rectangular coordinates as $a + b$i, or in polar coordinates as $re^{i\theta}$. Both representations can be represented as pairs: $(a \cdot b)$ or $(r \cdot \theta)$:

```
COMPLEX ::= RECTANGULAR | POLAR | REAL
RECTANGULAR ::= (REAL-PART . IMAG-PART)
POLAR ::= (MAGNITUDE . ANGLE)
REAL-PART, IMAG-PART, MAGNITUDE, ANGLE ::= REAL
```

These representations can coexist if we attach type tags. We begin by defining two new type expressions:

```
(define rectangular-type 'rectangular)
(define polar-type 'polar)
```

Next, we redefine constructors for polar and rectangular representations of complex numbers:

```
; = ((type . rectangular) . (rp . ip))
(define (make-rectangular rp ip)
   (if (and (real? rp) (real? ip))
       (put-type rectangular-type (cons rp ip))
       (error "bad input(s)" make-rectangular rp ip)))

; = ((type . polar) . (mag . ang))
(define (make-polar mag ang)
   (if (and (real? mag) (real? ang))
       (put-type polar-type (cons mag ang))
       (error "bad input(s)" make-polar mag ang)))
```

We can replace Scheme's classification predicates for complex numbers with our own:

```
(define (polar? val)
   (type=? (type val) polar-type))

(define (rectangular? val)
   (type=? (type val) rectangular-type))
```

```
(define (complex? val)
   (or (polar? val) (rectangular? val) (real? val)))
```

Defining selectors can get involved because the inputs can be polar or rectangular:

```
(define (real-part z)
   ; z' = untyped z
   (define z' (rem-type z)) ; works even if z is real!

   (cond ((rectangular? z) (car z'))
         ((polar? z) (* (car z') (cos (cdr z'))))
         ((real? z) z)
         (else (error "bad input" real-part z))))
```

We leave the remaining selectors as an exercise:

```
(define (imag-part z) ???)
(define (magnitude z) ???)
(define (angle z) ???)
```

The next step is to define coercions between polar and rectangular representations. One idea is simply to switch type tags:

```
(define (rectangular->polar z)
   (if (rectangular? z)
       (put-type polar-type (rem-type z))
       (error "bad input to rectangular->polar: " z)))
```

Retyping a value is called **casting**, and a procedure that merely retypes its input is called a **cast**.[2] For example, rectangular->polar casts the value ((type . rectangular) . (2 . 3)) to the value ((type . polar) . (2 . 3)).

Sometimes casts are useful, but in this situation it's not what we want because $2 + 3i$ is not equivalent in any mathematical sense to $2e^{3i}$. The right way to implement rectangular->polar is:

```
(define (rectangular->polar z)
   (if (rectangular? z)
       (make-polar (magnitude z) (angle z))
       (error "bad input" rectangular->polar z)))
```

The reverse coercion is left as an exercise:

```
(define (polar->rectangular z) ???)
```

Of course we can't read and write complex numbers, but we can define special coercions between complex numbers and strings, which can be used to implement complex I/O procedures:

---

[2] In C, coercions are called casts.

```
; = "a+bi", suitable for printing
(define (complex->string z)
   (if (complex? z)
       (string-append
         (number->string (real-part z))
         "+"
         (number->string (imag-part z))
         "i")
       (error "bad input" complex->string z)))
```

The reverse coercion is more difficult, so we leave it as an exercise:

```
(define (string->complex str) ???)
```

The advantage of having dual representations for complex numbers becomes apparent when we implement complex arithmetic. Implementing addition is easy if we assume a rectangular representation because:

$$a+bi + c+di = e+fi \text{ where } e = a + c \text{ and } f = b + d$$

Here's our definition:

```
; = z1 + z2
(define (complex+ z1 z2)
   (if (and (complex? z1) (complex? z2))
       (make-rectangular
         (+ (real-part z1) (real-part z2))
         (+ (imag-part z1) (imag-part z2)))
       (error "bad input(s)" complex+ z1 z2)))
```

Multiplying complex numbers is easier if we assume a polar representation because:

$$ae^{i\alpha} * be^{i\beta} = ce^{i\gamma} \text{ where } c = a * b \text{ and } \gamma = \alpha + \beta$$

Here's our definition:

```
; = z1 * z2
(define (complex* z1 z2)
   (if (and (complex? z1) (complex? z2))
       (make-polar
         (* (magnitude z1) (magnitude z2))
         (+ (angle z1) (angle z2)))
       (error "bad input(s)" complex* z1 z2)))
```

What will happen if the inputs to complex+ are of mixed types?

```
> (complex+ (make-rectangular 4 2) 8)
???
```

The remaining arithmetic procedures are left as an exercise:

```
(define (complex/ z1 z2) ???)
(define (complex- z1 z2) ???)
(define (complex=? z1 z2) ???)
```

4.6. Data-Driven Programming

We normally think of data as passive, dumb entities manipulated by active, intelligent entities called procedures. The data-driven programming paradigm reverses this view by regarding data as active, intelligent entities, while procedures are nothing more than messages requesting data objects to perform some action.

For example, let's reimplement the POINT ADT in the data-driven style. The basic idea is to represent a point as a message-dispatching procedure with a nonglobal defining environment. Information about the point, x-, y-, and z-coordinates, is stored inside the defining frame, accessible only to the message dispatcher:

```
(define (make-point xc yc zc)

   ; define message dispatcher
   (define (self msg)
     (case msg
        ((xc) xc)
        ((yc) yc)
        ((zc) zc)
        ((type) 'point)
        (else (error msg-err self msg))))

   (if (and (real? xc) (real? yc) (real? zc))
       self ; return dispatcher!
       (error "bad input(s)" make-point xc yc zc)))
```

where msg-err is a standard error message:

```
(define msg-err "unrecognized message")
```

The peculiar thing about the definition of make-point is that after it defines the message dispatcher (which is called "self" to maintain some similarity with C++ and Smalltalk), it doesn't call it; rather it returns it as a value!

To get a better picture of how make-point works, study the environment diagram in Figure 4.6 after the definition:

```
(define p1 (make-point 7 2 9))
```

Notice that while the bindings $xc = 7$, $yc = 2$, and $zc = 9$ are local and hence have local scopes (they are only available to self), they have global extents. This is because there is a permanent reference from p1 in the global environment, through DE, to the frame containing these bindings.

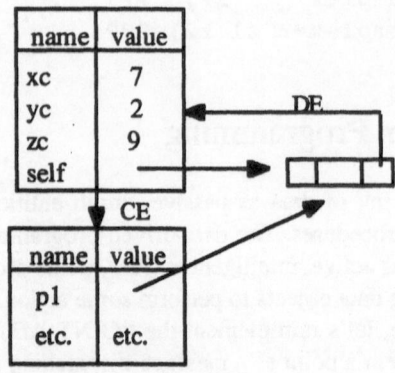

Global Environment

Figure 4.6

To use points we only need to complete the ADT by defining the selectors and a point? predicate. The following definitions use a technique called **message passing**. Although in the header it appears that *xc* is the name of a procedure and point is the name of a parameter, the body of *xc* shows these roles reversed. Now point is a procedure being applied to the message `*xc*:

```
(define (xc point)
   (if (point? val)
       (point `xc)
       (error "bad input" xc point)))
```

The remaining selectors are left as copying exercises:

```
(define (yc point) ???)
(define (zc point) ???)
```

Applying *xc* to p1 actually works:

```
> (xc p1)
7
```

How? Evaluating (*xc* p1) reduces to evaluating (p1 `*xc*). Remember, p1 is really a message-dispatching procedure called "self" in its defining environment. So the application (p1 `*xc*) is equivalent to the application (self `*xc*). The value of the case expression inside the self is the parameter *xc*, which is bound to 7 in the defining environment of p1.

Unfortunately, the point? predicate has a flaw. It properly returns #f if applied to any nonprocedural object. It also works properly if applied to any dispatch procedure that handles the `type message, but in other cases an error occurs at the point val is applied to the symbol `type:

```
(define (point? val)
   (and (procedure? val)
        (eq? 'point (val 'type))))
```

Now that our ADT is complete, we can use the vector arithmetic procedures without bothering to redefine them. For example, we can define p2 as the sum of p1 with itself:

```
(define p2 (point+ p1 p1))
```

The coordinates of p2 are as we would expect:

```
> (xc p2)
14
> (zc p2)
18
> (yc p2)
4
```

The only suspicious thing is Scheme's inability to display p2:

```
> p2
#[procedure self]
```

Of course we could implement our own point printer as an abstract procedure:

```
(define (display-point point)
   (writeln "(" (xc point) (yc point) (zc point) ")"))
```

Appendices

Appendix 4.1. Object-Oriented Programming

So far, our Scheme programs have been built out of procedures and data, but these are not the only possible building blocks. In object-oriented programming, components called **objects** are used as primitive elements.

Object-oriented programming is popular because software engineers often build models of **application domains** —the real world contexts their programs will work in — using objects (i.e., representations of people, organizations, places, events, and things). Translating these models into program designs and, ultimately, programs, is much easier if objects are also available in the **design** and **implementation domains**.

After a *very* brief introduction of the main concepts of object-oriented programming: **encapsulation, inheritance**, and **polymorphism**, we will construct a simple object system in Scheme called **SOS** (Scheme Object System).

Encapsulation

An **object** is a software component that encapsulates services (procedures or **methods**) and **attributes** (variables). The **attribute values** of an object, i.e., the current values of its attribute variables, taken together, form the object's **state**.

The basic interaction between two objects fits a client-server model. The **client** object (or a human user) requests a service from the **server** object. Requesting a service is called **service invocation, method invocation,** or **message passing.** The server object may respond with a result (Figure 4.7).

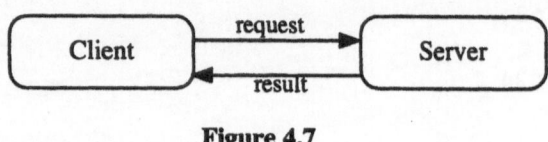

Figure 4.7

Assume smith is an employee object that encapsulates attributes such as name, salary, and social security number, and provides services for accessing and modifying these attributes. The following fragment of client code shows how these services are invoked in SOS using the send procedure:

```
> (send smith 'get-ssn)
111234321
> (send smith 'get-class)
employee
> (send smith 'set-salary 45000)
done
> (send smith 'get-salary)
45000
```

Classes

A **class** is a software component that constructs objects; it is an object factory. A class may be a special kind of object, or it may belong to a separate domain of software components. An object constructed by a class is called an **instance** of that class. All instances of a class provide the same services, but differ in their attribute values (i.e., their states).

For example, smith is an instance of the employee class. In SOS the employee class is identified with a constructor named employee and expecting the initial attribute values of the object to be constructed as arguments:

```
; specify name and ssn, initial salary = 0
(define smith (employee "Ian Smith" 111234321))
```

Inheritance

We can define a new class by extending an existing class. We call the new class the **derived class** or **subclass** and the existing class the **base class** or **super class**. We also say the derived class **extends** the base class.

The attributes and services of the base class automatically become attributes and services of the derived class. This is called **inheritance**. Inheritance is a **reuse mechanism** because it allows the implementor of a derived class to reuse the code defined in the base class.

A derived class often represents a subclass of the base class. For example, a secretary class would be a logical class to derive from our employee class. Instances of secretary would encapsulate attributes such as typing speed, and inherit attributes such as name, salary, and Social Security number.

```
; specify name & ssn, current typing speed = 60 wpm
(define jones (secretary "Jim Jones" 111223333 60))
```

Notice that jones provides set-salary and get-salary services inherited from the employee base class:

```
> (send jones 'set-salary 30000)
done
> (send jones 'get-salary)
30000
```

Association

Inheritance is a relationship between classes. A relationship between objects is called an **association**. For example, a person may play multiple roles in an application domain. Smith might be an employee *and* a customer. Therefore, it may be unwise to encapsulate personal information in an employee object if this same information will also need to be encapsulated and maintained in a customer object. A better strategy is to encapsulate employee attributes: salary, social security number, security clearance, etc. in an employee object and personal attributes: name, address, phone number, etc. in an associated person object:

```
(define smith (person "Smith" "(408) 555-4252"))
; emp1 is associated with smith:
(define emp1 (employee smith 111234321))
; associate smith with emp1:
(send smith 'set-role emp1)
```

If smith suddenly becomes a customer, we can create an associated customer object and quickly change Smith's role in the application domain:

```
; initial purchase = $120.45, person = smith
(define cust42 (customer 120.45 smith))
```

```
; re associate smith with cust42:
(send smith 'set-role cust42)
```

This makes more sense than trying to make smith an instance of the employee and customer classes.

Polymorphism

In the context of object-oriented programming, **polymorphism** means a client object
only needs to know the base class of a server object. This is accomplished by equipping
base classes with virtual procedures.

Virtual Procedures

The following client procedure prints each employee in its input list:

```
; staff = a list of employees
(define (print-staff staff)
   (define (virtual-print employee)
      (send employee 'print))
   (map virtual-print staff))
```

Assume programmer, secretary, and manager are among the classes derived from employee, and the following team of employees is assembled:

```
(define wong (manager ...))
(define jones (secretary ...))
(define morris (programmer ... ))
(define team (list wong jones morris))
```

Here's the output of print-staff applied to team:

```
> (print-staff team)
Name:        "Pat Wong"
SSN:         333224444
Salary:      90000
position:    manager
Secretary:   "Jim Jones"
Name:        "Jim Jones"
SSN:         111223333
Salary:      30000
Position:    secretary
WPM:         60
Name:        "Robert Morris Jr."
SSN:         123456789
Salary:      60000
Position:    programmer
Languages:   Scheme C++ Unix
```

Although map applied the same virtual-print procedure to each employee in the input list, the result was slightly different for each one. This is because each employee object responded to the print message according to its own specialized display-method. In other words, the employee object, not the virtual-print procedure determined what would happen.

We can think of this as a type of overloading, because the behavior of virtual-print depends on the type of its input. But unlike the overloaded procedures discussed earlier, which at least performed some sort of type dispatch, virtual-print doesn't really do any work other than send a message to its input. We call this type of procedure a **virtual procedure**.

Unlike overloaded procedures, a virtual procedure never needs to be changed, even when new subclasses are added to the application. At any point in the future we can add new subclasses of employee: accountant, intern, vice-president, etc., but we never need to change the definition of print-staff or virtual-print. Even if we forget to include specialized display-methods for these classes, the print message will be delegated to the employee parent object, where it will be handled by the default display-method.

In other words, the client code only needed to know the base class of the objects in the staff list: employee. We can think of print-staff as a logical description of how to print a list of employees. Once this logic is in place, it should never have to be changed, while the data-dependent details of how to display particular kinds of employees is encapsulated in each employee object. The print-staff procedure is reusable, even in the face of future system expansions.

SOS: A Scheme Object System

The step from data-driven programming to object-oriented programming is small. The main difference is the way unrecognized messages are handled by the dispatcher. In the POINT example given earlier the dispatcher raises an error in the else clause of the case-expression. A better idea is to **delegate** the message to another dispatcher, called the **parent**, that may know how to respond to the message. The parent is an associated object created by the base class constructor.

Assume *xxx* is a subclass of *yyy*. In SOS, the general format of an *xxx* object constructor is:

```
(define (xxx ...)
   (define parent (yyy ...))
 ; services and attributes go here
   (define (self . msg)
      (case (car msg)
         ; message handling goes here
         ((get-parent) parent)
         ((get-class) 'xxx)
         (else (delegate parent msg))))
   self)
```

It is similar to the POINT constructor, but we have made a few improvements. First, a local parent object is defined representing the associated instance of the super class, *yyy*.

Second, the msg parameter of the self procedure is an optional list. This allows for more complex messages, although (car msg) determines which case clause is evaluated.

Third, get-parent and get-class are included as standard messages. Because these messages are common, we introduce global names for them:

```
; some pre-defined messages:
(define get-parent 'get-parent)
(define get-class 'get-class)
```

Fourth, if msg is unrecognized, it is delegated to the parent object. The delegate procedure is just a synonym for Scheme's apply procedure:

```
(define delegate apply)
```

We introduce the send procedure to hide the fact that objects are merely dispatch procedures:

```
(define (send object . msg)
   (apply object msg))
```

Finally, we provide a base object to serve as the last stop for unrecognized messages. If a message is delegated all the way back to this object, it really is unrecognized, and an error is raised:

```
(define (base-object . msg)
   (case (car msg)
      ((get-parent) base-object)
      ((get-class) 'base-class)
      (else
         (error "unrecognized message"
                'base-object
                msg)))))
```

Example

We are now ready to implement the employee class and some of its subclasses.

The Employee Class

Because the employee class is at the top of our inheritance hierarchy, all employee instances inherit from the base-object. An instance of the employee class encapsulates attributes such as an employee's name, Social Security number, and salary.

Two employee services are provided. One displays information about the employee on the monitor, the other sets the employee's salary when it's time to give the employee a promotion or demotion. Notice that the message dispatcher invokes the display-method in response to several different messages:

```
(define (employee name ssn)
   ; attributes
   (define parent base-object)
   (define salary 0)

   ; services
   (define (display-method)
      (writeln "Name:" #\tab name)
      (writeln "SSN:" #\tab ssn)
      (writeln "Salary:" #\tab salary))

   (define (set-salary amt)
      (set! salary amt))

   (define (self . msg)
      (case (car msg)
         ((get-salary) salary)
         ((get-name) name)
         ((get-ssn) ssn)
         ((display print write show) (display-method))
         ((set-salary) (set-salary (cadr msg)))
         ((get-parent) parent)
         ((get-class) 'Employee)
         (else (delegate parent msg))))
   self)
```

Notice that the operand of set-salary is (cadr msg). Recall that the set-salary message is sent along with the new salary:

```
(send smith 'set-salary 90000)
```

This turns into the application: (self `set-salary 90000), which forms the parameter binding: msg = (set-salary 90000). Observe that (cadr msg) is 90000, the new salary.

Assignment Commands

The set-salary service uses set!, a Scheme assignment command. (We encountered set! in the last chapter where it was used by the receiver procedure to "redefine" the return procedure as the current continuation.) The syntax of a set! command is:

```
(set! NAME EXPRESSION)
```

Briefly, set! is used to "redefine" NAME to the value of EXPRESSION. This isn't quite accurate. The full story is the topic of Chapter 7. Assignment commands like set! don't belong to functional Scheme but play a useful role in object-oriented programming, hence they appear here. Outside of the context of object-oriented programming, readers should refrain from using assignment commands until they are properly introduced in Chapter 7.

The Secretary Class

We express the fact that secretary is a subclass of employee by defining the parent to be an instance of the employee super class. All unrecognized messages will be delegated to this object, creating the illusion that secretary objects can respond to employee messages.

Also, notice that display-method is redefined. When a secretary object receives a print message, it invokes its local display-method rather than delegating the message to its parent object. However, in addition to other things, the secretary display-method explicitly sends a print message to its parent. In this way the secretary display-method appears to extend the employee display-method:

```
(define (secretary name ssn speed)

   (define parent (employee name ssn))

   (define (display-method)
      (send parent print)
      (writeln "Position: " #\tab 'secretary)
      (writeln "WPM: " #\tab speed))

   (define (self . msg)
      (case (car msg)
         ((get-wpm) speed)
         ((display print write show) (display-method))
         ((get-parent) parent)
         ((get-class get-position) 'Secretary)
         (else (delegate parent msg))))
   self)
```

It might be useful to look at the environment diagram in Figure 4.8 after considering the definition:

```
(define jones (secretary "Jim Jones" 111223333 60))
```

The middle frame contains the secretary attributes and services. The name jones in the global environment is bound to the self procedure in this frame. The parent name in the secretary frame is bound to the self procedure in the employee frame at the top of the figure. This frame was implicitly created by the employee application inside the secretary constructor. It contains all of the employee attributes and services. The parent name in the employee frame is bound to the global base-object procedure.

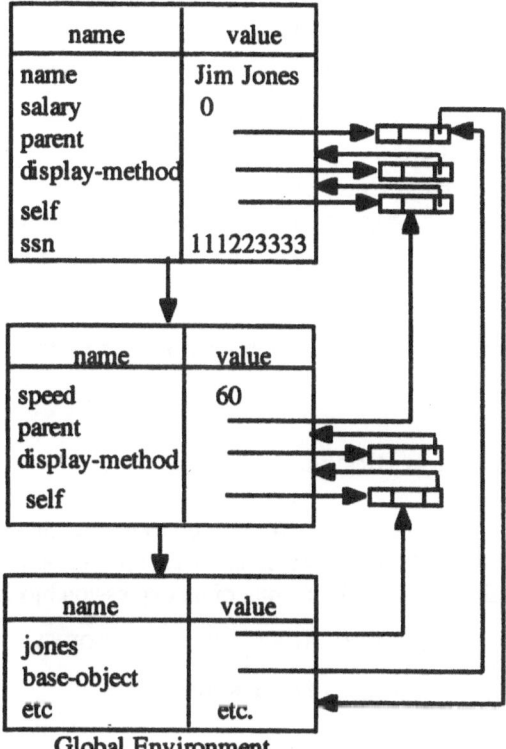

name	value
name	Jim Jones
salary	0
parent	
display-method	
self	
ssn	111223333

name	value
speed	60
parent	
display-method	
self	

name	value
jones	
base-object	
etc	etc.

Global Environment

Figure 4.8

The Manager Class

Like the secretary class, manager is a subclass of employee. It, too, extends the definition of display-method:

```
(define (manager name ssn)

   (define parent (employee name ssn))
   (define secretary base-object) ; for now

   (define (display-method)
      (define sec (send secretary 'get-name))
      (send parent print)
      (writeln "Position: " #\tab 'manager)
      (writeln "Secretary: " #\tab sec))

   (define (set-secretary sec)
      (set! secretary sec))
```

```
(define (self . msg)
   (case (car msg)
       ((get-secretary) secretary)
       ((set-secretary) (set-secretary (cadr msg)))
       ((display print write) (display-method))
       ((get-parent) parent)
       ((get-class get-position) 'manager)
       (else (delegate parent msg))))
   self)
```

Notice that instances of the manager class are associated with instances of the secretary class.

Appendix 4.2. Expression Blocks

We saw that procedure blocks can be used to restrict the scopes of procedures and data, but we can do even better. Scheme allows scopes to be restricted to a single expression using **expression blocks**. The format of an expression block is

```
BLOCK ::= (LET (DECLARATION ...) BODY)
```

BODY is simply a sequence of expressions:

```
BODY ::= EXPRESSION ...
```

and DECLARATION is a name paired with an expression:

```
DECLARATION ::= (NAME EXPRESSION)
```

Resolving a declaration creates a binding between NAME and the value of EXPRESSION. The scope of this binding extends to the end of the body, but no further. The beginning of the scope depends on the LET operator.

There are three variations of the LET operator:

```
LET ::= let | let* | letrec
```

Blocks formed with let are called **collateral blocks**. Declarations in a collateral block are resolved in parallel, hence the bindings they create are unavailable to each other. In other words, the scope of a binding created by a declaration inside a collateral block is exactly the body of the block (see Figure 4.9).

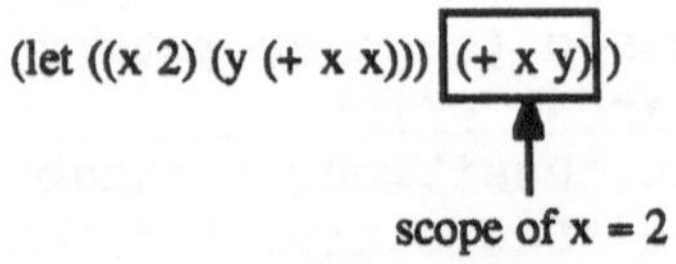

Figure 4.9

Blocks formed with let* are called **sequential blocks**. Declarations in a sequential block are resolved sequentially; hence the binding created by a declaration is available to the declarations that follow it. In other words, the scope of a binding created by a declaration inside a sequential block begins immediately after the declaration and extends to the end of the body (see Figure 4.10).

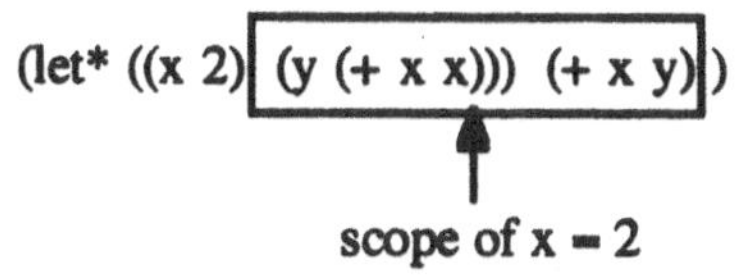

scope of x = 2

Figure 4.10

Blocks formed with letrec are called **recursive blocks**. Procedure declarations in a recursive block can refer to themselves or to procedure bindings created by subsequent declarations (see Figure 4.11).

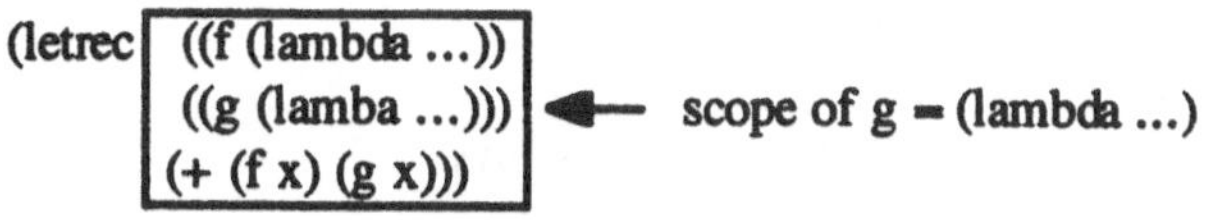

scope of g = (lambda ...)

Figure 4.11

Assume the following global declaration has been made:

```
(define x 100)
```

We can understand the difference between let and let* by studying the following evaluations:

```
> (let ((x 2) (y (+ x x))) (+ x y))
202
> (let* ((x 2) (y (+ x x))) (+ x y))
6
```

In the let expression the first declaration created the binding $x = 2$. Because the second declaration is resolved simultaneously, the $x = 2$ binding is unavailable at the time $(+ x x)$ is evaluated; hence x is assumed to refer to the global x, which is bound to 100, and the binding $y = 200$ is created. The scope of both local bindings is the body, $(+ x y)$. The value produced by this expression, 202, is the value produced by the let expression.

In the let* expression the first declaration also created the binding $x = 2$. The second declaration is resolved after this binding is created; hence the x in $(+ x x)$ is assumed to refer to the local x, which is bound to 2, thus the binding $y = 4$ is created. The scope of these two bindings extends over the body; hence the value of $(+ x y)$, and therefore the value of the let* expression, is 6.

Notice that sequential blocks are a redundant feature because we can accomplish the same effect by nesting collateral blocks:

```
> (let ((x 2)) (let ((y (+ x x))) (+ x y)))
6
```

In fact, collateral blocks are redundant because we can accomplish the same effect using a technique called **lambda lifting**. The idea is to trade declaration bindings for parameter bindings. For example, the expression block:

```
(let ((x 2) (y 3)) (+ x y 5))
```

is equivalent to the application:

```
((lambda (x y) (+ x y 5)) 2 3)
```

Suppose we wanted to include the definition of a recursive procedure inside an expression block. For example, the factorial procedure returns the product of all integers between 1 and its argument, n:

```
(fact n) = (* 1 2 3 ... n)
```

We cannot define fact inside a let* block:

```
> (let* ((fact (lambda (n)
                 (if (= n 0)
                     1
                     (* n (fact (- n 1)))))))
         (z 3))
    (fact z))
Error, undefined symbol: fact
```

The problem is that the scope of the binding fact = (lambda ...) begins immediately after the declaration (fact (lambda ...)). Unfortunately, the fact procedure is used inside its own declaration. Technically, this use of fact is out of the scope of the fact binding.

To remedy this situation, Scheme provides recursive expression blocks. Thus, the following expression can be evaluated:

```
> (letrec ((fact (lambda (n)
                   (if (= n 0)
                       1
                       (* n (fact (- n 1)))))))
           (z 3))
      (fact z))
6
```

Applications of Expression Blocks

Expression blocks have several advantages over procedure blocks. First, because procedure blocks aren't officially part of ANSI/IEEE Scheme, they may not be available in some implementations.

Second, expression blocks are ordinary expressions, hence they can be nested inside other expressions. Definitions are not expressions. They can only appear at the beginning of a procedure block. For example, assume we want to add input validation to the variance procedure defined earlier. The following definition illegally attempts to nest definitions inside of an if-structure:

```
(define (variance scores)
   (if (distribution? scores)
       (begin
         (define mu (mean scores)) ; NO!
         (define (deviation^2 score) ; NO!
            (square (- score mu)))
         (mean (map deviation^2 scores)))
       (error "bad input" variance scores)))
```

We could rename variance unsafe-variance and nest it inside a wrapper procedure called variance:

```
(define (variance scores)
   (define (unsafe-variance scores) ...)
   (if (distribution? scores)
       (unsafe-variance scores)
       (error "bad input" variance scores)))
```

The problem with this approach is that it requires an extra procedure application, which we now know incurs the overhead of extending and restoring environments. An economical alternative is to use an expression block, which can be nested inside an if-structure:

```
(define (variance scores)
   (if (distribution? scores)
       (let* ((mu (mean scores))
              (deviation^2
                  (lambda (score)
                      (square (- score mu)))))
         (mean (map deviation^2 scores)))
       (error "bad input" variance scores)))
```

(Why was let* used instead of let?)

Problems

Solutions to the following problems are to be given in functional Scheme; do not use procedures or special forms discussed in subsequent chapters. (You may use set! inside object constructors.) Do not use any of the I/O procedures discussed in the last chapter except to print error or diagnostic messages or unless you are specifically directed by the problem to use them. You may use the definitions given in this or previous chapters as well as solutions to other problems (although you will have to include these definitions in your definition file so you can test your definitions). You may also define any supporting procedures you need. You are required to validate inputs.

Problem 4.1.

You acquire a LISP interpreter from an FTP site. Unfortunately, the documentation is written in Latin. You know the interpreter accepts Scheme syntax, but you don't know if it uses the dynamic or static scope rule. How can you find out?

Problem 4.2.

Complete the following overloaded procedures. In each case the procedure generalizes the corresponding list procedure. Your procedures should work for strings, lists, vectors, and pairs if appropriate. You will need to decide for yourself how to handle simple inputs.

```
a. (define (val-length val) ???)
b. (define (val-append . vals) ???)
c. (define (val-ref val pos) ???)
d. (define (val-member item val) ???)
e. (define (val-tail val pos) ???)
```

Problem 4.3.

Modify the get-type procedure so it distinguishes between integers, reals, rationals, and complex numbers and distinguishes between input and output ports. Be careful of your clause order. Is the order of clauses in the unmodified definition important?

Problem 4.4.

Is the order of clauses in get-type important? Why?

Problem 4.5.

We can make our type expressions more elaborate by introducing composite type expressions:

```
TEXP ::= SIMPLE-TEXP | COMPOSITE-TEXP

SIMPLE-TEXP ::=
    number | char | symbol | string | port | boolean |
    value
```

```
COMPOSITE-TEXP ::=
   (pair TEXP TEXP) | (list TEXP) | (vector TEXP) | (map
TEXP ...)
```

Using these type expressions, state the types of the values denoted by following expressions:

```
a. sin               type = (map number number)
b. #((1 2 3) (4 5 6) (7 8 9))
c. quotient
d. string<?
e. floor
f. char?
g. '((a . 1) (b . 2) (c . 3))
h. '(t #t #\t "t")
```

Problem 4.6.

How could you modify get-type so it returns the pair type above? (Hint: get-type can call itself.) Do the other type expressions make sense in Scheme?

Problem 4.7.

How could you implement a value? predicate in Scheme?

```
(value? val)
   = #t if val is a Scheme value
   = #f, otherwise
```

Do you think this would be useful?

Problem 4.8.

Why isn't input validation important for polymorphic procedures?

Problem 4.9.

There are three kinds of type errors. One results when the types of the actual parameters don't match the types of the corresponding formal parameters, another results when the operand of an application isn't a valid procedure and the third results when the number of actual parameters is different from the number of formal parameters. Input validation guards against the first kind of type error. Why don't we need input validation to guard against the second and third kinds of type errors?

Problem 4.10.

Implement an *n*-ary version of ord<? (defined earlier).

Problem 4.11. The RATIONAL ADT

Assume Scheme did not supply rational numbers. We can represent rationals as pairs of integers:

```
RATIONAL ::= (INTEGER . POSITIVE)
```

where POSITIVE represents any positive integer.

We interpret the pair (*n . m*) as the rational *n/m*. Implement the necessary constructor, predicate, and selectors:

```
(define (make-rational num den) ???)
(define (numerator rat) ???)
(define (denominator rat) ???)
(define (rational? rat) ???)
```

Your constructor should perform reductions (use gcd) and should guarantee that the denominator will always be positive. For example:

```
> (make-rational 4 -8)
(-1 . 2)
> (make-rational 4 0)
error!
    Gripe: Zero Denominator
    Source: make-rational
```

Problem 4.12.

Given the rational ADT described earlier, implement the following procedures. Do not make any assumptions about how rationals are represented.

```
a. (define (rational+ rat1 rat2) ???)
b. (define (rational* rat1 rat2) ???)
c. (define (rational- rat1 rat2) ???)
d. (define (rational/ rat1 rat2) ???)
e. (define (rational=? rat1 rat2) ???)
f. (define (rational<? rat1 rat2) ???)
```

Problem 4.13. The REAL ADT

Assume Scheme did not supply real numbers. We can represent a real number as a pair of the form:

```
REAL ::= (INTEGER . NATURAL)
```

Recall:

```
NATURAL ::= 0 | 1 | 2 | 3 | etc.
INTEGER ::= [-]NATURAL
```

We interpret the pair (n . m) as the real $n*10^{-m}$. Define the necessary constructor and selectors for this ADT:

```
(define (make-real b e) ???)
(define (exponent real) ???)
(define (base real) ???)
```

Here are some sample constructions:

```
(define r32.0046 (make-real 320046 4))
(define r32.00460 (make-real 3200460 5))
(define r.00003 (make-real 3 5))
(define r99.0 (make-real 99 0))
```

Problem 4.14.

Implement the following procedures. Assume *a*, *b*, and *c* are members of the REAL domain defined in the previous problem. Except for the predicates, these problems return members of the REAL domain. Do not make any assumptions about how reals are represented.

```
a. (define (truncate a) ???)
b. (define (real* a b) ???)
c. (define (real+ a b) ???)
d. (define (real>? a b) ???)
e. (define (real=? a b) ???)
```

Problem 4.15.

Define a coercion from the REAL domain defined earlier to Scheme's domain of real numbers.

```
(define (real->real a) ???)
```

Problem 4.16. The INTEGER ADT

Assume Scheme supplied natural numbers, but not integers. An integer can be represented as a pair of the form:

```
INTEGER ::= (BOOLE . NATURAL)
```

We interpret the pair (#t . 42) as +42 and the pair (#f . 42) as −42. Notice that 0 has two representations: (#t . 0) and (#f . 0). Assuming a and b are members of this INTEGER domain, implement the following procedures:

```
a. (define (integer+ a b) ???)
b. (define (integer* a b) ???)
c. (define (integer<? a b) ???)
d. (define (zero? a) ???)
```

Problem 4.17. The NATURAL ADT

Assume Scheme did not supply any numbers. We can represent the natural number n as a list of n #t's:

```
NATURAL ::= (#t ... )
```

This is called a **unary representation** because only a single symbol is used. Assuming this representation, implement the following procedures. Remember, you are pretending Scheme does not support numbers of any sort, so the primitive arithmetic and ordering procedures are unavailable:

```
a. (define (natural+ a b) ???)
b. (define (natural* a b) ???)
c. (define (natural<? a b) ???)
d. (define (natural=? a b) ???)
```

Problem 4.18.

For convenience, implement coercions between unary and Scheme representations of natural numbers:

```
(define (natural->unary nat) ???)
(define (unary->natural uny) ???)
```

Problem 4.19. Readers and Writers

Assume the domain definitions given earlier. Implement the following coercions:

```
a.  (define (rational->string rat) ???)
b.  (define (rectangular->string z) ???)
c.  (define (integer->string int) ???)
d.  (define (real->string real) ???)
```

Problem 4.20.

Implement an ADT for rational numbers in the data-driven style. Test your implementation by defining procedures for adding, multiplying, subtracting, and dividing rationals. These procedures should be independent of the method used to represent rational numbers.

Problem 4.21. Registers, Counters, and Accumulators

A **register** is a small storage device capable of holding a natural number less than some given maximum. The primitive register operations are read and write.

Like a register, a **counter** also stores a number. Besides read and write, a counter provides users with procedures for incrementing and decrementing the stored number.

An **accumulator** is a counter that provides a procedure for adding any number to the stored number.

Accumulators are specialized counters, and counters are specialized registers. Using the tools and methods described in this chapter, define object-oriented constructors for registers, counters, and accumulators.

Only register objects should have a variable containing the integer value. Counter and accumulator objects will have to send read and write messages to their parent objects to access this data.

Problem 4.22.

Assume the following definitions have been made:

```
(define x 100)
(define y 200)
```

Evaluate the following Scheme expressions. Your answers should be consistent with the IEEE/ANSI specification. If the expressions contain errors or produce unspecified values, then say why.

```
1.  (let ((x 4) (y (+ x 1))) (* x y))
2.  (let* ((x 4) (y (+ x 1))) (* x y))
3.  (let ((f (lambda (g) (g x))))
       (let ((g (lambda (y) (+ y y))))
          (f g)))
4.  (let ((f (lambda (y) (+ x y)))))
```

```
(let ((x 50))
   (f x)))
```

Problem 4.23.

Rewrite the following sequential block as a collateral block:

```
(let* ((x 22) (y (+ x x)) (z (* y y))) (gcd x y z))
```

Problem 4.24.

Use lambda lifting to rewrite the following collateral block as an application of a lambda structure:

```
(let ((x 2) (y 3) (z 4)) (lcm x y z))
= ((lambda (???) ???) ???)
```

Problem 4.25.

Rewrite the variance procedure using expression blocks instead of procedure blocks.

Problem 4.26. Combinators

A procedure that defines an internal procedure but returns it as a value instead of evaluating it is called a **combinator**. Implement the following combinators:

```
a. (deriv proc)
      = approximates derivative of proc

b. (compose proc1 proc2)
      = proc3, where (proc3 x) = (proc1 (proc2 x))
```

Problem 4.27. Curried Procedures

A **unary** procedure expects a single input. **Binary** procedures expect two inputs, **3-ary** procedures expect three inputs, etc. In the 1930s the mathematician Haskell Curry devised a way of reducing all binary, 3-ary, 4-ary, etc. procedures to unary procedures. The corresponding unary procedure is said to be **curried**. For example, the binary procedure:

```
(define (avg x y) (/ (+ x y) 2))
```

can be reduced to the curried procedure:

```
(define (curried-avg x)
   (define (avg-x y) (/ (+ x y) 2))
   avg-x)
```

Make sure you understand the way curried-avg is used to average two numbers. Here is a sample transcript:

```
> (avg 2 4)
3
> ((curried-avg 2) 4)
3
> (define avg-2 (avg 2))
error: not enough inputs to avg
> (define avg-2 (curried-avg 2))
unspecified
> avg-2
avg-x
> (avg-2 4)
3
```

The disadvantage of curried procedures is the extra set of parenthesis needed to call them: ((curried-avg 2) 3) instead of (avg 2 3). The advantage of Curried procedures is that unlike unCurried procedures, they return something sensible when given fewer than the expected number of inputs. For example, (curried-avg 2) returned a procedure, avg-x, which when applied to any number y returns the result of averaging y with 2. By contrast, (avg 2) produced an error message.

Curried procedures are so useful that PC Scheme provides a syntax for defining them. For example, an alternative syntax for the definition of curried-avg is:

```
(define ((curried-avg x) y) (/ (+ x y) 2))
```

Define a curried version of a procedure that expects the lengths of the legs of a right triangle as input and returns the length of the hypotenuse as output.

Problem 4.28. The Fixed Point Combinator

One approach to getting rid of recursive procedures is to treat them as limits of successively better nonrecursive approximations. An **improver** expects an approximation of a recursive procedure as input and returns a better approximation as output. For example:

```
(define (fact-improver old-fact)

   (define (improved-fact n)
      (if (zero? n)
          1
          (* n (old-fact (sub1 n)))))

   improved-fact)
```

Starting with a crude approximation of the factorial procedure:

```
(define (fact-0 n) (if (= n 0) 1 0))
```

we can build incrementally better approximations:

```
(define fact-1 (fact-improver fact-0))
(define fact-2 (fact-improver fact-1))
(define fact-3 (fact-improver fact-2))
(define fact-4 (fact-improver fact-3))
```

Observe that:

```
(fact-k n)
  = n!, if 0 ≤ n ≤ k
  = 0, otherwise.
```

We can think of the true factorial procedure as the limit of these approximations. We can represent this limit, but we need a recursive iterator procedure to do it:

```
(define (iterate n improver init)
  (if (zero? n)
      init
      (improver (iterate improver (- n 1) init))))
```

Using iterator we can define the factorial procedure as follows:

```
(define (fact n)
  ((iterate fact-improver n fact-0) n))
```

We can trace a call to (fact 3) to see what's going on:

```
(fact 3)
((iterate fact-improver 3 fact-0) 3)
...
((fact-improver
   (fact-improver (fact-improver fact-0))) 3)
(fact-3 3)
6
```

Observe that the fact procedure defined earlier can't be further improved:

```
(define better-fact (fact-improver fact))
```

but for every n: (fact n) = (better-fact n). In other words, fact is a fixed point for fact-improver.

Unfortunately, our last approach to getting rid of recursive procedures wasn't completely successful because we needed the recursive iterator procedure. Another approach is to define self-improving improvers and apply them to themselves:

```
(define (self-improver old-self-improver)
```

```
(define (better-fact n)
   ((self old-self-improver) n))

(fact-improver better-fact))
```

```
(define fact (self self-improver))
```

This definition relies on the self application combinator:

```
(define (self f) (f f))
```

We can generalize self-improver by replacing fact-improver by a parameter. The resulting procedure is known as the **fixed point combinator**:

```
(define (fix improver)

   (define (self-improver old-self-improver)
      (define (better n)
         ((self old-self-improver) n))
      (improver better))

   (self self-improver))
```

Returning to our example, we can redefine fact as follows:

```
(define fact (fix fact-improver))
```

Notice that no recursion was used to define fact, fact-improver, or fix. We can employ this same strategy to replace all recursive definitions with nonrecursive definitions of the form:

```
(define foo (fix foo-improver))
```

Then, using our preprocessor, we can replace all occurrences of foo by (fix foo-improver). This eliminates the need of all definitions.

Use fix to define the triangle procedure from Chapter 3.

5
Iteration

The systems view looks at the world in terms of relationships and integration. Systems are integrated wholes whose properties cannot be reduced to those of smaller units. Instead of concentrating on basic building blocks or basic substances, the systems approach emphasizes basic principles of organization.

—Frijtof Capra, *The Turning Point*

The systems Capra is referring to are so ubiquitous that any definition would sound hopelessly vague (we'll try anyway). Electromechanical systems range from computer chips and vending machines to space shuttles and ocean liners, while biological systems range from viruses and amoebas to whales, brains, and redwoods. Some organisms form complex social systems such as ecosystems, beehives, ant hills, universities, corporations, armies, even nations. There are legal systems, economic systems, mathematical systems, problem-solving systems, solar systems, weather systems, hardware systems, and software systems. The whole universe is a system.

Systems are interesting to programmers and computer scientists for two reasons. First, computer models can be used to predict and control the behavior of a system. Many computer applications take this form. Computers are used to predict stock market behavior, control satellites, and track weather systems. Second, a computer executing a program is an example of a system. Predicting and controlling program behavior is not only the goal of program testing, but also the goal of many system-level programs, including operating systems, optimizers, interpreters, and debuggers.

5.1. Modeling Systems

At any moment a **system** S is in a particular **state**. The state of a system can be anything: temperature, velocity, volume, content, position, value, mass, structure, entropy, energy, etc. The domain of all possible states is called the system's **state space**:

```
STATE ::= all possible states of system S
```

Starting in an initial state, the system repeatedly changes its state until it enters a final state. The next state usually depends on the previous state, but may depend on other parameters as well. Next states are computed by an **update procedure**:

```
; = next state of system S
(define (update current-state ...) ...)
```

Final states are recognized by a final? predicate:

```
; = #t if state is a final state of system S
(define (final? state) ...)
```

The sequence of states a system passes through, beginning with an initial state, is called an **orbit**. A **convergent orbit** is an orbit that terminates in a final state. Not all orbits terminate. For example, an unchecked population just keeps growing. In this case we say the orbit **diverges**. An **oscillating orbit** perpetually bounces between several states (called an **attractor**) without ever reaching a final state.

The system is driven by a **control-loop**, which iteratively updates the state of the system until a final state is reached. Each iteration of update is called a **cycle**. The number of cycles needed to reach a final state (if a final state can be reached) will depend on the initial state. But how can we repeat the update procedure an unknown number of times?

5.1.1. Iterative Evaluation

Scheme provides an iterative structure called a **do-loop** that allows programmers to repeat the evaluation of several expressions until some condition becomes true (i.e., unfalse). Scheme's do-loop is similar to Pascal's repeat-until-statement or C's for-command. The do-loop is both a control structure and a block structure. It is a control structure because it allows programmers to control the flow of evaluation. It is a block structure similar to a let-expression because it establishes temporary bindings with local scopes.

The format of a do-loop is:

```
DO ::= (do (DECLARATION ...) EXIT-CLAUSE BODY)
```

BODY is just a sequence of zero or more expressions:

```
BODY ::= EXPRESSION ...
```

These expressions are evaluated on each repetition, although their values are discarded. (Normally these would be calls to output procedures like newline or display.)

EXIT-CLAUSE has the same form as the CLAUSE appearing in a cond-expression:

```
EXIT-CLAUSE ::= (CONDITION EXPRESSION ...)
```

When CONDITION is no longer #f, the remaining EXPRESSIONs in EXIT-CLAUSE are evaluated and the do-loop terminates. The value of the last EXPRESSION in EXIT-CLAUSE is the value of the do-loop. The values of the other EXPRESSIONs are discarded, so these would normally be calls to output procedures also.

DECLARATION is similar to the declaration appearing in an expression block, except two expressions are specified. The first expression, INIT, is initially bound to

NAME. The second expression, STEP, is bound to NAME after each subsequent iteration:

```
DECLARATION ::= (NAME INIT STEP)
```

INIT, STEP, and CONDITION are arbitrary Scheme expressions:

```
INIT, STEP, CONDITION ::= EXPRESSION
```

The evaluation of a do-loop is complicated:

1. A temporary environment is created containing bindings between each NAME and the value of the associated INIT expression. The evaluation order of the INIT expressions is unspecified.

2. CONDITION is evaluated relative to this environment.

3a. If the value of CONDITION is *not* #f, then each EXPRESSION in CLAUSE is evaluated. The value of the last one is the value returned by the do-expression. Otherwise:

3b. If the value of CONDITION is #f, then each EXPRESSION in BODY (if there are any) is evaluated. The values of all these expressions are discarded, so they are evaluated only for the side effects they produce.

4. Each STEP expression is evaluated relative to the temporary environment. The evaluation order of the STEP expressions is unspecified. After all the STEP expressions are evaluated, each NAME in rebound to the value of its associated STEP expression. The new bindings replace the old bindings in the temporary environment.

5. Go to Step 2.

It's easiest to understand how a do-loop works by studying an example:

```
(define (count-down n)
    (do ((i n (- i 1))            ; declaration
         ((< i 0) 'blast-off!)    ; exit clause
         (display i)              ; body
         (newline)))              ; body
```

The do-loop inside count-down has a single declaration:

```
(i n (- i 1))
```

When the do-loop is evaluated, a temporary frame containing a binding between *i* and *n* (INIT) extends the current environment. The scope of this binding extends only to the end of the do-loop body.

At the beginning of each subsequent iteration the STEP expression, $(- i\ 1)$, is evaluated relative to the temporary environment. The value of this expression is bound to i and replaces the old binding of i. Thus, each iteration of the do-loop replaces the old binding $i = j$ with a new binding $i = k$ where $k = j - 1$.

The EXIT-CLAUSE of the do-loop is:

```
((< i 0) 'blast-off!)
```

The CONDITION, $(< i\ 0)$, is evaluated on each iteration after the bindings are created. Eventually, i will fall below 0, $(< i\ 0)$ will then be #t, and the symbol blast-off! will be the value of the entire do-loop.

The BODY of the do-loop is the sequence:

```
(display i)
(newline)
```

These expressions are evaluated on each repetition assuming CONDITION is #f. The values of these expressions are discarded, but their side-effects can be seen as screen output.

Here are some sample evaluations of count-down:

```
> (count-down 3)
3
2
1
0
blast-off!

> (define x (count-down 3))
3
2
1
0
unspecified ;   = value of (define ...)
> x
blast-off!   ; blast-off! returned by do & count-down
```

5.1.2. Control Loops

Assume the initial state, update procedure, and final? predicate of a system S are given:

```
(define init-state ...) ; = initial state of system S

; = next state of system S
(define (update current-state) ...)
```

```
; = #t if state is a final state of system S
(define (final? state) ...)
```

We can implement the control loop as a do-loop:

```
(do ((state init-state (update state)))
    ((final? state) state))
```

This do-loop consists of a single declaration:

```
(state init-state (update state))
```

which initially binds state to init-state, and subsequently rebinds state to the value of (update state). The exit clause of this do-loop is:

```
((final? state) state)
```

When (final? state) is not #f, the current value of state is returned; otherwise state is re-bound to (update state) and the cycle repeats. Notice, this do-loop has no body. This could hardly make a difference because the values of expressions in the body are discarded anyway. We could formalize the control loop as a Scheme procedure:

```
(define (control-loop init-state)
   (do ((state init-state (update state)))
       ((final? state) state)))
```

Recall that a meta-procedure is a procedure that expects procedures as inputs or returns procedures as outputs. We have already seen several examples of meta-procedures: for-each, map, apply, lambda, and the object oriented constructors of the last chapter. Of course we are free to define our own meta-procedures. We can generalize our control loop procedure by treating the update procedure and final? predicate as ordinary parameters:

```
(define (control-loop init-state final? update)
   (do ((state init-state (update state)))
       ((final? state) state)))
```

We could make control-loop more useful by keeping track of the cycle and printing the current cycle and state in the body of the do-loop if an optional trace argument is supplied:

```
(define
   (control-loop init-state final? update . trace)
      (do ((state init-state (update state))
           (cycle 0 (+ cycle 1)))
          ((final? state) state)
          (if (not (null? trace))
             (begin
                (writeln "cycle = " cycle)
                (writeln "state = " state)))))
```

5.1.3. Example: A Digital Clock

A digital clock is a system with state given by a vector of the form:

```
TIME ::= #(HOUR MIN SEC)
```

where

```
HOUR ::= 0 | 1 | 2 | ... | 23
SEC, MIN ::= 0 | 1 | 2 | ... | 59
```

We can treat TIME as an abstract data type (ADT) by introducing appropriate time constructors and selectors:

```
(define (make-time hour min sec)
   (vector hour min sec))

(define (hour time) (vector-ref time 0))
(define (minute time) (vector-ref time 1))
(define (second time) (vector-ref time 2))
```

The state of a digital clock is updated every second by the update procedure:

```
; = time 1 second after input time
(define (update-time time)
   (update-hour (update-min (update-sec time))))
```

The update-sec procedure merely increments the second component of time modulo 60:

```
(define (update-sec time)
   (make-time (hour time)
              (minute time)
              (mod60+ 1 (second time))))
```

If (second time) is zero, then the update-min procedure increments the minute component modulo 60; otherwise it does nothing:

```
(define (update-min time)
   (if (zero? (second time))
       (make-time (hour time)
                  (mod60+ 1 (minute time))
                  (second time))
       time))
```

If both (second time) and (minute time) are zero, then update-hour increments the hour component modulo 24; otherwise it does nothing:

```
(define (update-hour time)
   (if (and (zero? (minute time))
            (zero? (second time)))
       (make-time (mod24+ 1 (hour time))
```

```
            (minute time)
            (second time))
    time))
```

The mod24+ and mod60+ procedures are simply modulo 24 and modulo 60 addition, respectively:

```
(define (mod24+ x y) (modulo (+ x y) 24))
(define (mod60+ x y) (modulo (+ x y) 60))
```

If we imagine our digital clock has an alarm, then we can define the final state to be the time at which the alarm rings. I have to set my clock for 6:30 A.M.:

```
(define (alarm? time)
    (and (= (hour time) 6)
         (= (minute time) 30)
         (= (second time) 0)))
```

Assume the initial state of the clock is 6:29:55

```
(define init-time (make-time 6 29 55))
```

The control loop iterates the update-time procedure for five "seconds:"

```
> (control-loop init-time alarm? update-time 'trace)
state = #(6 29 55)
cycle = 0
state = #(6 29 56)
cycle = 1
state = #(6 29 57)
cycle = 2
state = #(6 29 58)
cycle = 3
state = #(6 29 59)
cycle = 4
#(6 30 0)
```

Digital versus Analog Systems

Our example raises an important distinction. If we modeled an analog clock rather than a digital clock we would take states to be vectors of the form:

```
TIME ::= #(REAL REAL REAL)
```

where the components indicate the angle from 0 to 2π radians of the hour, minute, and second hands, respectively. More significantly, the state of the analog clock is updated continuously rather than at discrete one-second intervals. Systems like analog clocks that update their states continuously are called **continuous dynamical systems**. Systems like digital clocks that update their states at discrete intervals are called **discrete dynamical systems.**

Like digital clocks, digital computers are discrete dynamical systems, although analog computers do exist. (What is the state space of a computer?) As such, they are not very good for modeling continuous dynamical systems. The best they can do is discretely approximate continuous state change by updating the state every Δ seconds for very small values of Δ.

From now on we shall use the term **dynamical system** or just **system** to refer to discrete dynamical systems or discrete approximations of continuous dynamical systems.

5.1.4. Example: Compound Interest

A bank loan is repaid in monthly installments. Of course every month interest accumulates on the remaining debt. Eventually, if the principle is low enough, the debt is reduced to zero.

We can model bank loans as dynamical systems. The state space consists of all possible debts:

```
DEBT ::= REAL          ; = dollars owed
```

Assume the interest rate and monthly payments are fixed:

```
(define rate .01) ; monthly interest rate = 1%
(define pmt 50)   ; monthly payment = $50
```

(In reality, the monthly payment is adjusted to insure the loan can be repaid in a fixed amount of time.) Each month the new debt is the old debt, plus the interest on the old debt, less the monthly payment:

```
new-debt = debt + rate * debt - pmt
         = debt * (1 + rate) - pmt
```

We can express this equation as a Scheme procedure. To make book-keeping simpler, the new debt is rounded to the nearest dollar. This procedure is the update procedure for our system:

```
(define (new-debt debt)
   (round (- (* debt rate+1) pmt)))
```

where:

```
(define rate+1 (+ 1 rate))
```

The final state is reached when the debt becomes less than the monthly payment. At this point the bank customer repays the balance and the debt is canceled:

```
(define (paid? debt) (< debt pmt))
```

The control loop repeatedly updates the debt until the amount owed falls below the monthly payment:

```
> (control-loop 400 paid? new-debt 'trace)
state = 400
cycle = 0
state = 354
cycle = 1
state = 308
cycle = 2
state = 261
cycle = 3
state = 214
cycle = 4
state = 166
cycle = 5
state = 118
cycle = 6
state = 69
cycle = 7
20
```

5.1.5. Example: A Simple Interactive System

A mod-n counter is a simple memory device that stores a single integer called count. The count is always between 0 and some maximum integer, max-int:

0 ≤ count < max-int

Assume max-int is a fixed constant:

```
(define max-int 16)   ; max-int usually 2^n
```

We can model a counter as an **interactive procedure**. An interactive procedure is a procedure that engages the user in a dialog. In this case the procedure prompts the user for a command; the user enters a command through a keyboard, mouse, or some other input device; the procedure executes the command, displays the result, and the cycle repeats. This type of dialog should be familiar to readers because it is exactly the type of interaction that occurs between Scheme programmers and the Scheme control loop. In particular, the Scheme control loop can be regarded as a type of dynamical system.

Returning to the counter, the state of our system is the integer count together with a special final state:

```
COUNT ::= NATURAL | bye
```

The update procedure prompts users for a command, then executes the command. A counter provides commands for reading, resetting, incrementing, or decrementing the count. The result of executing any command, even in the case when the command is unrecognized, is always a count:

```
; = new value of count
(define (exec-cmmd count)

   ; prompt user and read command
   (define cmmd (get-cmmd))

   (case cmmd
      ((inc) (modulo (+ count 1) max-int))
      ((dec) (modulo (- count 1) max-int))
      ((get) (writeln "count = " count) count)
      ((set) 0)
      ((q quit exit) 'bye)
      (else
         (writeln "unrecognized command: " cmmd)
         count)))
```

The get-cmmd procedure displays a menu of options, then reads and returns the user's input. Notice the use of tab characters to format the menu:

```
; prompts user & returns command read
(define (get-cmmd)
   (writeln "command menu: ")
   (writeln #\tab "inc" #\tab "increments count")
   (writeln #\tab "dec" #\tab "decrements count")
   (writeln #\tab "get" #\tab "displays count")
   (writeln #\tab "set" #\tab "resets count to 0")
   (writeln #\tab "quit" #\tab "to quit")
   (display "command-> ")
   (read))
```

The final? predicate, called bye?, compares the state to the 'bye token:

```
(define (bye? state) (eq? state 'bye))
```

Here is a sample session:

```
> (control-loop 5 bye? exec-cmmd)    ; tracing disabled
command menu:
    inc        increments count
    dec        decrements count
    get        displays count
    set        resets count to 0
    quit       to quit
command-> inc
command menu:
    inc        increments count
    dec        decrements count
    get        displays count
```

```
    set       resets count to 0
    quit      to quit
command-> inc
command menu:
    inc       increments count
    dec       decrements count
    get       displays count
    set       resets count to 0
    quit      to quit
command-> get
count = 7
command menu:
    inc       increments count
    dec       decrements count
    get       displays count
    set       resets count to 0
    quit      to quit
command-> add1
error: unrecognized command: add1
command menu:
    inc       increments count
    dec       decrements count
    get       displays count
    set       resets count to 0
    quit      to quit
command-> q
bye
>
```

5.1.6. Example: Guess and Test

Problem solving is a good example of a dynamical system. Suppose a state space consists of all possible guesses at solutions to a given problem, some better than others:

```
GUESS ::= all guesses at solutions to a given problem
```

Unless we have some analytical way of deriving the desired solution, we will have to resort to searching the state space using the guess-and-test method (i.e., trial and error). More formally, suppose we have a method for improving guesses:

```
; = a better guess than input guess
(define (improve guess) ...)
```

and a predicate for recognizing when a guess is good enough:

```
; = #t if guess is close enough to the solution
(define (good-enuf? guess) ...)
```

Beginning with an initial guess, we iterate the guess improver, testing each guess to see if it is "good enough," until we produce a desirable solution state:

```
(control-loop init-guess good-enuf? improve)
```

We cannot predict how many times the control loop will iterate the guess improver. The iteration continues until a guess is produced that satisfies the good-enuf? test. Indeed, this may never happen and the control loop will go on iterating the improver forever.

Solving Equations

A solution of a real-valued procedure f is an input s satisfying:

```
(f s) = 0
```

We can use algebra to compute the solutions of some procedures, but for most we have to resort to guess-and-test. In this case the good-enuf? test is simply:

```
; = #t if guess is small, i.e., close to 0
(define (good-enuf? guess)
   (<= (abs (f guess)) delta))
```

where delta is a suitably small nonlocal constant:

```
(define delta 1e-10)
```

A bigger problem is defining the guess improver. Fortunately, the framer of the laws of mechanics, Sir Isaac Newton (1642-1727) developed a method using a little invention of his called calculus. Newton observed that if f was differentiable, and guess was a point on the x-axis near its intersection with f's graph, then a nearer point was the intersection of the x-axis and the line tangent to f's graph at the point (guess, (f guess)):

The point-slope form of the equation for this tangent line is:

$$y - y_0 = m(x - x_0)$$

where (x_0, y_0) is the tangent point:

```
(x0, y0) = (guess, (f guess))
```

and m, the slope of the line, is the derivative of f, df, evaluated at guess:

```
m = (df guess)
```

The point of intersection with the x-axis, i.e., the improved guess, is gotten by solving the line equation for x when y is set to 0:

```
improved guess = x = guess - f(guess)/df(guess)
```

We could base a Scheme procedure on this formula:

```
; = a better guess at f's solution than input
(define (improve guess)
   (- guess (/ (f guess) (df guess))))
```

But without knowing more about the *f* procedure, how can we compute its derivative? Again we have to dust off our calculus books. Recall the general formula for computing the derivative of a function *f*:

$$df(x) = \lim_{\delta \to 0} \frac{f(x + \delta) - f(x)}{\delta}$$

We can't expect to compute arbitrary limits in Scheme, but we can easily approximate the derivative of *f* using small values of delta:

```
(define (df x)
   (/ (- (f (+ x delta)) (f x)) delta))
```

Computing Square Roots

By cleverly choosing f, we can use Newton's method for finding square roots. Observe that $\sqrt{n}$ is the solution of $x^2 - n$. We can formalize this as a Scheme procedure:

```
(define (f x) (- (* x x) n))
```

To compute the square root of *n* we only need to call control-loop with an initial guess of 1.

We can encapsulate all of these definitions in a single procedure block:

```
(define (sqrt n)

   (define (f x)
      (- (* x x) n))

   (define delta 1e-10)

   (define (df x)
      (/ (- (f (+ x delta)) (f x)) delta))

   (define (good-enuf? guess)
      (< (abs (f guess)) delta))

   (define (improve guess)
      (- guess (/ (f guess) (df guess))))

   (control-loop 1 good-enuf? improve))
```

Computing nth Roots

We can use the model of our sqrt procedure to find the solution to any unary numeric procedure. We only need to change the definition of f inside. Unfortunately this can be awkward, especially if we need to solve two procedures simultaneously.

We confronted a similar situation when we generalized the control loop procedure by allowing update and final? to be parameters instead of specific predefined procedures. We can use the same trick here and generalize our square root procedure by treating f as a formal parameter:

```
(define (solve f)

   (define delta 1e-10)

   (define (df x)
      (/ (- (f (+ x delta)) (f x)) delta))

   (define (good-enuf? guess)
      (< (abs (f guess)) delta))

   (define (improve guess)
      (- guess (/ (f guess) (df guess))))

   (control-loop 1 good-enuf? improve))
```

We can use this procedure to define a cube root procedure as follows:

```
(define (cube-root n)

   (define (f x)
      (- (* x x x) n))

   (solve f))
```

5.2.   Computations as Data

The Scheme expression evaluator is an example of a dynamic system. In this case the state space is the domain of all Scheme expressions, the initial state is the input expression, literal expressions are the final states, apply is the update procedure, and an orbit is a computation.

Just as we might analyze the orbits of a vibrating string or a population of Wildebeest, we can analyze the orbits of the expression evaluator. Let's begin by fixing a generic example.

5.2.1. Predicting the Future

Assume the system, *S*, we are interested in modeling is a population of amoebas living in a pond. The state of system is the size of a population. Assume initially only a single amoeba lives in the pond, and during a cycle every amoeba in the pond divides into two amoebas. (Amoebas reproduce asexually by cellular division.)

```
(define init-state 1)    ; = size of initial population

; = population after one reproductive cycle
(define (update state) (* 2 state))
```

Suppose we want to predict the state of this system after *n* cycles:

```
; = state of system S after n cycles
(define (state n) ???)
```

Because the input to the state procedure is a natural number, we might try to develop a recursive algorithm. We ask two questions:

Base Case:
What is (state 0)?

Successor Case:
How can we use (state (- n 1)) to compute (state n)?

We answer these questions by working out a few examples. First note that (state 0), the state after 0 cycles, is just the initial state:

```
(state 0)    = init-state
```

Thereafter, each state is gotten by applying the update procedure to the previous state:

```
(state 1)    = (update init-state)
             = (update (state 0))

(state 2)    = (update (update state))
             = (update (state 1))

(state 3)    = (update (update (update state)))
             = (update (state 2))
```

Notice the general pattern in the return values when *n* > 0. We can describe it as a Scheme expression:

```
(state n)    = (update (state (- n 1)))
```

This suggests the following implementation of the state procedure:

```
; = state of system S after n cycles
(define (state n)
```

```
(if (zero? n)
    init-state
    (update (state (- n 1))))))
```

Let's declare update and state "interesting" and trace the computation generated by (state 4):

```
(state 4)
(update (state 3))
(update (update (state 2)))
(update (update (update (state 1))))
(update (update (update (update (state 0)))))
(update (update (update (update 1))))
(update (update (update 2)))
(update (update 4))
(update 8)
16
```

5.2.2. Measuring Computations

We can treat computations[1] like the one just given as ordinary data. Two important measurements of a computation are its length and width. Assume exp is any Scheme expression, and define:

```
|exp|
    = length of the computation generated by exp
```

```
[exp]
    = width of the computation generated by exp
```

The length of a computation is the number of steps (cycles) from exp to the final result. Note: Oscillating and divergent computations have infinite lengths.

The width of a computation is the size of the largest expression appearing in the computation. The size of an expression is the number of procedure applications appearing in the expression. For example, in the preceeding computation:

```
|(state 4)| = 10
[(state 4)] = 5
```

If we choose interesting procedures wisely, then lexpl is proportional to the amount of computer time required to evaluate exp and [exp] is proportional to the amount of memory needed to evaluate exp (this is because the Scheme evaluator maintains a frame for each pending procedure call).

---

[1] Technically this is a **trace**, which is a subsequence of a computation.

5.2.3. Measuring Efficiency

How do we measure the overall efficiency of a procedure, proc? If we regard n as a parameter, then |(proc n)| and [(proc n)] are both reasonable choices.

An important property of a measurement is order, the ability to say that one is bigger or smaller than another. This is especially important for measurements of efficiency, because two procedures might do the same thing, but one may be more efficient than the other. Unfortunately, |(proc n)| and [(proc n)] are functions, not numbers. How do we compare functions?

Although there is no general way of comparing two functions, we can often compare their growth rates. If f and g are functions, let $f = O(g)$ mean:

```
growth rate of f ≤ growth rate of g
```

More formally, $f = O(g)$ means we can fix a constant c such that for all large values of n:

```
f(n) ≤ c * g(n)
```

Equivalently:

$$\lim_{n \to \infty} \frac{f(n)}{g(n)} < \infty \text{ or } 0 < \lim_{n \to \infty} \frac{g(n)}{f(n)}$$

Next, we design a "measuring stick" marked by functions of known growth rates (see Figure 5.1).

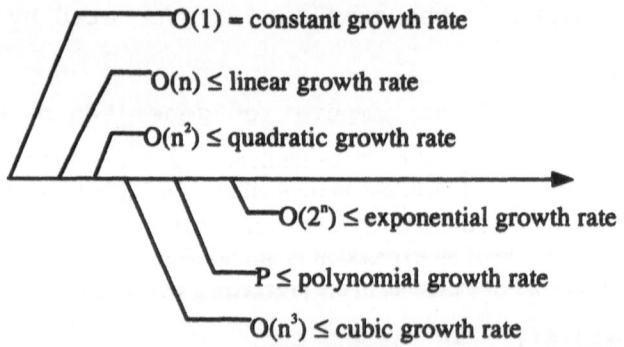

O(1) = constant growth rate

O(n) ≤ linear growth rate

O(n^2) ≤ quadratic growth rate

O(2^n) ≤ exponential growth rate

P ≤ polynomial growth rate

O(n^3) ≤ cubic growth rate

Figure 5.1

If |(proc n)| (or [(proc n)]) is a polynomial of degree k, then its position on the ruler is $O(n^k)$, i.e., |(proc n)| = $O(n^k)$, because the lower-order terms don't have much influence on growth rate for large values of n. (Use L'Hôpital's rule and the limit characterizations of $f = O(g)$ to prove this.) For example, |(state n)| = $2n + 2 = O(n)$, and [(state n)] = $n + 2$ = $O(n)$.

5.2.4. The Tyranny of Growth Rate

To gain some appreciation for our efficiency measures, assume four procedures: proc1, proc2, proc3, and proc4, compute the same function, only $|(\text{proc1 } n)| = O(n)$, $|(\text{proc2 } n)| = O(n^2)$, $|(\text{proc3 } n)| = O(n^3)$, and $|(\text{proc4 } n)| = O(10^n)$. Let's assume one step in a computation requires one microsecond (i.e., 10^{-6} seconds). If $n = 100$, then $(\text{proc1 } n)$ will consume $10^2 * 10^{-6} = 10^{-4}$ seconds, $(\text{proc2 } n)$ will consume $10^4 * 10^{-6} = 10^{-2}$ seconds, $(\text{proc3 } n)$ will consume $10^6 * 10^{-6} = 1$ second, and $(\text{proc4 } n)$ will consume $10^{100} * 10^{-6} = 10^{94}$ seconds. There are on the order of 10^7 seconds in a year, so this works out to about 13.4 years!

If we increase n to 1000, then $(\text{proc1 } n)$ consumes a reasonable $10^3 * 10^{-6} = 10^{-3}$ seconds, $(\text{proc2 } n)$ only consumes $10^6 * 10^{-6} = 1$ second, but $(\text{proc3 } n)$ consumes $10^9 * 10^{-6} = 10^3$ seconds. That's more than 16 minutes! $|(\text{proc4 } n)|$ is comparable to the known age of the universe!

5.3.   Finding Iterative Solutions

How can we improve the efficiency of the state procedure? We could reimplement state using a do-loop. We use local bindings to keep track of the state (result) and cycle (count). When $n \leq$ count, the final state s is returned:

```
(define (state n)
   (do ((count 0 (+ count 1))
        (result init-state (update result)))
       ((<= n count) result)))
```

It should be clear that $|(\text{state } n)| = O(n)$ because the do-loop generates n calls to the update procedure. However, the sizes of the expressions appearing in the computation generated by (state n) is constant, because the iterations of update are not nested. Therefore $[(\text{state } n)] = O(1)$, a big improvement over the recursive implementation.

Let's develop iterative solutions to the recursive procedures we developed in Chapter 3: nat-expt and make-list. Our make-list do-loop will use two loop control bindings. One will be a counter that counts from 0 to n, the other will be the list under construction. The list is updated on each cycle by consing val to the front of the previous list:

```
; = the length n list (val ... val)
(define (make-list n val)
   (if (not (natural? n))
       (error "bad input" make-list n)
       (do ((count 0 (+ count 1))
            (result '() (cons val result)))
           ((<= n count) result))))
```

We use the same strategy to implement nat-expt. The only difference is the method used to initialize and update result:

```
;  = b^n
(define (nat-expt b n)
   (if (not (and (number? b) (natural? n)))
       (error "bad input(s)" nat-expt b n)
       (do ((count 0 (+ count 1))
            (result 1 (* b result)))
           ((<= n count) result))))
```

It should be clear that while |(nat-expt n)| = O(n) and |(make-list n val)| = O(n), the same as the recursive implementations, [(nat-expt n)] = O(1) and [(make-list n val)] = O(1), an improvement over the O(n) efficiencies of the recursive implementations.

5.4.   Tail Recursion: Are do-loops Necessary?

Are do-loops redundant? It seems likely that a procedure implemented using a do-loop can be reimplemented as a recursive procedure, but will the recursive implementation always use more memory than the iterative implementation? Not necessarily.

Our plan is to simulate Scheme's do-loop with an ordinary recursive procedure called iter. Assume we want to simulate the do-loop:

```
(do ((count init0 (+ count 1))
     (result init1 (update result)))
    ((<= n count) result))
```

The parameters of our simulation will be the loop control variables count and result. A recursive call will simulate the looping action. The operands of the recursive call will be the STEP expressions. The recursion terminates when CONDITION becomes true. We call our simulation iter:

```
(define (iter count result)
   (if (<= n count)
       result
       (iter (+ count 1) (update result))))
```

The initial values of the loop control parameters are parameters:

```
(iter init0 init1)
```

For example, we can rewrite control-loop using iter:

```
(define (control-loop init final? update)

   (define (iter state)
      (if (final? state)
          state
          (iter (update state))))

   (iter init))
```

Here's an implementation of the state procedure using iter:

```
(define (state n)

   (define (iter count result)
     (if (>= count n)
         result
         (iter (+ count 1) (update result))))

   (if (not (natural? n))
       (error "bad input" state n)
       (iter 0 1)))
```

Let's trace the computation generated by (state 4), taking state, iter, and update to be our interesting procedures:

```
(state 4)
(iter 0 1)
(iter 1 (update 1))
(iter 1 2)
(iter 2 (update 2))
(iter 2 4)
(iter 3 (update 4))
(iter 3 8)
(iter 4 (update 8))
(iter 4 16)
16
```

It seems pretty clear that $|(\text{state } n)| = 2n + 3 = O(n)$, but notice the width of the computation remains constant. This would be true even if the input was very large. In other words, for all n: $[(\text{state } n)] = 2 = O(1)$, the same as the iterative solution!

This happens because the recursive call to iter was not nested inside a call to the update procedure, hence it was not necessary to save pending calls to the update procedure like the original recursive implementation of state did. (This is what made the computations get fat.)

A recursive procedure is **tail-recursive** if the recursive call is the last expression evaluated before the procedure terminates. This happens if the recursive call is not the input to another call (structures don't count), and if it is not part of a sequence (unless it's the last expression in the sequence). The Scheme interpreter is designed to reuse the frame created by a call to a tail-recursive procedure for all subsequent calls; therefore computations generated by calls to tail-recursive procedures consume a constant (i.e., $O(1)$) amount of memory.

Here is a tail-recursive implementation of make-list:

```
; = the length n list (val ... val)
(define (make-list n val)
```

```
(define (iter count result)
   (if (<= n count)
       result
       (iter (+ count 1) (cons val result)))))

(if (not (natural? n))
    (error "bad input" make-list n)
    (iter 0 '()))))
```

The tail-recursive implementation of nat-expt is also straightforward:

```
; = b^n
(define (nat-expt b n)

   (define (iter count result)
      (if (<= n count)
          result
          (iter (+ count 1) (* b result)))))

   (if (not (and (number? b) (natural? n)))
       (error "bad input(s)" nat-expt b n)
       (iter 0 1)))
```

5.5. Finding Elementary Solutions

Sometimes we can use tracing to find **elementary** (i.e., nonrecursive, noniterative) solutions. For example, assume the initial value and update procedure of a system are given by:

```
(define init-state 1)    ; = initial state of system S

; = next state of system S
(define (update state)
   (- (* 4 state) 1))
```

Assume state is defined as before:

```
; = state of system S after n cycles
(define (state n)
   (if (zero? n)
       init-state
       (update (state (- n 1))))))
```

Let's trace a call to (state n), for any $n > 0$. Notice how each step of the computation builds a term in a geometric series:

```
(state n)
(- (* 4 (state (- n 1))) 1)
(- (* 4 (- (* 4 (state (- n 2))) 1) 1)
(- (* 16 (state (- n 2))) (+ 4 1))
(- (* 16 (- (* 4 (state (- n 3))) 1)) (+ 4 1))
(- (* 64 (state (- n 3))) (+ 16 4 1))
...
```

$$(- (* 4^k (state (- n k))) (+ 4^{k-1} 4^{k-2} ... 4^0))$$

```
...
```

After the last call to state, we are left with a geometric series:

$$(- (* 4^n (state 0)) (+ 4^{n-1} ... 4^0))$$
$$= (- 4^n (+ 4^{n-1} ... 4^0))$$

Recall the formula for computing the sum of a geometric series:

$$\sum_{i=0}^{k} r^i = \frac{1 - r^{k+1}}{1 - r}$$

Hence $(+ 4^{n-1} ... 4^0)$ is $(4^n - 1)/3 = (4^n - 1)/3$. This suggests the following elementary implementation of the state procedure:

```
.; = next state of system S after n cycles
(define (state n) (/ (- (expt 4 n) 1) 3))
```

The amount of space and time consumed by this implementation of state is independent of n:

```
|(state n)| = O(1)
[(state n)] = O(1)
```

The situation is analogous with the situation in physics. An analog system is initially modeled by a differential equation much the same way a recursive procedure models a digital system. This is satisfactory for predicting future states of the system, but the physicist doesn't claim the system is "understood" until the differential equation can be solved, i.e., replaced by a closed-form equation.

Appendices

Appendix 5.1. The Hyper-Exponential Hierarchy

In Figure 5.1 we began constructing a measuring stick marked by functions of known growth rates. We stopped at $O(2^n)$ because if $|(proc\ n)|$ or $[(proc\ n)]$ is beyond this point, then proc would be too wildly inefficient to be useful. Despite this, it's still interesting to study functions beyond the $O(2^n)$ growth rate. (Sometimes "useful" and "interesting" are different!)

Pick an implementation of 2^n:

```
; = 2^n
(define (exp2 n)
   (if (zero? n)
       1
       (double (exp2 (- n 1))))))
```

where

```
(define (double n) (* 2 n))
```

Notice (exp2 n) works by iterating double n times. Following this pattern, define a recursive procedure that iterates exp2 n times:

```
(define (hyper-exp n)
   (if (zero? n)
       1
       (exp2 (hyper-exp (- n 1))))))
```

Let's trace (hyper-exp 4):

```
(hyper-exp 4)
(exp2 (hyper-exp 3))
(exp2 (exp2 (hyper-exp 2)))
(exp2 (exp2 (exp2 (hyper-exp 1))))
(exp2 (exp2 (exp2 (exp2 (hyper-exp 0)))))
(exp2 (exp2 (exp2 (exp2 1))))
(exp2 (exp2 (exp2 2)))
(exp2 (exp2 4))
(exp2 16)
65536
```

For $n > 1$, (hyper-exp n) = $2^{(\text{hyper-exp} (- n 1))}$, hence (hyper-exp 3) is a stack of three twos:

$$(\text{hyper} - \text{exp} \, 4) = 2^{2^2}$$

In fact, exp2 = O(hyper-exp), but hyper-exp ≠ O(exp2), so we can take O(hyper-exp) as the next point on our measuring stick.

Next, define a recursive procedure that iterates hyper-exp:

```
(define (hyper^2-exp n)
   (if (zero? n)
       1
       (hyper-exp (hyper^2-exp (- n 1))))))
```

Let's trace (hyper^2-exp 4):

```
(hyper^2-exp 4)
(hyper-exp (hyper^2-exp 3))
(hyper-exp (hyper-exp (hyper^2-exp 2)))
```

```
(hyper-exp (hyper-exp (hyper-exp (hyper^2-exp 1))))
(hyper-exp (hyper-exp (hyper-exp
                        (hyper-exp (hyper^2-exp 0)))))
(hyper-exp (hyper-exp (hyper-exp (hyper-exp 1))))
(hyper-exp (hyper-exp (hyper-exp 2)))
(hyper-exp (hyper-exp 4))
(hyper-exp 65536)
```
$2^{(\text{hyper-exp } 65535)}$ = ?

The result of this computation is quite a staggering number, a stack of 65,536 twos! A stack of five twos is already 2^{65536}. This is far larger than the number of atoms in the universe. It can be proved that hyper-exp = O(hyper^2-exp), but hyper^2-exp ≠O(hyper-exp), so we can take hyper^2-exp as the next marker on our measuring stick.

Unimpressed? Let's iterate hyper^2-exp n times:

```
(define (hyper^3-exp n)
   (if (zero? n)
       1
       (hyper^2-exp (hyper^3-exp (- n 1))))))
```

The reader shouldn't be surprised to learn that hyper^2-exp = O(hyper^3-exp), but not vice-versa.

We can continue to mark our measuring stick with hyper^4-exp, hyper^5-exp, etc. as shown in Figure 5.2.

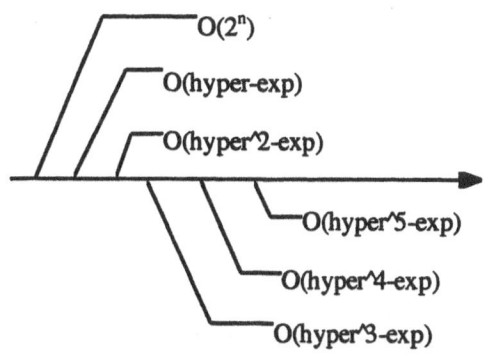

Figure 5.2

We can combine all the procedures in the hyper-exponential hierarchy into a single procedure:

```
; = hyper^m-exp n)
(define (exp* m n)
   (cond ((zero? n) 1)
         ((zero? m) (exp2 n))
         (else (exp* (- m 1) (exp* m (- n 1)))))))
```

The exp* procedure is much more convenient to use than the hyper-exponentials:

```
(exp* 0 n)  = (exp2 n)
(exp* 1 n)  = (hyper-exp n)
(exp* 2 n)  = (hyper^2-exp n)
(exp* 5 n)  = (hyper^5-exp n)
etc.
```

It boggles the mind to think of the sizes of the outputs produced by the exp* procedure, even for small values of m. But this didn't intimidate the German mathematician W. Ackermann. In 1928 he observed that diagonalizing[2] exp* produced a procedure that eventually grows faster than all of the hyper-exponentials:

```
(define (ack n) (exp* n n))
```

To see why, observe that (ack n) = (exp* n n) > (exp* m n) when $n > m$. In other words, O(ack) lies beyond O(hyper^n-exp) for all n!

Of course we can continue beyond O(ack) by iterating ack:

```
(define (hyper-ack n)
   (if (zero? n)
       1
       (ack (hyper-ack (- n 1))))))
```

```
(define (hyper^2-ack n) ...) .
(define (hyper^3-ack n) ...)
etc.
(define (ack^2 n) (ack* n n)) ; = (hyper^n-ack n)
(define (ack^3 n) (ack^2* n n))
etc.
```

Appendix 5.2. Undecidability

> I will here and now construct a Demon of the Second Kind, and you will see for yourself the wondrous perfection of that metainformationator! All you have to do is find me a box —any size will do, but it must be airtight. We'll put a little pinhole in it and sit the Demon over the opening; perched there it will let out only significant information, keeping in the non-sense. For whenever a group of atoms accidentally arranges itself in a meaningful way, the Demon will pounce on that meaning and instantly record it. ...
>
> —Stanislaus Lem, *The Cyberiad*

---

[2] Place applications of exp* in an infinite matrix so the row m, column n entry is (exp* m n). The diagonal entries are of the form (exp* n n).

If we set aside questions of efficiency, can we at least claim that every well-defined problem can be solved by a computer? Surprisingly, the answer is No; there are fairly straightforward problems that can never be solved by a computer. We are *not* saying that a computer solution to these problems has not yet been found, we *are* saying that a computer solution can *never* be found!

A problem that can't be solved by a computer is called **undecidable**. One such problem is called the **halting problem**:

> Determine if an arbitrary procedure applied to an arbitrary list of inputs eventually returns a value (i.e., halts or converges) or not.

To solve this problem we would need to implement the following procedure:

```
(convergent? proc val...)
  = #t, if (apply proc (list val...)) returns a value
  = #f, otherwise
```

Unfortunately, this procedure can *never* be implemented. To see why, assume otherwise; assume convergent? *can* be implemented:

```
(define (convergent? proc . vals) ???)
```

Once it has been defined, it can be called by other procedures, such as the famous **diagonalization procedure**:

```
(define (diag proc)
  (if (convergent? proc proc)
      (undef)
      'done))
```

where undef is a nasty, nonterminating tail-recursion:

```
(define (undef) (undef))    ; runs forever
```

Basically, (diag proc) diverges if the computation generated by applying proc to itself—(proc proc)—converges, and that it converges if (proc proc) diverges.

Applying a procedure to itself may seem a bit weird, but if proc is a meta-procedure, then it expects a procedure as input, and this procedure could be proc itself. For example, the identity procedure can handle procedure inputs:

```
(define (id p) p) ; the identity procedure
```

Applying the identity procedure to itself produces the identity procedure as output:

```
(id id)  = id
```

Because this computation returns a value, we would expect (diag id) to call undef and diverge.

Like id, convergent?, and apply, diag is a meta-procedure. So what happens when diag is applied to itself?

```
(diag diag) = ?
```

This depends on the outcome of:

```
(convergent? diag diag)
```

If this returns #t, then the undef procedure is called, and the computation drags on for eternity. In other words, the computation diverges, contradicting the fact that (convergent? diag diag) returned #t.

To avoid this contradiction we must assume (convergent? diag diag) returns #f. But in this case the done token is returned and the computation halts, contradicting the assumption that (convergent? diag diag) returned #f.

We seem to be caught in a paradoxical situation. If (convergent? diag diag) returns #t, then it should have returned #f. If it returns #f, then it should have returned #t. Unfortunately, the only way out of the paradox is to assume that (convergent? diag diag) diverges, contradicting the assumption that we could implement convergent?, so it *always* gave correct answers.

Appendix 5.3. Chaos

The philosopher-mathematician Pierre Laplace (1749-1827) viewed the universe as a huge dynamical system with an update procedure specified by Newton's laws. Knowing the state of the universe at any moment —i.e., the position, velocity, acceleration, and mass of every particle —we could accurately predict any future or past state. (Of course, knowing the state of the universe at any moment would be difficult; there are many particles and each has many properties that must be taken into account.)

In 1930 German physicist Werner Heisenberg's (1901-1976) uncertainty principle put a small knot in Laplace's dream. Because properties of small particles could only be estimated, iterating a Newtonian (or Einsteinian) update procedure would only yield estimates of future states. In other words, if the initial state of the universe is init0, but our estimate of this state is init1, then after n iterations, our predicted state would be:

```
state0   = (update (update ... (update init0) ... ))
```

while the true state would be:

```
state1   = (update (update ... (update init1) ... ))
```

Laplace might have speculated that if init0 is at least close to init1, then state0 should be close to state1. More formally, for each small δ, there should be a corresponding small ε such that

```
|init0 - init1| < δ implies |state0 - state1| < ε
```

Sadly, this isn't necessarily true. In 1960 the MIT meteorologist Edward Lorenz discovered the **butterfly effect**. Like the universe, Earth's atmosphere is a huge dynamical system, but with an update procedure specified by the laws of fluid mechanics. Given an estimate of the atmosphere's state at any moment —say the temperature, humidity, and pressure of every cubic meter— we should be able to estimate the weather at any future date. Why then are the predictions of modern meteorologists only marginally better than Willard Scott's?

Lorenz discovered simple dynamical systems that were highly sensitive to their initial conditions. In these systems even if |init0 - init1| < δ, for large enough n, |state0 − state1| would be very large. Because Lorenz's systems were simplified atmospheric models, he concluded that small differences in the state of the atmosphere, such as a butterfly flapping its wings in Brazil, could produce large differences later, such as a tornado in Texas!

Although the sensitivity of Lorenz's model seems to imply the unpredictability of future states, this isn't exactly true. We can predict *which* future states will occur, just not *when* they will occur. For example, we can safely say that at some future date the weather will be sunny, but we can't safely predict a specific date. In other words, the set of all possible future weather states is well known: it seldom snows in Cairo, hurricanes in Topeka are infrequent, and Arctic heat waves are virtually unknown. Regardless of slight variations in the initial state, weather system orbits almost always settle into predictable patterns, but the sequence of states varies unpredictably.

We say two orbits of a system S are nearby if their initial states are close in the system's state space. If nearby orbits tend to settle into the same limit or attractor (i.e., fixed point, cycle, or other set of states), we say the system is *not* sensitive to initial conditions. (Fixed points and cycles can be attractors, but more complex limits can also be attractors.) If the system S has an attractor but is also sensitive to initial conditions, we call the attractor **strange**. Thus, the set of all normal weather states for a given region is a strange attractor. If a system S has a strange attractor, we say it exhibits **chaos**.

Example: The Devil's Pitchfork

The logistic function is a simple example of a system with a strange attractor.

```
; = next state of system S
(define (logistic state)
    (* const (- 1 state) state))
```

The classical example of a system with the logisitic function as its update procedure is a self-limiting population. As the population, i.e., state, grows, the food supply dwindles and the growth rate, i.e., (* const (− 1 state)), becomes smaller, even becoming negative. This causes the population to decline, which causes the food supply to increase; hence the growth rate increases and the cycle repeats. Will the population eventually reach equilibrium or settle into a simple growth and decay cycle?

We can display the logistic function's attractors by displaying the last few states generated after a large number of cycles. For example, we might display the states generated by the last 20 of 520 cycles of logistic. Hopefully the orbit will have settled into an attractor by then. To make our display procedure more useful, we will treat the constant factor appearing in the logistic procedure as a parameter:

```
; = displays attractor of logistic procedure
(define (show-log-attractor const)
```

```
; the logistic function
(define (logistic state)
    (* const (- 1 state) state))

; 0 <= init-state <= 1 & init-state <> .5
(define init-state .2)

; control-loop:
(do ((cycle 0 (+ cycle 1))
     (state init-state (logistic state)))
    ((> cycle 520) 'done)
    (if (> cycle 500)
        (show-state const state))))
```

For now show-state is simply:

```
(define (show-state const state)
    (display (cons const state))
    (newline))
```

If we use show-log-attractor to display attractors for small values of const, say const < 3, we discover that the attractors are single states. This is called a *fixed point*:

```
> (show-log-attractor 2.5)
(2.5 . .6)
(2.5 . .6)
(2.5 . .6)
(2.5 . .6)
(2.5 . .6)
(2.5 . .6)
etc.
```

As const approaches 3, the attractor is a two-cycle. The orbit perpetually oscillates between two states:

```
> (show-log-attractor 3)
(3 . .6561)
(3 . .6769192740696468)
(3 . .6561)
(3 . .6769)
(3 . .6561)
(3 . .6769)
etc.
```

At const = 3.5 the attractor is a four-cycle:

```
> (show-log-attractor 3.5)
(3.5 . .5008842103072181)
```

```
(3.5 . .8749972636024641)
(3.5 . .38281968301732416)
(3.5 . .8269407065914386)
(3.5 . .5008842103072181)
(3.5 . .8749972636024641)
(3.5 . .38281968301732416)
(3.5 . .8269407065914386)
etc.
```

Finally, for 3.7 < const < 4, the attractor begins to look random:

```
> (show-log-attractor 3.99)
(3.99 . .4691998052029333)
(3.99 . .9937148785218463)
(3.99 . 2.4920018717372792e-2)
(3.99 . 9.695305542414934e-2)
(3.99 . .34933711026760395)
(3.99 . .9069297676933606)
(3.99 . .33678857501845993)
(3.99 . .8912145027144256)
(3.99 . .3868353393349597)
(3.99 . .9464031007104995)
(3.99 . .2023898439874461)
(3.99 . .6440984982023515)
(3.99 . .9146501350351492)
(3.99 . .31148040940617666)
(3.99 . .8556968522097255)
(3.99 . .49268419981909)
(3.99 . .9972864514801749)
(3.99 . 1.0797678845279992e-2)
(3.99 . .0426175450175684)
(3.99 . .16279714659823327)
```

In fact, the attractors have a complex fractal structure that can only be seen if we actually plot the states and const values on a co-ordinate system, as in Figure 5.3.

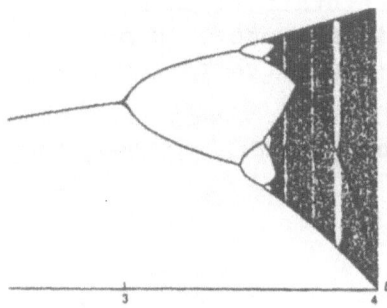

Figure 5.3

Some implementations of Scheme provide special libraries of graphics procedures. In graphics mode the screen is regarded as an *n*-by-*m* grid of points called pixels (pixel = PICture ELement). Each pixel is identified by its column and row number, these are called its **screen coordinates**. The most basic graphics procedure allows programmers to set the color of an individual pixel. For example, UG/PC-Scheme provides an easy-to-use, fairly standard graphics library called BGI. The color of a pixel is set by:

```
(put-pixel (x . y) 'color)
   = returns an unspecified value. As a side effect, sets
   color of pixel with screen co-ordinates (x, y) to 'color.
```

Here is our reimplementation of show-state:

```
(define (show-state const state)
   (put-pixel (cons const state) 'white))
```

The structure created by plotting a large number of attractors for 1 < const < 4 is called the **devil's pitchfork**, because it forks wildly as const becomes large. Also, magnifying the devil's pitchfork reveals that it is composed of tiny devil's pitchforks. Magnifying these reveals still tinier pitchforks, and so on. A self-similar structure with fractional dimension, like the devil's pitchfork, is called a **fractal**.

To be able to magnify the pitchfork we will treat the start and finish values of const as parameters. The number of attractors displayed will be controlled by a constant called slices. We begin by initializing the graphics mode and setting the top-left and bottom-right screen co-ordinates. Fortunately, BGI provides procedures for this purpose. The body of the procedure is a do-loop that iteratively increments const and calls show-log-attractor:

```
(define (pitchfork start finish)

   (define slices 75)    ; # of attractors shown

   (define delta (/ (- finish start) slices))

   (init-graph)          ; enter graphics mode

   (do ((const start (+ const delta)))
       ((< finish const) 'done)
       (show-log-attractor const)))
```

Try (pitchfork 1 4) to see the whole picture, then investigate tiny slices of the pitchfork, for example, (pitchfork 3.8 3.81). Type (close-graph) to return to text mode.

Problems

Solutions to the following problems are to be given in functional Scheme; do not use procedures or special forms discussed in subsequent chapters. Do not use any of the I/O procedures discussed in this chapter except to print error or diagnostic messages or unless you are specifically directed by the problem to use them. You may use the definitions given in this or previous chapters as well as solutions to other problems in this or previous chapters (although you will have to include these definitions in your definition file so you can test your definitions). You may also define any supporting procedures you need. You are required to validate inputs.

Problem 5.1.

Compute the values of the following expressions. If the values are unspecified, if the expressions contain errors, or if the expressions result in a nonterminating evaluation, explain:

```
a. (* 2 (do ((x = 1 1) (y 1 (+ y 1))) ((< 50 y) x)))

b. (do ((x 1 (do ((y x (* 2 y))
                  (i 0 (+ i 1)))
                 ((< 20 i) y))
        ((i 0 (+ i 1)))
        ((< 10 i) x))

c. (do () ())
```

Problem 5.2.

Find iterative and tail-recursive implementations of the factorial function:

```
(fact n)
   = 1, if n = 0
   = 1 * 2 * ... * n, otherwise
```

Problem 5.3.

Find O limits on |(fact n)| and [(fact n)].

Problem 5.4.

Find iterative and tail-recursive implementations of triangle.

Problem 5.5.

For each implementation of triangle in the previous problem, find O limits for |(triangle n)| and [(triangle n)].

Problem 5.6.

The Fibonacci sequence is:

0 1 1 2 3 5 8 13 21 34 etc.

The Fibonacci numbers are interesting because they are ubiquitous in nature. Implement iterative and tail-recursive versions of a procedure that calculates Fibonacci numbers.

Problem 5.7.

The harmonic series is $\sum_{k=1}^{\infty} \frac{1}{k}$ Write iterative and tail-recursive Scheme procedures that compute the partial sums of this series:

$$\text{(harmonic-sum } n) = \sum_{k=1}^{n} \frac{1}{k}$$

Problem 5.8.

Recall from calculus that the fixed point of the derivative procedure is $f(x) = e^x$. The exact value of e is given by the series:

$$e = \sum_{k=0}^{\infty} \frac{1}{k!}$$

Write iterative and tail-recursive Scheme procedures that approximate e to any accuracy by computing partial sums of this series.

Problem 5.9.

Write iterative and tail-recursive Scheme procedures called sum that expect an unsigned integer input n and return the following partial sum:

$$\text{sum(n)} = \sum_{i=1}^{n} \frac{(-1)^i}{2i}$$

Problem 5.10.

Assume Scheme did not supply * but did supply +. Of course, * is an overloaded procedure, but most variants can be defined in terms of nat*, which multiplies two natural numbers. Find iterative and tail-recursive implementations of nat* that don't use *.

Problem 5.11.

Assume Scheme did not supply +, but did supply add1 and sub1:

```
(add1 z) = z + 1
(sub1 z) = z - 1
```

(If your version of Scheme doesn't provide add1 and sub1 you'll have to define them using +.) Of course + is an overloaded procedure, but most variants can be defined in terms of nat+, which adds two natural numbers. Find iterative and tail-recursive implementations of nat+ that don't use +.

Problem 5.12.

Reimplement the hyper iterators and Ackermann's function using do-loops.

Problem 5.13.

Write a procedure that computes the amount in your savings account after n years assuming:

(i) An initial deposit of $1000 at 8% interest compounded quarterly.

(ii) An initial deposit of $200 at 6% interest compounded monthly.

Problem 5.14.

Write a procedure that computes the balance after n months of a $100,000 loan assuming the interest rate is 8% compounded monthly and the monthly payment is $1200. How long will it take to pay off this loan?

Problem 5.15.

When a plant or animal dies the amount of radioactive carbon-14 in its tissue begins decaying into nonradioactive carbon. The half-life of carbon-14 is 5700 years (i.e., half decays after 5700 years).

(i) Write a recursive procedure that determines the amount of radioactive carbon in a tissue sample after *n* years assuming the initial amount was 100 grams.

(ii) Using the procedure given earlier, determine the age of a specimen assuming 83% of the original carbon-14 is present.

(iii) Replace the recursive procedure used in part i with an equivalent elementary procedure.

Problem 5.16.

Find elementary implementations of the following procedures:

```
a.  (define (mystery1 n)
    (if (= n 0)
        0
        (+ 3 (mystery1 (- n 1))))))
```

```
b.  (define (mystery2 n)
    (if (= n 0)
        1
        (* 3 (mystery2 (- n 1))))))
```

```
c.  (define (mystery3 n)
    (if (<= n 0)
        0
        (+ 3 (mystery3 (- n 2))))))
```

```
d.  (define (mystery4 n)
    (if (= n 0)
        10
        (+ 5 (+ 3 (mystery4 (sub1 n)))))))
```

Problem 5.17.

Write a well-designed procedure called control-loop that perpetually prompts the user for an unsigned integer, then displays the binary, octal, decimal, and hexadecimal representations of the integer. (Use number->string for this.) Your procedure should be modeled after the counter control-loop discussed earlier.

Problem 5.18.

Write a procedure that displays all Scheme characters and their numeric codes.

```
>  (display-chars)
    0       #\?
    1       #\?
...
    127     #\?
```

Problem 5.19.

Modify the control-loop used in the digital clock example so that:

a. states are updated at approximately one-second intervals.

b. the computer's bell rings when the final state is reached.

c. HOUR ::= 1 | 2 | ... | 12

Problem 5.20.

Use iteration and tail recursion combined with car, cdr, and cons to implement the following procedures. Do not use coercions.

Problem 5.20.1.

Assume *m* and *n* are natural numbers. Find iterative and tail-recursive implementations of:

```
(m-to-n m n)    = (m ... n) if m < n
                = () otherwise
```

Problem 5.20.2.

Assume *n* is a natural number. Implement:

```
(nest 0) = ()
(nest 1) = (())
(nest 2) = ((()))
etc.
```

Problem 5.20.3.

Assume Scheme did not provide list-ref or length. How could you implement these using iteration and tail recursion?

Problem 5.20.4.

Assume vals is a list and n is a natural number. Find iterative and tail-recursive implementations of the following procedure:

```
(rem-nth vals n)
   = vals with the item in position n removed
```

Problem 5.20.5.

Assume vals is a list and n is a natural number. Find iterative and tail-recursive implementations of the following procedure:

```
(put-nth vals val n)
   = vals with val inserted in position n.
```

Problem 5.21.

Use the solve procedure to write a procedure that computes fifth roots. In other words, $(\text{fifth-root } n)^5 = n$.

Problem 5.22.

Use the solve procedure to write a procedure that computes nth roots. In other words, $(n\text{th-root } m \ n)^m = n$.

Problem 5.23. Fixed Points

Assume f is a procedure that expects a number as an input and returns a number as a value. A number z is a fixed point for f if $f(z) = z$. For example, 0 and 1 are fixed points for square. Use the solve procedure to implement:

```
(fix f)
   = a fixed point for f if one exists,
   = unspecified otherwise.
```

Problem 5.24.

Assume $h = O(g)$ and $g = O(f)$. Show $h = O(f)$.

Problem 5.25.

Find two different functions f and g such that $O(f) = O(g)$.

Problem 5.26.

Prove: $O(n) \subset O(n^2) \subset O(2^n)$, but $O(2^n) \not\subset O(n^2) \not\subset O(n)$.

Problem 5.27.

This problem shows why the hyper-exponentials form a hierarchy:
Let hyper^n-exp denote the nth procedure in the hyper-exponential hierarchy. Show that if $n < m$, then

```
hyper^n-exp = O(hyper^m-exp)
```

but

```
hyper^m-exp ≠ O(hyper^n-exp)
```

Show that for all n:

```
hyper^n-exp = O(ack)
```

but

```
ack ≠ O(hyper^n-exp)
```

Problem 5.28.

Modify the show-log-attractor procedure to investigate the attractors generated by the update procedure $x^2 + c$ for $-2 < c < 0.25$.

Problem 5.29.

Give an example of an oscillating computation with finite width. Can you find an example of a divergent computation with finite width?

Problem 5.30.

Some versions of Scheme provide a more general iteration structure called a **named let**. The syntax of a named let is similar to a let structure:

```
NAMED-LET ::= (let NAME (DEC ...) EXP ...)
```

Essentially, this structure creates a procedure called NAME with formal parameters identical to the local variables and body identical to EXP..., then it calls NAME with the values of the local variables. This means NAME can be recursively called inside EXP.... . For example, the following expression:

```
(let count-down ((x 10))
   (writeln x)
   (if (<= x 0)
       'done
       (count-down (- x 1))))
```

is equivalent to:

```
(letrec
   ((count-down
       (lambda (x)
           (writeln x)
           (if (<= x 0) 'done (count-down (- x 1)))))))
   (count-down 10))
```

Why is letrec necessary in this definition? Why is a named let more general than a do-loop? Reimplement the control-loop procedure defined earlier using a named let instead of a do-loop.

Problem 5.31.

It seems like it wouldn't be hard to define convergent? What's wrong with this:

```
(define (convergent? proc vals)
   (define val (apply prov vals))
   (if (or val (not val)) #t #f))
```

6
Recursive Domains

Like procedures, domains can have recursive definitions. For example, the VALUE and EXPRESSION domains defined in Chapter One were recursive. The VALUE domain consisted of simple and composite values:

```
VALUE ::= SIMPLE | COMPOSITE
```

The COMPOSITE domain consisted of lists, vectors, strings, and pairs:

```
COMPOSITE ::= LIST | VECTOR | STRING | PAIR
```

But the definitions of the LIST, VECTOR, and PAIR domains recursively referred back to the VALUE domain:

```
LIST ::= (VALUE ...)
VECTOR ::= #(VALUE ...)
PAIR ::= (VALUE . VALUE)
```

The EXPRESSION domain consisted of literals, symbols, applications, and structures:

```
EXPRESSION ::=
    LITERAL | SYMBOL | APPLICATION | STRUCTURE
```

But the definition of the APPLICATION and STRUCTURE domains recursively referred back to the EXPRESSION domain. For example:

```
APPLICATION ::= (EXPRESSION EXPRESSION ...)
```

We can find more direct recursive definitions for some domains. For example, we normally define the LIST domain as a sequence of zero or more values bracketed by parenthesis:

```
LIST ::= (VALUE ...)
```

but because every nonempty list is really a pair, we can also use the following recursive definition of the LIST domain:

```
LIST ::= () | (VALUE . LIST)
```

6.1.   Recursive Domains as Hierarchies

In the last chapter we devoted considerable energy to finding nonrecursive implementations of recursive procedures. In the name of efficiency and understandability we sought iterative implementations, tail-recursive implementations, even elementary (i.e., nonrecursive, noniterative) implementations. In the same spirit we now ask: Are recursive definitions of domains necessary? Is there some way to redefine these domains to avoid the recursion?

One technique is to "unfold" the recursive domain into a hierarchy of nonrecursive subdomains. For example, the LIST domain has a natural hierarchical structure, which is revealed by unfolding the recursive definition given earlier:

```
LIST₀ ::= ()
LIST₁ ::= LIST₀ | (VALUE . LIST₀)
LIST₂ ::= LIST₁ | (VALUE . LIST₁)
LIST₃ ::= LIST₂ | (VALUE . LIST₂)
...
LISTₙ ::= LISTₙ₋₁ | (VALUE . LISTₙ₋₁)
etc.
```

Notice that each $LIST_n$ is a nonrecursive domain. It's pretty easy to see:

```
LISTₙ ::= all lists of length ≤ n
```

We can now give a nonrecursive definition of the LIST domain as the infinite union of all $LIST_n$ domains:

```
LIST ::= LIST₀ ∪ ... ∪ LISTₙ ∪ ...
```

Alternatively, we can think of LIST as the limit of the $LIST_n$ domains as n tends to infinity:

$$LIST = \lim_{n \to \infty} LIST_n$$

We call the $LIST_n$ domain level n of the LIST hierarchy. (Of course, our definition of LIST is still recursive because it refers to the VALUE domain, and the definition of the VALUE domain refers back to the LIST domain. To really get rid of the recursion we will have to apply the unfolding technique to the entire VALUE domain; this is left as a problem at the end of the chapter.)

We can also define the STRING and VECTOR domains as hierarchies of nonrecursive domains:

$$VECTOR ::= \lim_{n \to \infty} VECTOR_n$$

$$STRING ::= \lim_{n \to \infty} STRING_n$$

where:

```
VECTORₙ ::= all vectors of length ≤ n
STRINGₙ ::= all strings of length ≤ n
```

6.1.1. Recursion over Hierarchies

We can generalize our method for writing recursive procedures that operate on natural numbers to recursive procedures that operate on members of any hierarchy $H = \lim_{n \to \infty} H_n$.

We only need to modify the basic questions:

Base Case:
What is (proc v) for v in H_0?

Successor Case:
How can we use (proc v) for some v in H_{n-1} to compute (proc w) for w in H_n?

6.2.   List Recursion

In the case of lists, the technique for writing recursive procedures can be restated as follows:

Base Case:
What is (proc '())?

Successor Case:
How can we use (proc (cdr x)) to compute (proc x)?

This works because if x is nonempty, then the length of (cdr x) is less than the length of x. In other words, if x is in LIST$_n$ for $n > 0$, then (cdr x) is in LIST$_{n-1}$. (Of course, in some cases we may also need to apply our recursive assumption to other sublists of x.)

6.2.1.   Application: Are Lists Necessary?

Recall the definition of Necessary Scheme:

> Necessary Scheme = IEEE/ANSI Scheme - redundant features

We have already seen that all string and vector procedures can be implemented in terms of list procedures using the appropriate coercions and the corresponding primitive list procedures. We have seen that every nonempty list can be represented as a pair. In the exercises of the previous chapter we saw that many primitive list procedures could be implemented in terms of the primitive pair procedures (car, cdr, and cons) using number recursion. The remaining list procedures can be implemented using list recursion.

Example: length

As a simple example, let's implement the length procedure. We can answer the Base Case questions by observing:

```
(length '())   = 0
```

As for the Successor Case, clearly the length of a nonempty list is 1 more than the length of its tail:

```
(length vals)  = (+ 1 (length (cdr vals)))
```

This suggests the following implementation of length:

```
(define (length vals)
   (if (null? vals)
       0
       (+ 1 (length (cdr vals))))))
```

If we want to include input validation, we should rename length unsafe-length and nest it inside an input-validating wrapper procedure:

```
(define (length vals)
   (define (unsafe-length vals) ...)
   (if (list? vals)
       (unsafe-length vals)
       (error "bad input" length vals)))
```

We can get an idea of why length (i.e., unsafe-length) works by tracing a call:

```
(length '(6 9 3))
(+ 1 (length '(9 3)))
(+ 1 (+ 1 (length '(3))))
(+ 1 (+ 1 (+ 1 (length '()))))
(+ 1 (+ 1 (+ 1 0)))
(+ 1 (+ 1 1))
(+ 1 2)
3
```

It's pretty simple to show that the amount of time and memory consumed by the length procedure is proportional to the size (i.e., length) of its input. Suppose vals is a list of length n. Then:

```
|(length vals)| = O(n)
[(length vals)] = O(n)
```

We could seek an iterative implementation. Each iteration increments a counter and removes an item from the original input list. When all items have been removed, the value of the counter should be the length of the original list:

```
(define (length vals)
   (if (not (list? vals))
       (error "bad input" length vals)
       (do ((count 0 (+ 1 count))
            (tail vals (cdr tail)))
           ((null? tail) count))))
```

As expected, this implementation will be more frugal with memory:

```
|(length vals)| = O(n)
[(length vals)] = O(1)
```

We leave it as an exercise to the reader to find a tail-recursive solution. To obtain an elementary (i.e., nonrecursive, noniterative) solution we would have to include the length in the representation of every list and modify cons and cdr to increment and decrement this component. For example, the list (a e i o u) could be represented internally as the pair: ((a e i o u) . 5), and the empty list could be represented internally as the pair: (() . 0).

Recognizing Lists

PC Scheme doesn't provide a list? predicate. How can we define one? From the recursive definition of LIST we know a list is either the empty list or a pair whose cdr is again a list:

```
LIST ::= () | (VALUE . LIST)
```

This suggests the following definition:

```
(define (list? val)
   (cond ((null? val) #t)
         ((pair? val) (list? (cdr val)))
         (else #f)))
```

Notice that this definition is tail-recursive. If val is a length n list, then

```
|(list? val)| = O(n)
[(list? val)] = O(1).
```

6.2.2. Application: Association Lists

Recall that an association list (alist) is a list of pairs called associations:

```
ALIST ::= () | (ASSOCIATION . ALIST)
```

An **association** is any pair of values. We tend to think of the car of an association as an attribute and the cdr as the attribute value:

```
ASSOCIATION ::= (ATTRIBUTE . VALUE)
```

For example:

```
((eyes . blue) (age . 50) (name . "Picard"))
```

Association lists are useful for representing records, tables, and graphs. Recall that Scheme provides three primitive procedures for searching alists: assoc, assq, and assv:

```
(ass* PROP ALIST)
    = left-most ASSOCIATION in ALIST such that PROP is
    equivalent to (car ASSOCIATION) in the sense of equal?,
    eqv?, or eq? depending on *.
    = #f, otherwise
```

These procedures are somewhat unsatisfactory and incomplete. A more complete set of procedures for operating on association lists would include methods for getting (i.e., searching), removing, and putting associations, as well as constructing association lists:

```
(get PROP ALIST)
    = (cdr a) where a is the unique association in ALIST such
    that (equal? PROP (car a))
    = unspecified if there are multiple ASSOCIATIONs a in
    ALIST such that (equal? PROP (car a))
    = fail, otherwise

(rem PROP ALIST)
    = alist obtained by removing all associations a such that
    (equal? PROP (car a))

(put PROP VAL ALIST)
    = alist obtained by placing (PROP . VAL) in (rem PROP
    ALIST)

(make-alist PROPS VALS)
    = an alist. The nth association is the nth member of
    PROPS paired with the nth member of VALS.
```

where fail is a special token used to distinguish a failed search from a found value of #f:

```
(define fail 'fail)
```

Of course, we could define equivalent procedures based on eq? and eqv?: getq, getv, putq, putv, remq, and remv.

Searching for Associations

The get procedure is similar to the primitive assoc procedure, except get returns attribute values rather than associations. Thus, a quick implementation of get would be:

```
(define (get prop alist)
   (let ((association (assoc prop alist)))
       (and association (cdr association))))   ;?!
```

Of course, we are trying to show that assoc is unnecessary, so we shouldn't use it in our implementation. Instead, we search for a recursive solution:

```
(define get prop alist)

   (define (unsafe-get prop alist) ???)

   (if (alist? alist)
       (unsafe-get prop alist)
       (error "bad input" get alist)))
```

Observe that unsafe-get always returns fail if alist is empty:

```
(unsafe-get prop '())   = fail
```

If the attribute we are given is the car of the first association:

```
(equal? prop (car (car alist)))
```

then the value we seek is the cdr of the first association:

```
(cdr (car alist))
```

Otherwise, we can recursively apply unsafe-get to (cdr alist).

Our implementation uses (caar x) and (cdar x) as abbreviations of (car (car x)) and ·(cdr (car x)):

```
(define (unsafe-get prop alist)
   (cond ((null? alist) fail)
         ((equal? prop (caar alist)) (cdar alist))
         (else (unsafe-get prop (cdr alist)))))
```

A short sample computation might help explain how get works:

```
(get 3 '((1 . a) (2 . b) (3 . c)))
(unsafe-get 3 '((1 . a) (2 . b) (3 . c)))
(unsafe-get 3 '((2 . b) (3 . c)))
(unsafe-get 3 '((3 . c)))
c
```

Notice that unsafe-get is tail-recursive. The width of the computation does not depend on the size of the input, hence the amount of memory consumed is constant. Of course, if alist contains n associations, then the length of the computation will be proportional to n:

```
|(unsafe-get prop alist)|  = O(n)
[(unsafe-get prop alist)]  = O(1)
```

Removing Associations

A quick method for removing an association of the form (PROP . VAL) is to install a new association of the form (PROP . fail) at the beginning of the alist:

```
(define (rem prop alist)
  (if (alist? alist)
      (cons (cons prop fail) alist)
      (error "bad input" rem alist)))
```

This actually works because get searches the alist from left to right. If we search for
PROP, the attribute fail will be returned before VAL. This is exactly the behavior we expect when (PROP . VAL) has been removed from the alist.

This implementation has two defects. First, it depends on the fact that get searches
from left to right, but this is not part of the specification of get. Second, imagine a poor
customer who deletes associations from a large database to free space on his hard disk.
The more he deletes, the fuller the disk becomes! Let's look for another implementation.

```
(define (rem prop alist)

  (define (unsafe-rem prop alist) ???)

  (if (alist? alist)
      (unsafe-rem prop alist)
      (error "bad input" rem alist)))
```

At first, removing an association seems similar to searching for an association. We recursively move through alist searching for an association with a matching attribute, then we
snip the association away using cdr. Here's an adaptation of the unsafe-get procedure:

```
(define (unsafe-rem prop alist)
  (cond ((null? alist) alist)
        ((equal? prop (caar alist)) (cdr alist))
        (else (unsafe-rem prop (cdr alist)))))
```

Unfortunately, this doesn't work. We can see why by tracing a computation:

```
(rem 2 '((1 . a) (2 . b) (3 . c)))
(unsafe-rem 2 '((1 . a) (2 . b) (3 . c)))
(unsafe-rem 2 '((2 . b) (3 . c)))
((3 . c))
```

The problem is in the recursive step. We know the first association did not contain a
matching attribute, but we discarded it anyway! Instead, we must cons this association
back onto the result of recursively applying rem to (cdr alist):

```
(define (unsafe-rem prop alist)
  (cond ((null? alist) alist)
        ((equal? prop (caar alist)) (cdr alist))
        (else (cons (car alist)
                    (unsafe-rem prop (cdr alist))))))
```

This procedure doesn't quite work either. To see why, imagine removing an association
from an alist with two identical associations:

```
(rem 2 '((1 . a) (2 . b) (2 . b)))
(unsafe-rem 2 '((1 . a) (2 . b) (2 . b)))
(cons '(1 . a) (unsafe-rem 2 '((2 . b) (2 . b))))
(cons '(1 . a) '((2 . b)))
((1 . a) (2 . b))
```

Just because the attribute matches (caar alist) in the third cond clause doesn't mean we can stop the removal process. We must continue to remove associations from (cdr alist). This can be accomplished by an additional recursive call:

```
(define (unsafe-rem prop alist)
   (cond ((null? alist) alist)
         ((equal? prop (caar alist))
            (unsafe-rem prop (cdr alist)))
         (else
            (cons (car alist)
                  (unsafe-rem prop (cdr alist))))))
```

Unlike unsafe-get, unsafe-rem is not tail-recursive. The recursive call to unsafe-rem in the else clause is nested inside a call to cons. This means we will have to build a deep nest of pending calls to cons:

```
(rem 4 '((1 . a) (2 . b) (3 . c)))
(unsafe-rem 4 '((1 . a) (2 . b) (3 . c)))
(cons '(1 . a) (unsafe-rem 4 '((2 . b) (3 . c))))
(cons '(1 . a)
   (cons '(2 . b) (unsafe-rem 4 '((3 . c)))))
(cons '(1 . a) (cons '(2 . b) (cons '(3 . c) '())))
(cons '(1 . a) (cons '(2 . b) '((3 . c))))
(cons '(1 . a) ' ((2 . b) (3 . c)))
((1 . a) (2 . b) (3 . c))
```

Clearly, if alist contains n associations, then

```
|(unsafe-rem prop alist)| = O(n)
[(unsafe-rem prop alist)] = O(n)
```

Our iterative implementation traverses alist. Each iteration either adds (cons) a non-matching association from alist to the result or does nothing to the result if the next association should be removed. The iteration halts when traversal of the alist is complete:

```
(define (rem prop alist)
   (if (not (alist? alist))
       (error "bad input" rem alist)
       (do ((tail alist (cdr tail))
            (result (if (equal? prop (caar tail))
                        result
                        (cons (car tail) result))))
           ((null? tail) (reverse result)))))
```

A tail-recursive implementation of rem is left as an exercise.

Installing Associations

Installing a new association is simple: Make the association, then cons it onto the result of removing conflicting associations from the alist:

```
(define (put prop val alist)
   (define assoc (cons prop val))
   (if (alist? alist)
       (cons assoc (rem prop alist))
       (error "bad input" put alist)))
```

Is it necessary to remove conflicting associations? Yes! Remember, the description of get doesn't specify in which direction alists are searched. Our put and rem procedures must work with implementations of get that search from right to left or left to right.

Constructing Association Lists

Given a list of attribute names and a corresponding list of attribute values, we would like to produce an alist using a single constructor instead of repeatedly applying put starting with the empty list:

```
(define (make-alist props vals) ???)
```

For example:

```
> (make-alist '(a b c) '(1 2 3))
((a . 1) (b . 2) (c . 3))
> (make-alist '() '())
()
```

The make-alist procedure first validates its inputs, then it uses the map procedure with the binary cons to zip the attribute and value lists together:

```
(define (make-alist props vals)
   (if (and (list? props)
            (list? vals)
            (= (length props) (length vals)))
       (map cons props vals)
       (error "bad input(s)" make-alist props vals)))
```

Recognizing Association Lists

To finish things off, we need a predicate for recognizing alists. Our predicate is similar to the tail-recursive list? predicate defined earlier, except we add a check to make sure each element of the input list is a pair:

```
(define (alist? val)
   (cond ((null? val) #t)
         ((pair? val)
```

```
            (and (pair? (car val))
                 (alist? (cdr val)))))
      (else #f)))
```

6.3.   The Signal Processing Paradigm[1]

Computer, telephone, and television networks are all examples of **communication networks**. A communication network is a network of transmitters and receivers connected by communication channels (e.g., wires); see Figure 6.1.

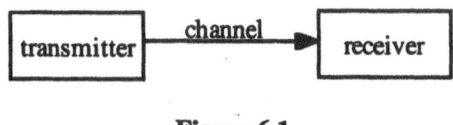

Figure 6.1

A transmitter encodes input data into a **signal**—a sequence of short **messages**, frames, packets, cells, etc.—that can be propagated through the channel, as in Figure 6.2.

Figure 6.2

The receiver reverses the process, decoding message sequences (signals) into the original data.

Unfortunately, signals can get distorted as they travel through the channel, causing the output data produced by the receiver to differ from the input data sent by the transmitter. The two major causes of **distortion** are **noise** (e.g. static) and **attenuation** (decay).

The effects of attenuation can be mitigated by inserting amplifiers into the channel. An **amplifier** restores or strengthens each message that passes through it. The effects of noise can be diminished by inserting filters into the channel. Filters remove messages that have been corrupted by static; these will have to be retransmitted. Figure 6.3 shows a simplified model of a communication channel with a filter and an amplifier.

---

[1] Also called the **Pipe and Filter architecture**.

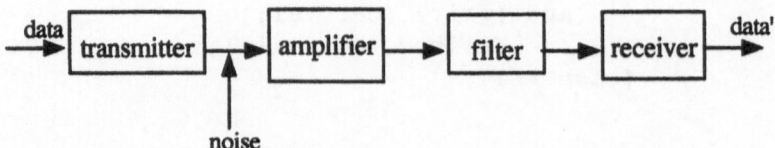

Figure 6.3

This suggests a **paradigm**, or computational model, for list processing: View lists as lists of messages and list procedures as communication channels composed of procedures that mimic transmitters, amplifiers, filters, and receivers.

6.3.1. Filters

The output of a filter is the input message list with **noise** removed. We define noise to be corrupted messages among the input messages. We rely on the user to provide as a parameter a predicate for recognizing noisy messages:

```
(define (noise? msg) ...)
```

The filter procedure first validates inputs, then it calls a recursive unsafe-filter internal procedure:

```
(define (filter noise? msgs)

   (define (unsafe-filter noise? msgs) ???)

   (if (and (procedure? noise?) (list? msgs))
       (unsafe-filter noise? msgs)
       (error "bad input(s)" filter noise? msgs)))
```

Unfortunately, Scheme does not provide a unary-predicate? procedure.
  Here are some sample evaluations:

```
> (filter odd? '(1 2 3 4 5 6 7 8 9))
(2 4 6 8)
> (filter prime? '(1 2 3 4 5 6 7 8 9))
(1 4 6 8 9)
```

Clearly, the result of filtering noise from the empty list is the empty list:

```
(unsafe-filter noise? '()) = ()
```

Assume (unsafe-filter noise? (cdr msgs)) returns x, a list of filtered messages, and y is (car msgs). If (noise? y), then x is the value returned by (unsafe-filter noise? msgs); otherwise (cons y x) is returned:

```
(define (unsafe-filter noise? msgs)
   (cond
```

```
  ((null? msgs) '())
  ((noise? (car msgs))
     (unsafe-filter noise? (cdr msgs)))
  (else
     (cons (car msgs)
           (unsafe-filter noise? (cdr msgs))))))
```

As an example, suppose we have a predicate that recognizes prime numbers:

```
; = #t if n is prime
(define (prime? n) ...)
```

(Recall that a natural number n is **prime** if it is bigger than 1 and its only divisors are 1 and n.) A **composite** number is a number that is not prime:

```
(define (composite? n)
   (and (natural? n) (not (prime? n))))
```

We can use this predicate to filter all composite numbers from a list of integers:

```
(define (primes ints) (filter composite? ints))
```

Let's trace a sample computation:

```
(primes '(13 15 17 19 21 21))
(filter composite? '(13 15 17 19 21 21))
(unsafe-filter composite? '(13 15 17 19 21 21))
(cons 13 (unsafe-filter composite? '(15 17 19 21)))
(cons 13 (unsafe-filter composite? '(17 19 21)))
(cons 13
   (cons 17 (unsafe-filter composite? '(19 21))))
(cons 13
   (cons 17
      (cons 19 (unsafe-filter composite? '(21)))))
(cons 13
   (cons 17 (cons 19 (unsafe-filter composite? '()))))
(cons 13 (cons 17 (cons 19 '())))
(cons 13 (cons 17 '(19)))
(cons 13 '(17 19))
(13 17 19)
```

This computation suggests that the length and width of computations generated by calls to filter are proportional to the length of the input list. In other words, if msgs has length n, then

```
|(filter pred? msgs)| = O(n)
[(filter pred? msgs)] = O(n)
```

We can find a more memory efficient iterative implementation by traversing the message list. Each message encountered that is determined not to be noise is added (cons) to a result list. When we reach the end of the message list, the result list is reversed and returned:

```
(define (filter noise? msgs)
   (if (or (not (procedure? noise?))
           (not (list? msgs)))
       (error "bad input(s)" filter noise? msgs)
       (do
          ((tail msgs (cdr tail))
           (result
             '()
             (if (noise? (car tail))
                 result
                 (cons (car tail) result))))
          ((null? tail) (reverse result)))))
```

A tail-recursive implementation is left as an exercise.

6.3.2. Amplifiers (Map)

Recall the primitive map procedure introduced in Chapter 2:

```
(map proc vals ...)
   = the list of values obtained by applying proc to each
   member of vals. If proc requires n inputs, then n vals
   lists are specified.
```

For example:

```
> (map square '(2 4 6))
(4 16 36)
> (map cons '(a b c) '(0 0 0))
((a . 0) (b . 0) (c . 0))
```

In the signal processing paradigm, the map procedure is analogous to an amplifier. Each message in the output list is a "strengthened," or "amplified," version of the corresponding message in the input list.

Assume Scheme did not provide a map procedure. How can we implement our own? Let's begin with a simplified version that expects a unary procedure of the form:

```
(define (amp msg) ...)
```

and a single list of messages as input:

```
(define (unary-map amp msgs)

   (define (unsafe-map amp msgs) ???)
```

```
(if (and (procedure? amp) (list? msgs))
    (unsafe-map amp msgs)
    (error "bad input(s)" unary-map amp msgs)))
```

Unfortunately, Scheme does not provide a unary-procedure? predicate.

If msgs is empty, unsafe-map returns the empty list:

```
(unsafe-map amp '()) = ()
```

Assume (unsafe-map amp (cdr msgs)) returns a valid list of amplified messages. The only job is to apply amp to (car msgs) and cons the result to this list:

```
(cons (amp (car msgs)) (unsafe-map amp (cdr msgs)))
```

The complete definition is:

```
(define (unsafe-map amp msgs)
  (if (null? msgs)
      '()
      (cons (amp (car msgs))
            (unsafe-map amp (cdr msgs)))))
```

Note: We really don't need to supply amp as a parameter to unsafe-map because this is always the same as the amp parameter of the encapsulating unary-map procedure, which is therefore available to unsafe-map as a nonlocal.

The iterative solution traverses msgs, applying amp to each member and consing the value onto a list of results. When the end of msgs is reached, the result is reversed and returned:

```
(define (unary-map amp msgs)
  (if (or (not (procedure? amp)) (not (list? msgs)))
      (error "bad input(s)" unary-map amp msgs)
      (do ((tail msgs (cdr tail))
           (result
             '()
             (cons (amp (car tail)) result)))
          ((null? tail) (reverse result)))))
```

A tail-recursive implementation is left as an exercise.

n-ary Map

The real version of map is an *n*-ary procedure that expects an *m*-ary amplifier procedure as input together with *m* message lists, one corresponding to each of the expected inputs of *m*-amp. This suggests the following implementation:

```
(define (map m-amp . m-msgs)

  (define (unsafe-map m-msgs) ???)
```

```
(if (and (procedure? amp) (all? list? m-msgs))
    (unsafe-map m-amp m-msgs)
    (error "bad input(s)" map m-amp m-msgs)))
```

Here we are using the all? predicate developed in Chapter 2 to verify that all members of the *m*-msgs parameter are lists. Note: To be perfectly safe, we should also verify that these lists all have the same length. Also, we are not passing *m*-amp as a parameter to unsafe-map because it will be available as a nonlocal.

The definition of unsafe-map doesn't follow our usual pattern of recursion. Instead of calling (unsafe-map (cdr *m*-msgs)) in the recursive application, we use

```
(unsafe-map (unary-map cdr m-msgs))
```

In other words, what gets smaller is not the length of *m*-msgs, but the length of the lists contained in *m*-msgs. Similarly, instead of terminating the recursion by asking (null? *m*-msgs), we ask:

```
(some? null? m-msgs)
```

where some? is also defined in Chapter 2. In other words, if any of the lists in *m*-msgs becomes empty, then the recursion will terminate. (If all the lists have the same length, then when one becomes empty, they all become empty.)

(It should be pointed out that the some? and all? predicates defined in Chapter 2 used map. To avoid a nonterminating recursion, all? and some? should be reimplemented using unary-map.)

The last piece of the puzzle is to apply m-amp to the first element of each list in *m*-msgs, and then cons this result onto the list returned by the recursive call. We can form a list of cars by again using unary-map:

```
(unary-map car m-msgs)
```

We can use the apply procedure to apply *m*-amp to this list:

```
(define (unsafe-map m-msgs)
  (if (some? null? m-msgs)
      '()
      (let ((first
              (apply m-amp (unary-map car m-msgs))))
        (cons first
              (unsafe-map (unary-map cdr m-msgs))))))
```

An iterative implementation is left as an exercise.

6.3.3. Receivers (Accumulators)

Like the other signal-processing devices we have seen, the input of an **accumulator** is a list of messages. However, unlike filters and amplifiers, the output of an accumulator is not a list of messages, but rather an interpretation of the signal gotten by combining every message in the signal into a single value. In a sense, an accumulator is analogous to a receiver, which decodes message lists into data.

How are the input messages to be combined? This will have to specified as a binary procedure parameter of the form:

```
(define (combiner first rest) ...)
```

What will be the result of combining the messages in an empty list? This, too, will have to be specified as a parameter. We call this initial value parameter init. The form of accum is:

```
(define (accum combiner init vals)

    (define (unsafe-accum combiner init vals) ???)

    (if (and (procedure? combiner) (list? vals))
        (unsafe-accum combiner init vals)
        (error "bad input(s)" accum combiner vals)))
```

Here are some sample calls:

```
> (accum + 0 '(1 2 3 4 5))
15
> (accum * 1 '(2 4 6 8))
396
> (accum cons '() '(a e i o u))
(a e i o u)
```

Let's turn to an implementation of unsafe-accum. By definition:

```
(unsafe-accum combiner init '()) = init
```

For the successor case, let's try to generalize from an example. Assume:

```
(define x '(1 2 3 4 5))
```

We know:

```
(unsafe-accum + 0 x) = 15
```

We can assume accum already works on (cdr x):

```
(unsafe-accum + 0 (cdr x)) = 14
```

To get 15 from 14 we only need to add 1, i.e., (car x), to the recursive call. In general:

```
(combiner
    (car msgs)
    (unsafe-accum combiner init (cdr msgs)))
```

The final form of unsafe-accum is:

```
(define (unsafe-accum combiner init msgs)
   (if (null? msgs)
       init
       (combiner
         (car (msgs))
         (unsafe-accum combiner init (cdr msgs)))))
```

An iterative accumulator initializes a loop variable called result to init. As the message list is traversed, each message is combined to result using the combiner procedure:

```
(define (accum combiner init msgs)
   (if (or (not (procedure? combiner))
           (not (list? msgs)))
       (error "bad inputs to accum: " combiner msgs)
       (do ((tail msgs (cdr tail))
            (result
              init
              (combiner (car tail) result)))
           ((null? tail) result))))
```

As a simple example of accum, we can use it to quickly compute the average of a list of test scores:

```
(define (avg . scores)
   (/ (accum + 0 scores) (length scores)))
```

6.3.4. Transmitters (Generators)

Generators, the last signal-processing component we need, are analogous to transmitters. A generator is the opposite of an accumulator. It takes a value as input and turns it into a list of messages. For now we will be content to define a simple generator that produces an arithmetic sequence from a specified length. This is accomplished by initializing a counter, i, to n. Each time through the loop, (* scale i) is added (using cons) to the message list, then decremented by step:

```
(define (m-to-n m n)

   (define step 1)    ; decrement amount
   (define scale 1)   ; scaling factor

   (if (not (and (real? m) (real? n)))
       (error "bad input(s)" m-to-n m n)
       (do ((i n (- i step))
            (msgs '() (cons (* scale i) msgs)))
           ((< i m) msgs))))
```

Here are some sample evaluations:

```
> (m-to-n -3 5)
(-3 -2 -1 0 1 2 3 4 5)
> (m-to-n 5 -3)
()
```

6.3.5. Applications

Many types of list recursions are embodied by the signal-processing procedures. In effect, we can use these procedures to "hide" recursive and iterative definitions.

To sum the odd squares between 1 and n^2 we can set up a simple communication channel as in Figure 6.4.

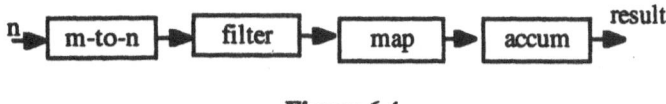

Figure 6.4

m-to-*n* will generate the list (1 2 ... *n*), and filter will remove the even numbers, producing the list (1 3 ...). The map procedure amplifies each member with square. Finally, accum is used to sum the list:

```
(define (sum-odd-squares n)
   (accum + 0
      (map square
         (filter even?
            (m-to-n 1 n)))))
```

The beauty of this definition is that it doesn't appear to be recursive. If accum, m-to-n, filter, and map were primitive procedures, programmers could implement many powerful procedures before they ever had to write a recursive definition. Indeed, the availability of map as a primitive procedure allowed us to write powerful procedures like all? and some? in applicative Scheme (Chapter 2), before recursion was available to us. For example, the recursive and iterative length and rem procedures defined earlier can be replaced with nonrecursive, noniterative, stream-processing implementations:

```
(define (length vals)
   (define (combiner m n) (+ n 1)) ; ignores m!
   (accum combiner 0 vals))

(define (rem prop alist)
   (define (noise? association)
      (equal? prop (car association)))
   (filter noise? alist))
```

Of course, the nonrecursiveness of these procedures is merely an illusion. If we count filter and accum as single steps in a computation, then |(length vals)| = O(1) and |(rem prop alist)| = O(1), but if we count the cons and cdr operations inside filter and accum, then |(length vals)| = O(n) and |(rem prop alist)| = O(n), where length of vals = length of alist = n.

6.4.   Trees and Tree Recursion

Sometimes it is useful to picture a list as a tree-like structure. For example, the list (a e i o u) can be represented as the tree shown in Figure 6.5.

Figure 6.5

The root node of the tree is labeled by the parenthesis surrounding the list, and the nodes immediately below the root node are labeled by the members of the list.

We can represent the empty list and nonlist values as single-node trees:

```
()      42      #(a e i o u)    "hello world"    #t
```

The tree representation is especially useful for picturing nested lists. For example, the list:

```
(((1 2 3) 4) (5 6) (((7))))
```

can be represented by the tree in Figure 6.6.

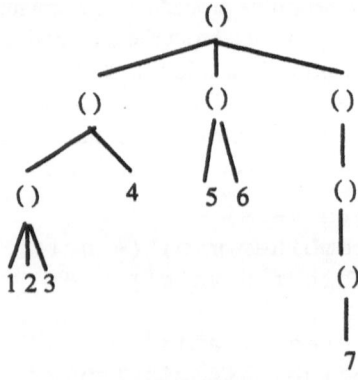

Figure 6.6

6.4.1. Terminology

Trees are useful structures for organizing hierarchical data. Directories, procedure-dependency graphs, parse trees, expressions, computations, and organizational charts are all examples of trees. The members of a tree are called **nodes**. The nodes immediately below a node N are called the **children** of N. A node with children is called a **parent** node. A node with no children is either an empty tree or a **leaf** node. The top-most node is called the **root** node. In all our examples, parent nodes will always be empty lists and leaf nodes will always be values other than nonempty lists.

6.4.2. The TREE Domain

We can formalize our notion of tree as a domain:

```
TREE ::= () | LEAF | PARENT
```

where:

```
PARENT ::= (TREE ... )
```

A leaf can be just about anything other than a pair:

```
LEAF ::= SIMPLE | STRING | VECTOR
```

We can make trees into an ADT (abstract data type) by introducing the obvious selectors, predicates, and constructors. We don't need a constructor for leafs or the empty tree. The make-parent constructor is simply a pseudonym for the Scheme list constructor:

```
(define make-parent list)
```

In some situations we need to construct a tree by grafting a new subtree under the root of an existing tree. Because the grafted subtree becomes a new child of the root, we call this **adoption**. Adoption is just a pseudonym for cons:

```
(define adopt cons)
```

In the interests of data abstraction, let's use a standard symbol to denote the empty tree:

```
(define the-empty-tree '())
```

We need predicates to distinguish between the three types of trees. A list can be anything other than a pair (i.e., a nonempty list):

```
(define (leaf? val) (not (pair? val)))
```

The empty-tree? predicate is a pseudonym for null? and the parent? predicate is a pseudonym for list?:

```
(define empty-tree? null?)
(define parent? list?)
```

For now, our selectors will operate on parents by selecting the left child (car) and all but the left child (cdr), respectively:

```
(define left car)
(define but-left cdr)
```

6.4.3. Tree Recursion

We can organize the TREE domain into a ramified hierarchy (i.e., a hierarchy of hierarchies). First, observe that parent trees are lists, so it makes sense to talk about the **length** of a tree. For example, the length of the tree (() (a e i o u)) is 2 because the list contains two lists. Obviously the length of the empty tree is 0. We can extend the notion of length to leafs by agreeing that all leafs have length 1.

Second, we define the **depth** of a parent tree to be the length of its longest branch. A **branch** is any path of nodes from the root to a leaf, and the length of a branch is the number of nodes along the path. For example, the depth of (a e i o u) is 2. The depth of the tree shown in Figure 6.6 is 5, the length of the branch from the root to 7. Let's agree that the empty tree and leafs have depth 1.

We define the hierarchy of trees by:

```
TREE ::= TREE₀ ∪ TREE₁ ∪ ... ∪ TREEₙ ∪ ...
```

where

```
TREEₙ ::= all depth ≤ n trees
```

$TREE_n$ is itself a hierarchy:

```
TREEₙ ::= TREEₙ⁰ ∪ TREEₙ¹ ∪ ... ∪ TREEₙᵐ ∪ ...
```

where

```
TREEₙᵐ ::= all depth ≤ n, length ≤ m trees
```

According to our definitions:

```
TREE₀ ::= empty
TREE₁⁰ ::= ()
TREE₁ⁿ ::= LEAF for all n > 0
TREE₁ ::= () | LEAF
TREE₂ ::= all nonempty, nonnested lists
```

The TREE hierarchy gives us a method for defining recursive procedures that operate on trees:

Base Case:
How can we compute (proc tree) for leafs and the empty tree?

Successor Case:
How can we compute (proc tree) assuming (proc (left tree)) and (proc (but-left tree)) are available?

This works because if tree is in $TREE_n^m$, then (left tree) is in $TREE_{n-1}$ and (but-left tree) is in $TREE^{m-1}$.

Example: Tree Depth

For our first example of a tree recursion, let's write a procedure for calculating the depth of a tree:

```
(define (depth tree) ??? )
```

We can take the Base Case values directly from the definition of depth:

```
(depth the-empty-tree)  = 1
(depth leaf)   = 1
```

Next we ask: How can we compute (depth tree) assuming values of depth are available for (left tree) and (but-left tree)?

If the longest branch of tree is in the but-left part of the tree, then (depth tree) = (depth (but-left tree)). If the longest branch goes through (left tree), then (depth tree) = 1 + (depth (left tree)) (we add 1 to count the root, which is not part of the left child). Therefore, (depth tree) is the maximum of:

```
(+ 1 (depth (left tree)))
(depth (but-left tree))
```

Our final procedure is:

```
(define (depth tree)
   (cond ((empty-tree? tree) 1)
         ((leaf? tree) 1)
         ((parent? tree)
            (max (+ 1 (depth (left tree)))
                 (depth (but-left tree))))
         (else (error "bad input" depth tree))))
```

Note: Our current definitions of empty-tree?, leaf?, and parent? practically make depth polymorphic. What Scheme value is not a tree? Consequently, control will never be passed to the else clause. We leave it in place in case we decide in the future to limit the concept of tree.

To understand how a recursive procedure works, we trace a few sample computations. In the past, traces (and computations) have always been linear sequences of Scheme expressions. The situation is different for tree recursions. In the preceeding example, there are two recursive calls to depth in the same clause. This means the computation will be a binary tree instead of a sequence. Let's draw the computation generated by the call (depth '((1) 2 (3))). We will only show applications of the depth procedure. The value returned by each call is shown next to the application. This is the max of the value of the right call value and 1 more than the value of the left call (see Figure 6.7).

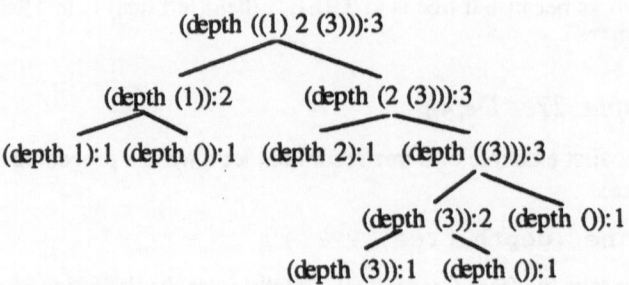

Figure 6.7

Notice that the value ultimately returned is 3, exactly what we would expect.

Example: Tree Flattening

Flattening a tree means collecting all its leafs into a list. Here's a sample call:

```
> (flatten '((a b) (a c (a)) a b c)))
(a b a c a a b c)
```

We want to complete the definition:

```
(define (flatten tree) ??? )
```

The Base Cases are easy:

```
(flatten ())   = ()
(flatten leaf) = (leaf)
```

We ask: How can we compute (flatten tree) assuming (flatten (left tree)) and (flatten (but-left tree)) are available? The answer is to append the recursive calls:

```
(append (flatten (left tree))
        (flatten (but-left tree)))
```

Our final procedure is:

```
(define (flatten tree)
   (cond ((empty-tree? tree) '())
         ((leaf? tree) (list tree))
         ((parent? tree)
            (append (flatten (left tree))
                    (flatten (but-left tree))))
         (else (error "bad input" flatten tree)))
```

Here's the computation generated by the call (flatten '((a) b (c))). Only calls to flatten are shown. As before, the return values are indicated next to the calls in Figure 6.8.

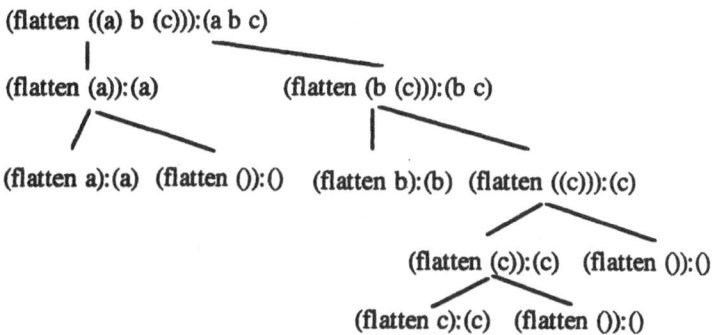

Figure 6.8

The value ultimately returned is as we expect, the list (*a b c*).

Example: Tree Substitution

Sometimes we want to substitute all occurrences of a subtree with another tree. For example:

```
> (tree-sub 'a 'b '((a b) (a c (a)) a b c))
((b b) (b c (b)) b b c)
```

We want to complete the definition:

```
(define (tree-sub old-item new-item tree) ???)
```

In this case, there are three parts to the Base Case. If tree is empty or a leaf, then there is no substitution to be performed, and tree is the result returned. However, if tree *is* old-item, then the entire tree is replaced by new-tree, which is returned as a value:

```
(tree-sub a b leaf)  = leaf
(tree-sub a b ())  = ()
(tree-sub a b a)   = b
```

How can we compute (tree-sub *a b c*) assuming (tree-sub *a b* (left *c*)) and (tree-sub *a b* (but-left *c*)) are available? After we apply the substitution to the left (i.e., car) and but-left (i.e., cdr), we can combine the return values using adopt (i.e., cons):

```
(adopt (tree-sub old-item new-item (left tree))
       (tree-sub old-item new-item (but-left tree)))
```

The general case and three Base Cases suggest we should use a five-way cond-expression:

```
(define (tree-sub old-item new-item tree)
   (cond
      ((equal? old-item tree) new-item)
      ((empty-tree? tree) tree)
```

```
((leaf? tree) tree)
((parent? tree)
  (adopt
      (tree-sub old-item new-item (left tree))
      (tree-sub
          old-item new-item (but-left tree))))
(else (error "bad input" tree-sub tree))))
```

Notice the use of equal? in the first clause. This was used instead of the more specialized equality predicates because we have no way of telling what types of trees we will need to compare.

Also, notice that the order of clauses is crucial. If the first clause is switched with the third clause, the call (tree-sub *a b a*) will return *a* instead of *b*.

Example: Tree Removal

The remove procedure for trees expects two inputs, an item to be removed and a tree to remove the item from. Here is a sample call:

```
> (rem 'a '((a b) (a c (a)) a b c))
((b) (c ()) b c)
```

It's interesting to compare this with the rem-item procedure defined in Problem 6.5.:

```
> (rem-item 'a '((a b) (a c (a)) a b c))
((a b) (a c (a)) b c)
```

Notice that rem-item only removes children of the root that match /a. Occurrences of /a at lower levels are ignored. Sometimes tree recursion is called **deep recursion** because it not only processes members of lists, but also members of members, members of members of members, and so on.

We want to complete the definition:

```
(define (tree-rem item tree) ??? )
```

Working out the Base Cases is tricky. What is left behind when we remove a tree from itself?

```
(tree-rem tree tree) = ???
```

Ideally, we would like the procedure to return nothing, but this will only be possible on recursive calls to tree-rem. For now, let's agree that the result of removing a tree from itself is the empty tree. The other two Base Cases are obvious:

```
(tree-rem-tree tree tree)  = ()
(tree-rem-tree item ()) = ()
(tree-rem-tree item leaf)  = leaf
```

Assume *b* is a parent tree. How can we compute (tree-rem *a b*) assuming (tree-rem *a* (left *b*)) and (tree-rem a (but-left *b*)) are available? We could use the tree-sub strategy: apply

tree-rem to left and but-left, then combine the results using adopt, but there is a problem
we can see by tracing a computation generated by this algorithm:

```
(tree-rem b (a b c))
(adopt a (tree-rem b (b c)))
(adopt a (adopt (tree-rem b b) (tree-rem b (c))))
(adopt a (adopt () (tree-rem b (c))))
(adopt a (adopt () (adopt c ())))
(adopt a (adopt () (c)))
(adopt a (() c))
(a () c)
```

We would like the result to have been (*a c*) instead of (*a* ( ) *c*). The ( ) crept into our result from the recursive call: (tree-rem *b b*), which returns ( ) as a value. This is the correct
value if *b* is a root node, but not if it is a left node. When we encounter a parent, we need
to peek at the left child to see if it is the same as the item being removed and to leave the
left child completely out of the result construction if it is. This suggests the following algorithm:

```
(tree-rem x (a b ... ))
  = (adopt (tree-rem x a) (tree-rem x (b ...))) if x ≠_a
  = (tree-rem x (b ...)) otherwise.
```

This can be translated into Scheme as follows:

```
(if (equal? item (left tree)
    (tree-rem item (but-left tree))
    (adopt (tree-rem item (left tree))
           (tree-rem item (but-left tree))))
```

The final form of our procedure is:

```
(define (tree-rem item tree)
  (cond
     ((equal? item tree) the-empty-tree)
     ((empty-tree? tree) tree)
     ((leaf? tree) tree)
     ((parent? tree)
        (if (equal? item (left tree)
            (tree-rem item (but-left tree))
            (adopt (tree-rem item (left tree))
                   (tree-rem item (but-left tree)))))
     (else (error "bad input" tree-rem tree))))
```

6.4.4. Efficiency of Tree Recursions

Recall the time consumed by a procedure proc was proportional to |(proc n)|. This doesn't quite make sense in the case of a tree recursion like depth or flatten. First, these procedures expect trees, not numbers, as inputs. Second, |(proc n)| was defined as the length of the computation generated by (proc n). This makes sense if computations are sequences, but what does it mean if computations are trees?

Assume proc is a procedure that operates on trees. We redefine |(proc tree)| as the number of nodes in the computation tree generated by (proc tree). This seems logical because each node corresponds to a step the evaluator must make; hence an amount of computer time consumed. It also agrees with our previous definition if the tree happens to consist of a single branch.

Looking at the example computations, we can see:

```
|(depth '((1) 2 (3)))|   = 16
|(flatten '((a) b (c)))|   = 17
```

In general, it is difficult to find |(proc t)| when t is a parameter, but we can find a general O bound. First observe that if t is a binary tree, then |t| = the number of nodes in t, is no more than 2^d - 1, where d = the depth of t.

Second, notice that the depth of a computation tree is related to the size of the input tree. For example, the depth of both the computation trees here is 6, which is the same as the number of nodes in the input trees $((1)$ 2 $(3))$ and $((a)$ b $(c))$. Rather than working out the details, we simply assert that if the input tree consists of n nodes, then the computation tree will consist of $c * n$ nodes for some fixed constant c.

Combining these two observations, we conclude that if |t| = n, then:

```
|(depth t)|  = O(2ⁿ)
|(flatten t)|  = O(2ⁿ)
```

Tree recursions are very inefficient. Each call to depth or flatten spawns two more calls. In each case frames for calls to + or append are created but can't be deallocated until all of the downstream recursions terminate. This suggests:

```
[(depth t)]  = O(2ⁿ)
[(flatten t)]  = O(2ⁿ)
```

Appendices

Appendix 6.1. Promises

When the sultan wanted someone to teach his pet donkey to read and write, Goha volunteered. He said the task would take three years, and to accomplish it he would need a villa with servants. The sultan agreed, and the next day Goha and the donkey moved into a splendid mansion. Time passed. Goha's friends came to visit him and found him lounging about in great comfort while the donkey roamed happily over the gardens. They warned him time and again that if he failed to come up with a literate donkey at the end of three years, he would surely lose his head. But Goha was unperturbed.

"I shall not give up hope," he said. "After all, one of four things might happen: the sultan may die, I may die, the donkey may die or —who knows? —the donkey may learn to read and write."

—Turkish Folk Tale

We have already seen a structure that uses delayed (i.e., lazy) evaluation. Recall:

```
(lambda (PARAM ...) BODY)
```

delays evaluation of BODY, freezing it inside a procedure that is the value returned by lambda.

Scheme provides another structure that uses delayed evaluation called **delay**. Delay is similar to lambda except that no parameters are involved. The "frozen" expression returned by delay is called a **promise**.[2]

```
(delay exp) = {exp} = a promise constructed from exp
```

We use the notation {exp} to represent the promise constructed from the expression exp. This notation is not standard, and will not be understood or produced by Scheme interpreters. It is only a convenient notation we use in this text.

Recall that an expression frozen inside a procedure was eventually "thawed" (i.e., evaluated) when the procedure was applied to arguments. Scheme also provides a mechanism for thawing (i.e., evaluating) promises:

```
(force {exp}) = value of exp.
```

For example:

```
> (define promise
        (delay (begin (writeln "hello world") 42)))
unspecified
> promise
promise ; = {(begin (writeln "hello world") 42)}
> (force promise)
hello world
42
```

Notice that the side effect produced by (writeln "hello world") wasn't seen until promise was forced.

Application: Lazy Procedures

Recall the definition of Lazy Evaluation given at the beginning of Chapter 3:

---

[2] Some programmers call promises thunks, said by some to be the noise made by data being pushed onto a stack.

1. Evaluate operator.
2. Replace parameters in body by unevaluated operands.
3. Evaluate body.

This algorithm has two problems. First, what if the operands contain symbols that are local to the procedure? This could cause unintended interpretations of these symbols. For example, assume the following definition has been made:

```
; = #t, if z near 0
(define (small? z)
   (define delta 1e-20)
   (<= (abs z) delta))
```

Unless the programmer and user are the same person, there's a good chance the user doesn't know about the local variable delta. Without this knowledge, the user may create his or her own global variable called delta and pass it to the small? predicate:

```
> (define delta 100000)
unspecified
> (small? delta) ; should be #f
?
```

If the lazy evaluation algorithm described earlier is used, then the unevaluated operand, delta, is substituted for z in the body of small?, and the body:

```
(<= (abs delta) delta)
```

is evaluated. In the local environment both occurrences of delta are assumed to refer to the local delta, and contrary to the user's expectation, #t is returned.

The second problem with our lazy evaluation algorithm has to do with efficiency. Suppose a parameter is needed several times inside the procedure body. Does this mean the corresponding operand will have to be evaluated multiple times? For example, the parameter z will be needed three times inside cube:

```
(define (cube z) (* z z z))
```

If our lazy evaluation algorithm is used to evaluate (cube (exp 1000)), then the unevaluated expression (exp 1000) will be substituted for all three occurrences of z in the body of cube:

```
(* (exp 1000) (exp 1000) (exp 1000))
```

Evaluating this expression forces us to compute (exp 1000) three times!

To solve these problems, let's modify the lazy evaluation algorithm as follows:

1. Evaluate operator.
2. Replace parameters in body by delayed operands.
3. Evaluate body. Force delayed operands if and when they are encountered.

(Sometimes the first lazy evaluation algorithm is called **normal order evaluation** to distinguish it from this algorithm.)

Although Scheme uses eager evaluation to evaluate applications of user-defined procedures, it is possible to define **lazy procedures** (also called **nonstrict** procedures) that use the lazy evaluation algorithm. Lazy procedures assume all their parameters are promises that need to be explicitly forced.[3] For example, here are lazy versions of small? and cube:

```
(define (lazy-small? promise)
   (define delta 1e-20)
   (<= (abs (force promise)) delta))

(define (lazy-cube promise)
   (* (force promise)
      (force promise)
      (force promise)))
```

Unfortunately, these procedures pass the burden of explicitly delaying operands to the poor user. For example, to cube 10, the user must type: (lazy-cube (delay 10)). In Chapter 8 we will see how to solve this problem using macros.

How does the new lazy evaluation algorithm solve the two problems associated with the old algorithm? In fact, (small? delta) returns the expected result:

```
> (define delta 100000)
unspecified
> (lazy-small? (delay delta))  ; should be #f
#f
```

If we trace this application, we see that the promise, {delta}, replaces the parameter in the body of lazy-small?:

```
(lazy-small? (delay delta))
(<= (abs (force {delta})) delta)
```

In some ways the promise {delta} is similar to the parameterless procedure (lambda () delta). Notice that delta would be considered a nonlocal in (lambda () delta); hence the static scope rule would dictate that the value of delta be determined by the procedure's defining environment rather than its calling environment. The same is true for promises. If symbols occur inside a promise, then the delaying environment, not the forcing environment, is used to determine their values.

In the preceding example, delta was delayed in the global environment. When the promise {delta} is forced in the body of lazy-small?, the delta = 10^{-20} binding in the local environment is ignored in favor of the global binding delta = 100,000.

Memoization

How is the efficiency problem associated with the first lazy evaluation algorithm solved by the second algorithm? If we trace the application (lazy-cube (exp 1000)), we see that

---

[3] All procedures are lazy in functional languages like Gofer.

after substitution, the promise {(exp 1000)} is forced three times in the body of lazy-cube:

```
(lazy-cube (delay (exp 1000)))
(* (force {(exp 1000)})
   (force {(exp 1000)})
   (force {(exp 1000)}))
```

Evaluating the first operand of the multiplication (assuming operands are evaluated left to right) forces us to compute e^{1000}. Here is where promises differ from parameterless procedures. The first time a promise is forced, it "remembers" its value by storing it in a hidden variable. If the promise is forced again, it merely returns the value stored in the hidden variable and doesn't bother evaluating its body. This technique is called **memoization**. For example, the promise {(exp 1000)} can be viewed as shorthand for the value produced by the expression:

```
(let ((value '())
      (first-time #t))
   (lambda ()
      (if first-time
         (begin
            (set! value (exp 1000))
            (set! first-time #f)))
      value))
```

(Recall that set! is a Scheme assignment operator used to "redefine" names. Please avoid using assignment commands until they are properly introduced in Chapter 7.)

Example: switch

Lazy procedures are useful when we want to avoid evaluating operands unless we need them. For example, suppose we want to create a procedure with four parameters that returns one of its last three parameters depending on the value of its first parameter. Because this is vaguely related to the C switch command, we call this procedure lazy-switch:

```
(lazy-switch key case1 case2 case3)
   = case1, if key < 0
   = case2, if key is even
   = case3, if key is odd
```

If we define lazy-switch as a lazy procedure, i.e., if we assume all parameters are promises, then only key and one case parameter will need to be evaluated:

```
(define (lazy-switch key case1 case2 case3)
   (define key-val (force key))
   (cond ((< key-val 0) (force case1))
         ((even? key-val) (force case2))
         (else (force case2))))
```

For now, users of lazy-switch must explicitly delay its inputs. Assume a global constant x has been defined:

```
(lazy-switch
   (delay x)
   (delay (exp 500)) ; = e^500, yikes!
   (delay (fact 40)) ; = (* 40 39 ... 1), yikes!
   (delay 100))
```

Like Goha, we hope, $x < 0$ here, and we can avoid computing (exp 500) or (fact 40) altogether.

Appendix 6.2. Streams

Some implementations of Scheme provide a STREAM domain.[4] Logically, streams and lists are identical. If (a e i o u) is a list, then we use $(a e i o u) to denote the equivalent stream. (This is analogous to using #(a e i o u) to denote the equivalent vector.) Of course, Scheme does not recognize $(a e i o u) as a valid literal or printable value. This notation is only used in this text to make the analogy between lists and streams clear.

Internally, there is an important difference between lists and streams. Like a list, a nonempty stream is a pair, but the cdr of the pair is a promise made from an expression that produces the tail of the stream:

```
STREAM ::= $() | (HEAD . {TAIL})
```

Every list procedure can be turned into an equivalent stream procedure by replacing car, cdr, cons, and so on with the corresponding stream procedures:

```
head = stream version of car
tail = stream version of cdr
cons-stream = stream version of cons
the-empty-stream  = $() = stream version of ()
empty-stream?  = stream version of null?
stream?  = stream version of list?
```

We could literally identify some of the stream procedures with their list counterparts:

```
(define head car)
(define the-empty-stream '())
(define empty-stream? null?)
```

But we have to be careful with cons-stream and tail. Because the cdr of a stream is a promise, tail needs to force it before returning it:

```
(define (tail stream) (force (cdr stream)))
```

Cons-stream is trickier because it must delay its second input before forming a pair:

---

[4] An implementation of streams is presented in the Macro section of Chapter 8.

```
(define (cons-stream head tail)
   (cons head (delay tail)))
```

Unfortunately, this doesn't work because eager evaluation will cause tail to be fully evaluated before we have a chance to freeze it. The correct implementation of cons-stream will have to wait until Chapter 8.

The definition of stream? is complicated by the fact that IEEE/ANSI Scheme does not provide a predicate for recognizing promises. (Fortunately, stream? is a primitive predicate in PC Scheme.)

Example: stream-ref

Let's implement a procedure for selecting members from a stream. This procedure will be analogous to list-ref, so we'll call it stream-ref:

```
(define (stream-ref stream n) ???)
```

We can use PC Scheme's stream? predicate and the natural? predicate developed earlier to validate the inputs of stream-ref:

```
(define (stream-ref stream n)

   (define (unsafe-stream-ref stream n) ???)

   (if (and (natural? n) (stream? stream))
       (unsafe-stream-ref stream n)
       (error "bad input(s)" stream-ref stream n)))
```

Remember, the first item in a list, vector, string, or stream is always in position 0. Therefore, if $n = 0$, unsafe-stream-ref returns (head stream). If the input stream is empty, then an "n out of range" error message is produced:

```
(define (unsafe-stream-ref stream n)
   (cond
     ((empty-stream? stream)
       (error "out of range" stream-ref n))
     ((zero? n) (head stream))
     (else (unsafe-stream-ref
              (tail stream)
              (- n 1)))))
```

Of course, we can seek a more efficient iterative implementation of stream-ref. To do this, we replace (unsafe-stream-ref stream n) in the body of stream-ref with a do-loop. The do-loop has two loop-control variables, an integer called count that is initially n, and a stream called members that is initially stream. Each time through the do-loop, count is decremented by one and the first element of members is removed. When count reaches 0 or when members becomes empty, the iteration stops and the head of members or an error message is returned:

```
(do ((count n (- count 1))
     (members stream (tail members)))
    ((or (zero? count) (empty-stream? members))
     (if (empty-stream? members)
         (error "out of range" stream-ref n)
         (head members)))))
```

Example: Creating Streams

We can create streams starting with the-empty-stream by repeated applications of cons-stream. A faster method is to coerce a list into a stream. The list->stream and stream->list coercions also show the close relationship between lists and streams. The list->stream coercion replaces the empty list by an empty stream. Assuming list->stream already converts (cdr vals) into an equivalent stream, we only need to add (car vals) to the beginning of this stream. This is done using cons-stream:

```
(define (list->stream vals)
   (if (null? vals)
       the-empty-stream
       (cons-stream
         (car vals)
         (list->stream (cdr vals)))))
```

Here are some sample calls:

```
> (list->stream '(a e i o u))
$(a e i o u)
> (list->stream '())
$()
```

The inverse coercion is left as an exercise.

Streams as Signals

We can represent signals as streams of messages rather than lists of messages. Translating map and filter into equivalent stream procedures is straightforward. For reasons that will be clear later, we do not define a stream version of accum.

The recursive, unary version of unsafe-stream-map mirrors safe-map:

```
(define (unsafe-stream-map amp msgs)
   (if (empty-stream? msgs)
       the-empty-stream
       (cons-stream
         (amp (head msgs))
         (unsafe-stream-map amp (tail msgs)))))
```

The iterative version is less obvious because we lack stream versions of reverse and append.

The recursive version of unsafe-stream-filter mirrors unsafe-filter:

```
(define (unsafe-stream-filter noise? msgs)
  (cond
    ((empty-stream? msgs) the-empty-stream)
    ((noise? (head msgs))
       (unsafe-stream-filter noise? (tail msgs)))
    (else (cons-stream
             (head msgs)
             (unsafe-stream-filter
               noise?
               (tail msgs))))))
```

Infinitely Long Streams

Given two real number inputs, the following procedure generates the stream of reals from m to n:

```
(define (m-to-n m n)
  (if (> m n)
      the-empty-stream
      (cons-stream m (m-to-n (+ m 1) n))))
```

Here are some sample calls:

```
> (m-to-n -3 5)
$(-3 -2 -1 0 1 2 3 4 5)
> (m-to-n 5 -3)
$()
> (m-to-n 5.2 5.2)
$(5.2)
```

The definition of m-to-n seems odd. Normally, our successor assumption would be that the values of m-to-n are available for inputs smaller than m, but in this case the input to the recursive call is $(+\ m\ 1)$ instead of $(-\ m\ 1)$. This works because the distance between $(+\ m\ 1)$ and n is smaller than the distance between m and n. Eventually, when m passes n, the recursion will terminate. This can be seen by tracing a call to m-to-n:

```
(m-to-n 3 5)
(cons-stream 3 (m-to-n 4 5))
(cons-stream 3 (cons-stream 4 (m-to-n 5 5)))
(cons-stream 3
   (cons-stream 4 (cons-stream 5 (m-to-n 6 5))))
(cons-stream 3 (cons-stream 4 (cons-stream 5 $())))
(cons-stream 3 (cons-stream 4 $(5)))
(cons-stream 3 $(4 5))
$(3 4 5)
```

Actually, this isn't what happens. Recall that cons-stream delays its second input. Hence, the real computation terminates after the third step:

```
(m-to-n 3 5)
(cons-stream 3 (m-to-n 4 5))
(3 . {(m-to-n 4 5)})
```

Like Goha, *m*-to-*n* has lazily put off the remaining calls to *m*-to-*n*, hoping they won't be necessary. If a persistent user wants to see the tail of this stream, *m*-to-*n* will unfold the recursion one more step:

```
(tail (3 . {(m-to-n 4 5)}))
(force {(m-to-n 4 5)})
(m-to-n 4 5)
(4 . {(m-to-n 5 5)})
```

Notice how lazy *m*-to-*n* is. It refuses to unfold any more of the recursion than is absolutely necessary.

This example brings up several interesting points. First, assume a simple value occupies four bytes of memory, and the amount of memory occupied by a pair (*x . y*) is the sum of the bytes occupied by *x* and *y*. Because the list (1 2 3) is equivalent to the pair (1 . (2 . (3 . ()))), it occupies 16 bytes of memory. By the same reasoning, the list (1 2 3 ... 100) occupies 404 bytes of memory. However, the stream $(1 2 3) is equivalent to a pair of the form (1 . {tail}), which occupies just 8 bytes of memory. Here's the interesting part: The stream $(1 2 3 ... 100) is also equivalent to a pair of the form (1 . {tail}), and so it too occupies only 8 bytes of memory!

The second interesting feature of the *m*-to-*n* example is this: because *m*-to-*n* lazily refuses to unfold any more of the recursion than is absolutely necessary, why does the recursion need to terminate? Why does the recursion need a Base Case? This motivates the following definition:

```
(define (from-m m)
   (cons-stream m (from-m (+ m 1))))
```

In any other language, this definition would be a disaster: (from-*m* 0) calls (from-*m* 1) calls (from-*m* 2) calls (from-*m* 3), etc. In Scheme, however, (from-*m* 0) immediately returns the pair:

```
(0 . {(from-m 1)})
```

Like Walt Disney, the troublesome infinite recursion is safely frozen inside a promise. This raises the question: What stream is represented by (from-*m* 0)? We can only imagine that this represents the infinite stream of all natural numbers:

```
$(0 1 2 3 ...)
```

This motivates the following definition:

```
(define nats (from-m 0))
```

The reader can verify that this is indeed the stream of all natural numbers by using stream-ref to select from nats

```
> (stream-ref nats 50)
50
> (stream-ref nats 1000)
1000
```

How can we generate other infinite streams? There are two techniques. The first is to imitate the method used for generating nats. For example, the infinite stream of all natural numbers divisible by 9 is:

```
$(0 9 18 27 36 ...)
```

To generate this stream, we first modify from-m:

```
(define (from-m m)
   (cons-stream m (from-m (+ m 9))))
```

Finally, we define our stream by calling (from-m 0):

```
(define nines (from-m 0))
```

The second technique uses stream-map and stream-filter to modify the nats stream. For example, an origin is a vector of zeros: #(0 ... 0). How can we generate the infinite stream of all even-length origins:

```
$(#() #(0 0) #(0 0 0 0) #(0 0 0 0 0 0) ...)
```

More specifically, how can we modify the nats stream to produce this stream? We can use stream-filter to eliminate the odd numbers from nats:

```
(define evens (stream-filter odd? nats))
```

Evens represents the infinite stream of all even numbers:

```
$(0 2 4 6 8 ...)
```

How can we amplify the even number n into a length n origin? We can base our amplifier on Scheme's make-vector procedure:

```
(define (make-origin n) (make-vector n 0))
```

To produce our final result we apply stream-map to evens using make-origin as an amplifier:

```
(define even-origins (stream-map make-origin evens))
```

Problems

Solutions to the following problems are to be given in functional Scheme. Try to restrict yourself to the necessary features within functional Scheme. Avoid coercions, strings, vectors, and list operations other than null?, car, cdr, and cons unless stated otherwise. You may use the definitions given in this chapter as well as solutions to other problems in this chapter (although you will have to include these definitions in your program files so you can test your definitions). You may also define any supporting procedures you need. Validate all inputs to monomorphic and overloaded procedures.

Problem 6.1.

How could you define a nonrecursive domain $NATURAL_n$ so that

$NATURAL ::= NATURAL_0 \cup \ldots \cup NATURAL_n \cup \ldots$

(Recall, NATURAL ::= all unsigned integers.)

Problem 6.2.

How could you define a nonrecursive domain $VALUE_n$ so that

$VALUE ::= VALUE_0 \cup \ldots \cup VALUE_n \cup \ldots$

Problem 6.3.

Trace the computations generated by the following calls assuming the definitions given earlier:

```
a. (accum cons '() '(3 4 5))
b. (list-ref '(a b c d e) 3)
c. (map square '(3 4 5))
```

Problem 6.4.

What function is computed by the following procedure? Reimplement it as an efficient, understandable, nonrecursive procedure using a do-loop. Can it be reimplemented in IEEE/ANSI Scheme without recursion or iteration?

```
(define (mystery vals)
   (if (null? vals)
       '()
       (append (mystery (cdr vals))
               (list (car vals))))))
```

Problem 6.5.

Implement the following procedures:

a. `(put-nth vals item n)`
   = vals with item inserted in position n

b. `(rem-nth vals n)`
   = vals with item at position n removed

c. `(rem-item item vals)`
   = vals with first occurrence of item removed

d. `(rem-item-all item vals)`
   = vals with all occurrences of item removed

e. `(rem-items items vals)`
   = vals with all occurrences of members of items
   list removed

Problem 6.6.

Assume vals is any list and test? is any unary predicate. Implement the following procedures:

a. `(all? test? vals)`
   = #t, if all members of vals pass test?
   = #f, otherwise

b. `(some? test? vals)`
   = #t, if some members of vals pass test?
   = #f, otherwise

Problem 6.7.

Assume vals is any list and n is a natural number. Implement the following procedures:

a. `(take vals n)`
   = a list containing the first n items in vals

b. `(drop vals n)`
   = a list containing all but the first n items in vals

Problem 6.8.

The zip procedure interleaves its two input lists into a single output list. Here are some examples:

```
(zip (1 2 3) (4 5 6)) = (1 4 2 5 3 6)
(zip (1 2) (3 4 5 6)) = (1 3 2 4 5 6)
(zip (1 2 3 4 5) (6)) = (1 6 2 3 4 5)
```

Implement the zip procedure without using map.

Problem 6.9.

Using the card ADT developed in Chapter 4, implement a procedure that expects no inputs but produces as output a list of all 52 playing cards.

Using only high-level procedures (zip, take, drop, etc.), write an update procedure called shuffle that shuffles a card-list input once. A list of cards is shuffled by splitting them in half, then interleaving the cards in the first half with the cards in the second half.

Write a procedure that allows users to iterate shuffle n times.

What's the period of shuffle, i.e., how many applications of shuffle lead back to the original order?

Problem 6.10.

Recall the definition of e given earlier:

$$e = \sum_{k=0}^{\infty} \frac{1}{k!}.$$

Write a procedure that expects no inputs, but produces a stream consisting of all the partial sums of this series. Using stream-ref to sample this stream at position n yields arbitrarily good approximations of e.

Problem 6.11.

In implementations of Scheme that provide eval, another possible implementation of the switch procedure is:

```
(define (switch key case1 case2 case3)
   (define key-val (eval key))
   (cond ((< key-val 0) (eval case1))
         ((even? key-val) (eval case2))
         (else (eval case3))))
```

Users could call switch by first quoting the inputs:

```
(switch 'i '(exp 50) '(fact 40) '10)
```

How could this produce different behavior from the earlier version? Hint: What environment is used by (eval *x*)? What environment is used by (force *x*)?

Problem 6.12.

Assume Scheme did not provide a member procedure. Implement one.

Problem 6.13.

Assume Scheme did not provide an append procedure. Implement one.

Problem 6.14.

Implement stream versions of member, take, and drop called stream-member, stream-take, and stream-drop. What problems would you expect from stream-append, a stream version of append?

Problem 6.15.

Compare the lengths of the computations generated by the expressions:

```
a.  (list-ref
        (filter even? (map square (m-to-n 1 n))) k)

b.  (stream-ref
      (stream-filter
          even? (stream-map square (m-to-n 1 n)))
    k)
```

Problem 6.16.

Write a procedure called orbit that, given an update procedure and an initial state as input, generates a stream representation of the orbit generated by iterating the update infinitely many times starting in the given initial state:

$(init (update init) (update (update init)) ...)

Here's a stub for orbit:

```
(define orbit init update) ???)
```

Problem 6.17.

Assuming a stream representation of an orbit, write a procedure called periodic? that returns #t if its orbit input is periodic.

Problem 6.18.

Recall the convergent? procedure from Chapter 5. We said that this procedure could not be implemented, but it is possible to implement loop detectors. Given a procedure proc and a list of values, vals, as input, a loop detector traces the computation gotten by applying proc to vals, storing the computation as a stream. Before each intermediate expression in the computation is added to the stream, the loop detector uses the periodic? predicate defined in the last problem to determine if any expression has appeared twice in the computation. If so, then the computation is oscillating and will never halt, so the loop detector returns #t. If the computation eventually halts, the loop detector returns #f.

We might try to use a loop detector to implement the convergent? predicate:

```
(define (convergent? proc vals)
   (if (loop-detect proc vals) #f #t))
```

Assuming loop-detector can be implemented, and it can, criticize this definition.

Problem 6.19.

Assume f is a function that operates on real numbers. The graph of f is the set of all pairs of the form $(n . (f n))$. We can represent the graphs of f as an infinite stream:

```
$((0 . (f 0)) (1 . (f 1)) (2 . (f 2)) ...)
```

Implement the meta-procedure:

```
(graph f)
   = the stream representation of the graph of f.
```

Problem 6.20.

Assume strings is a list of strings sorted in increasing order according to string<?; assume string is any string. Implement:

```
(insert string strings)
   = the sorted result of inserting string into strings.
```

Assume strings is an unsorted list of strings. Use insert to implement the following procedure:

```
(sort strings)
   = the result of sorting strings in increasing order
       using string<?
```

Problem 6.21.

If Scheme did not provide string-comparing procedures like string<? but did provide character-comparing procedures like char<?, how could you implement string<? (Recall char<? was implemented in terms of < earlier.)

Problem 6.22.

The level procedure extracts all leafs at a given level from a given tree. For example, assume tree *t* has the form in Figure 6.9.

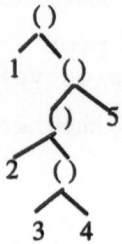

Figure 6.9

Implement level. Here are some sample calls:

```
(level 0 t) = ()
(level 1 t) = (1)
(level 2 t) = (5)
(level 3 t) = (2)
(level 4 t) = (3 4)
(level 5 t) = ()
```

Problem 6.23.

The size of a tree is the number of nodes. The empty node and leafs have size 1. Implement a size procedure.

Reimplement this procedure assuming the empty tree has size 0.

Problem 6.24.

Implement the following procedures using the signal-processing procedures: map, filter, accum, and *m*-to-*n*.

Your definitions should not be recursive or iterative. There are no restrictions on the amplifiers, combiners, and noise? procedures.

a. `make-alist, length, zip, cars`

b. `(prod-even-cubes n)`
     `= product of even cubes from 1 to n`^{3}.

c. `(primes n)  = a list of all primes between 2 and n.`

d. `(fact n) = n factorial.`

Problem 6.25.

Implement the stream->list coercion.

Problem 6.26.

Find a tail-recursive implementations of list?.

Problem 6.27.

Find iterative implementations of rem, make-alist, stream-filter, and map

Problem 6.28.

A geometric sequence has the form:

`(ar`^{0}` ar`^{1}` ar`^{2}` ... ar`^{n}`)`

where *a* and *r* are both arbitrary real numbers. Implement a generator for geometric sequences:

`(geom-seq a r n)  = (ar`^{0}` ... ar`^{n}`)`

Problem 6.29.

Generate the following infinite streams:

```
a. $(0 1 1 2 3 5 8 13 21 ...) ; Fibonacci sequence
b. $(1 1 1 1 ...)
c. $(1 1/2 1/3 1/4 ...)
d. $(0 1 0 1 0 1 0 ...)
e. $(1 -1 1 -1 1 -1 ...)
f. $(-1 -2 -3 -4 -5 ...)
g. $(.1 .01 .001 .0001 ...)
h. $(2 3 5 7 11 13 17 19 ...) ; Prime number sequence
i. $((0) (0 1) (0 1 2) (0 1 2 3) ...)
j. $("0" "000" "00000" ...)
k. $($() $(0) $(0 0) $(0 0 0) ...)
l. $(() (()) ((())) ...)
m. $(0 0 1 2 3 1 2 3 1 2 3 ...)
n. $(1e-1 1e-2 1e-3 1e-4 ...)
```

Problem 6.30.

Draw the tree representation of the following list:

```
(cons (+ x (* 2 y)) (cons a "hello"))
```

Problem 6.31.

Recall the Fibonacci sequence:

```
0, 1, 1, 2, 3, 5, 8, 13, 21, ...
```

Also recall the recursive definition of the Fibonacci procedure that computes the nth number in the Fibonacci sequence:

```
(define (fib n)
   (cond ((<= n 0) 0)
         ((= n 1) 1)
         (else (+ (fib (- n 1)) (fib (- n 2)))))))
```

Although this procedure does not operate on trees, we consider it a tree recursion because it generates binary-tree-shaped computations. This is because each call to fib can generate two more calls to fib. Draw the computation tree generated by the call (fib 5). Only show calls to fib. Indicate the return values using the notation used in the examples given earlier.

Problem 6.32.

Define tree-map, an analogue of the map and stream-map procedures. For example:

```
> (tree-map square '((2 3) 4 ((5))))
((4 9) 16 ((25)))
```

Problem 6.33.

Define tree-filter, an analogue of filter and stream-filter. For example:

```
> (tree-filter even? '((2 3) 4 ((5))))
((3) ((5)))
```

Problem 6.34.

Define tree-accum, an analogue of accum. For example:

```
> (tree-accum + 0 '((2 3) 4 ((5))))
14
```

Problem 6.35.

Recall that a rational number can be represented as an infinite repeating decimal. For example:

1/7 = .142857142857142857142857142857...
1/8 = .12500000000000000000000000000...

We can represent 1/7 and 1/8 as infinite digit streams:

$(1 4 2 8 5 7 1 4 ...)
$(1 2 5 0 0 0 0 0 ...)

Implement a procedure that expects two integers m and n as input and generates the stream representation of the infinite decimal expansion of m/n as output:

```
(define (rational->stream m n) ???)
```

Also implement the inverse procedure:

```
(define stream->rational expansion n) ???)
```

For example:

```
(stream->rational (rational->stream 1 7) 3) = 142
```

Note: This technique could be expanded to give us a way to exactly represent certain irrational numbers as streams. (This is related to the way e was represented earlier as a stream of partial sums.) Irrationals that can be represented in this way are called **recursive reals**. Clearly, rationals (and therefore integers) are recursive reals. Sadly, if we remove all nonrecursive reals from the number line, what remains has length 0.

Problem 6.36.

If vals is a length-n list, then |(length vals)| = $O(2n)$ because vals must be traversed once when (list? vals) is called, and again when (unsafe-length vals) is called. Of course, $O(2n)$ = $O(n)$, so one might argue that for large lists the difference is negligible. Still others might object to traversing a long list twice. We can incorporate input validation and length calculation into a single list traversal merely by verifying vals is a pair before computing (cdr vals):

```
(define (length vals)
   (cond ((null? vals) 0)
         ((pair? vals) (+ 1 (length (cdr vals))))
         (else (error "bad input" length vals)))
```

Copy the style of this definition to modify the definitions of filter, map, accum, get, put, and rem to avoid traversing their input lists twice.

Problem 6.37.

Redefine the list? predicate without using conditionals. Use and and or instead. Do you think this new definition is still tail-recursive?

7
Variables

7.1. Stores

In addition to the Global Environment, the Scheme evaluator maintains another structure called the **global store**. A **store** is an array of data containers called **cells**. A value that can be contained in a cell is called a **storable value**. Not all values are storable; for now we will identify storable values with simple values (numbers, Booles, chars, symbols, etc.) and the empty list:

```
STORABLE ::= () | SIMPLE
```

All stores provide basic read, write, and erase procedures. Assume val is a storable value then:

```
(read store xxx)
   = the value stored in cell specified by xxx

(write! store xxx val)
   = an unspecified value. As a side effect stores val
      in the cell specified by xxx

(erase! store xxx)
   = an unspecified value. As a side effect, erases
      contents of the cell specified by xxx
```

Stores differ in how cells are specified (i.e., *xxx*). Cells in **random access stores** are specified by addresses. Cells are specified in **associative stores** by the data they can contain. Cells are specified implicitly in **sequential stores**, **stacks**, and **queues**. All of these types of stores offer trade-offs between complexity and speed. Often the choice of which type of store to use is dictated by the algorithm.

Scheme's global store is a type of random access store called a **heap**. Each cell in a heap can be identified by a unique unsigned integer called its **location** or **address**. The heap shown in Figure 7.1 consists of eight cells. The cells at locations L_2 and L_7 contain the FREE token, indicating they are currently not in use.

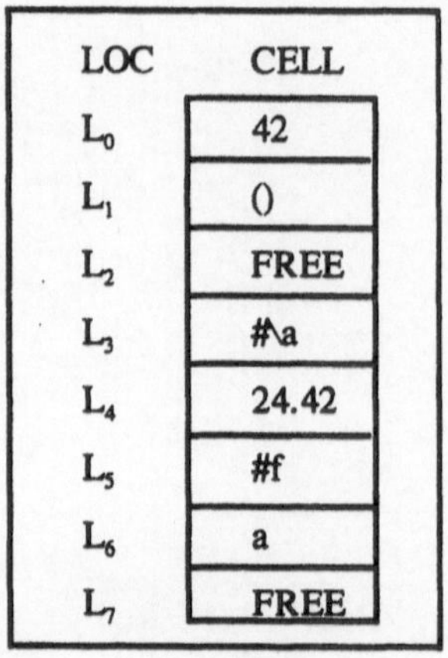

LOC	CELL
L_0	42
L_1	()
L_2	FREE
L_3	#\a
L_4	24.42
L_5	#f
L_6	a
L_7	FREE

Figure 7.1

We are now ready to tell the real story of what goes on inside the Scheme interpreter. When (define x 42) is resolved, what really happens is this:

1. A cell c at location L_0 is allocated from the Global Store.
2. The content of c is updated to 42.
3. L_0, the location of c, is bound to x.
4. The binding $x = L_0$ is installed in the Global Environment.

Figure 7.2 shows the **environment-store context** after the definition.

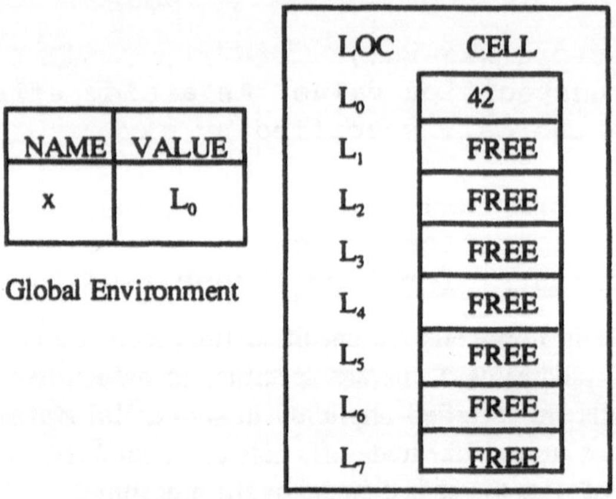

NAME	VALUE
x	L_0

Global Environment

LOC	CELL
L_0	42
L_1	FREE
L_2	FREE
L_3	FREE
L_4	FREE
L_5	FREE
L_6	FREE
L_7	FREE

Global Store

Figure 7.2

When the symbol x is evaluated, the evaluator searches the global environment for the location bound to x, then returns the value stored at this location in the global store.

7.2.   Variables and References

How are composite values such as pairs, vectors, strings, and lists stored? Obviously we will have to use multiple cells. A group of one or more cells that hold a single value (simple or composite) is called a **variable**. A **simple variable** is the same as a single cell. A **composite variable** is several cells that hold the components of a composite value. Normally, composite variables that hold pairs, strings, or vectors are composed of consecutive cells for fast access, while variables that hold lists may consist of non-consecutive cells.

How do we describe the location of a variable? Obviously the location of a simple variable is its cell location, but what about composite variables? One solution is to describe the location of a group of consecutive cells by a corresponding group of consecutive cell locations. For example, the location of a pair is given by a pair of consecutive locations, and the location of a vector is given by a vector of consecutive locations. A string will be equated with a character vector and a list will be equated with a nested pair, so we don't need special locations for these types of variables. A location or a sequence of locations is called a **reference**. More formally:

```
LOCATION ::= L₀ | L₁ | L₂ | etc.

REFERENCE ::= LOCATION |
              (LOCATION . LOCATION) |
              #(LOCATION LOCATION...)
```

Assume the following definitions are made:

```
(define a (vector #\r #\a #\s))
(define b (list 'c #t))
```

After these definitions the environment-store context in Figure 7.2 looks like the environment-store context shown in Figure 7.3.

NAME	VALUE
x	L_0
a	$\#(L_1\ L_2\ L_3)$
b	$(L_4 . L_5)$

Global Environment

LOC	CELL
L_0	42
L_1	#\r
L_2	#\a
L_3	#\s
L_4	c
L_5	$(L_6 . L_7)$
L_6	#t
L_7	0

Global Store

Figure 7.3

Unlike strings, vectors, and pairs, lists can grow and shrink. For this reason, we choose not to store lists in consecutive cells. Recall that the list (c #t) is equivalent to the nested pair (c . (#t . ( ))). We can depict (c #t) as a nested pair if we allow references to be storable values:

```
STORABLE ::= () | SIMPLE | REFERENCE
```

In this example the symbol x is bound to L_0, a reference to a simple variable containing the value 42. The symbol a is bound to #(L_1 L_2 L_3), a reference to a composite variable containing the vector #(#\r #\a #\s), and the symbol b is bound to (L_4 . L_5), a reference to a composite variable containing the list (c #t).

Sometimes it's easier to represent locations as **arrows** and references as **forks**. Figure 7.4 shows Figure 7.3 redrawn using this technique.

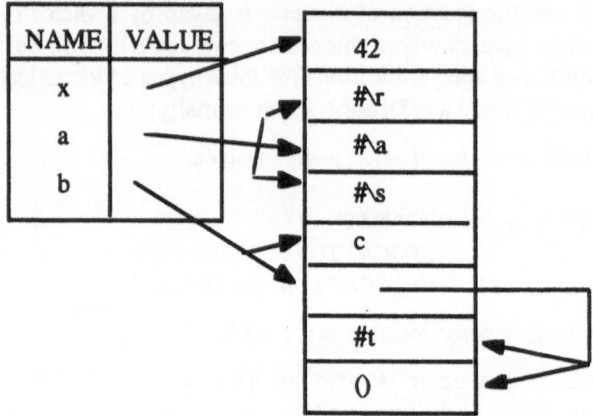

Figure 7.4

Another technique is to use **box and pointer diagrams** to represent long lists. For example, assume the following definition is made:

```
(define vowels '(a e i o u))
```

Internally, vowels is the nested pair:

```
(a . (e . (i . (o . (u . ()))))))
```

Each pair corresponds to a pair of consecutive cells in the global store. The first cell of each pair (i.e., the car cell) contains a vowel. The second cell of each pair (i.e., the cdr cell) contains a reference to the next pair of cells. This will be a reference of the form (L_n . L_{n+1}). Of course the cell pairs need not be consecutive; they can be scattered throughout the store. Box and pointer diagrams only depict the cell pairs involved in the actual list without indicating their relative position in the store. Figure 7.5 shows a box and pointer diagram for vowels.

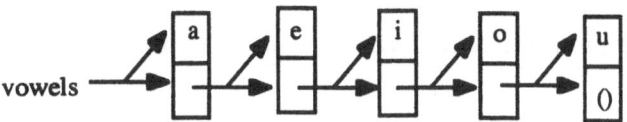

Figure 7.5

Box and pointer diagrams can get complicated. For example, the definition:

```
(define animals '("cat" "bat" "rat"))
```

creates a nested pair of the form:

```
("cat" . ("bat" . ("rat" . ())))
```

The car cell of each cell pair contains a reference to a string (i.e., vector) variable containing a string. Figure 7.6 shows the corresponding box and pointer diagram.

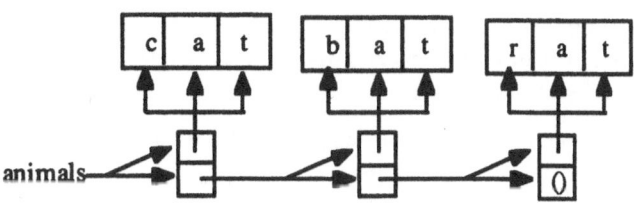

Figure 7.6

7.3.   Commands

Why are stores necessary? It seems like stores only make things more complicated.

We need stores to explain the action of commands. A **command** is a procedure or structure that returns an unspecified value but updates a variable as a side effect. By convention, names of Scheme commands usually end with an exclamation point. Scheme provides seven primitive commands. Assume *var* denotes a reference to any variable, *pair* denotes a reference to a pair variable, and *str* and *vec* denote references to length-n string and vector variables, respectively. Assume *val* is any value, i is any natural number less than n, and char is any character:

```
(set! var val) =
```
    an unspecified value. As a side effect updates var to
    val.

```
(set-car! pair val) =
```
    an unspecified value. As a side effect updates the car
    cell of pair to val.

```
(set-cdr! pair val) =
```
   an unspecified value. As a side effect updates the cdr
   cell of var to val.

```
(vector-set! vec i val) =
```
   an unspecified value. As a side effect updates the ith
   cell of vec to val.

```
(vector-fill! vec val) =
```
   an unspecified value. As a side effect updates each cell
   of vec to val.

```
(string-set! str i char) =
```
   an unspecified value. As a side effect, updates the ith
   cell of str to char.

```
(string-fill! str char) =
```
   an unspecified value. As a side effect updates each cell
   of str to char.

To illustrate, assume the following definitions have been made:

```
(define x 0)
(define y '(a e i o u))
(define z "hello world")
```

Here are some sample evaluations:

```
> (set! x (* 6 7))
unspecified
> x
42
> (set-car! (cdr y) 'y)
unspecified
> y
(a y i o u)
> (string-set! z 0 #\*)
unspecified
> z
"*ello world"
> (string-fill! z #\$)
unspecified
> z
"$$$$$$$$$$$"
```

What happens if the first input to a command is a literal? For example, how should the
evaluator evaluate the expressions:

```
(set! 4 0)
(set-car! '(a . b) 0)
(vector-fill! #(x y z) 'a)
```

Literals denote themselves, not references to variables; therefore all of these expressions should result in errors. It is illegal for the first input of a command to be a literal. (Note that some implementations of Scheme do not report errors for these expressions.)

7.4. *L*-Value versus *R*-Value

It should be clear why command semantics require us to carefully distinguish between a variable and its content. To make the point even clearer, think about the interpretation of the expression:

```
(set! x (+ 1 x))
```

Assume the environment-store context is as shown in Figure 7.3. We can interpret the x inside $(+ 1 x)$ to denote 42, the content of cell at location L_0, and therefore $(+ 1 x)$ denotes 43. But it doesn't make sense to interpret the left-hand occurrence of x to denote 42. What would the interpretation of the set! expression be in this case, "change 42 into 43"?

We can only make sense of this expression if we interpret the left-hand occurrence of x as the reference L_0. The interpretation of the entire expression becomes "change the content of the variable referenced by x to one plus its current content."

Deciding to interpret a symbol as a variable reference or a variable content depends on the symbol's context. If the symbol occurs as the left operand of a primitive command, then we interpret it as a variable reference. If the symbol occurs in the right operand of a primitive command (or in any other context), then we interpret it as a variable content. For this reason, we call the variable reference denoted by a symbol its **L-value** (L for left), and the corresponding variable content its **R-value** (R for right).

7.5. Aliasing

The L-value and R-value of a symbol may seem like a distinction of interest to theory-types only, but the presence of commands introduces a whole new class of problems called **aliasing bugs**.

For example, the definitions:

```
(define x (cons 1 2))
(define y (cons 0 x))
(define z (cons 4 x))
```

cause x, (cdr y), and (cdr z) to denote the same variable. We say that (cdr y) and (cdr z) are **aliases** of x. Figure 7.7 shows the environment-store context after these definitions are made. (Empty cells are free.)

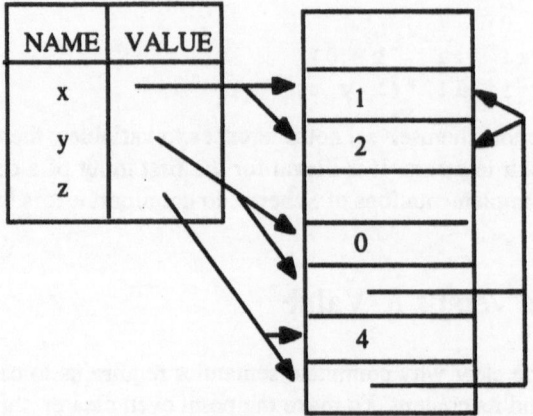

Figure 7.7

This causes no problem unless the content of the variable is changed by a command. To see why, imagine x, y, and z belong to three modules: X, Y, and Z, being developed by three programmers: Lars, Al, and Rölf respectively. The three programmers have long forgotten—or perhaps never knew—that (cdr y) and (cdr z) were aliases of x. Lars believes that x denotes the pair (1 . 2), Al thinks that y denotes the pair (0 . (1 . 2)), and Rölf is certain that z denotes the pair (4 . (1 . 2)).

One night Lars changes x:

```
> (set-car! x 0)
unspecifed
```

The new environment-store context is shown in Figure 7.8.

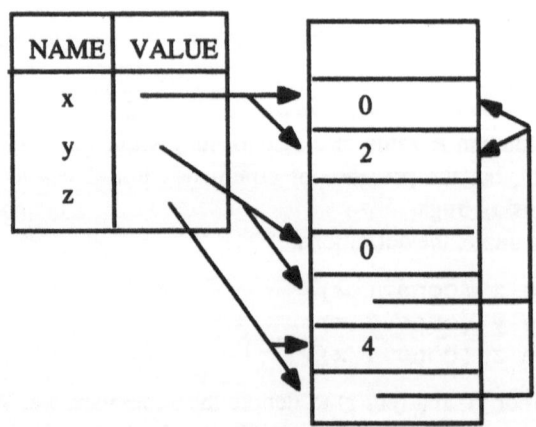

Figure 7.8

The next day Rölf and Al arrive at work and discover the code that tested bug-free the day before has suddenly developed problems. Mysteriously, *y* now seems to denote (0 . (0 . 2)), and *z* seems to be bound to (4 . (0 . 2)). It may take weeks before they discover Lars mutated *x* to 1 using set-car! instead of redefining *x* using define.

7.6.   Define Versus Assign

It's important to understand the difference between changing the content of a variable using a command and rebinding a name to a new variable reference using a definition. Assume the following definitions are made:

```
(define x 0)
(define y (cons 5 0))
```

The first definition allocates a simple variable *c* containing 0, and the second definition allocates a composite variable *k* containing the pair (5 . 0). The environment-store context is shown in Figure 7.9.

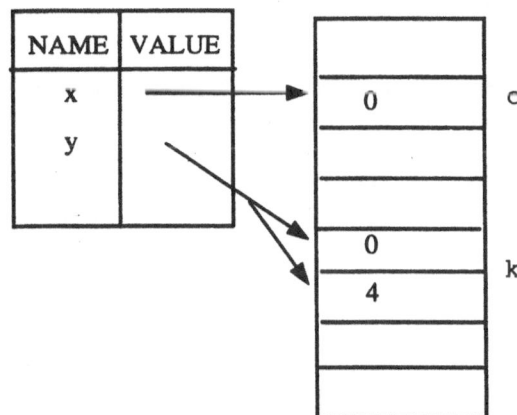

Figure 7.9

The following commands alter the content of *c* and *k*:

```
> (set! x 20)
unspecified
> (set-car! y 0)
unspecified
> (set-cdr! y 4)
?
```

After these commands the environment-store context in Figure 7.9 changes to the one shown in Figure 7.10.

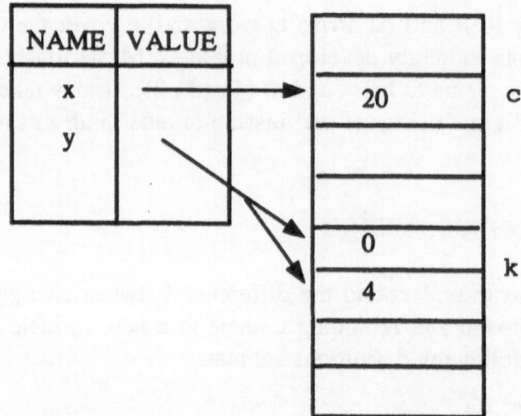

Figure 7.10

Now assume x and y are redefined:

```
> (define x 100)
unspecified
> (define y (cons 50 30))
unspecified
```

In this case, new variables c′ and k′ are allocated containing 100 and (50 . 30), respectively. Figure 7.11 shows the new environment-store context.

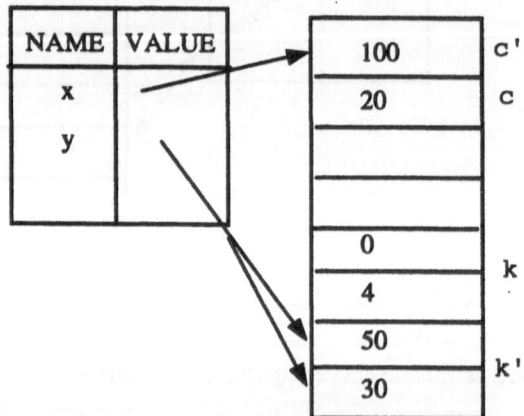

Figure 7.11

Notice the old variables c and k still exist. If no other chain of references leads from a global symbol to c or k, we say c and k are **unreferenced** or, to use a more colorful expression, c and k are **garbage**. When the store runs low on cells the evaluator will be temporarily interrupted by a program called the **garbage collector**. The garbage collector recycles (i.e., applies dealloc-loc!) to all unreferenced cells so they can be reallocated, and then allows the evaluator to resume evaluating.

There are other important differences between define and set!. The set! command can't be used to initially define variables. The command:

```
(set! xx 10)
```

may cause an undefined symbol error if *xx* hasn't previously been introduced by a definition or as a formal parameter.

Lastly, definitions can occur at the beginning of a procedure block, but definitions can't be nested inside arbitrary Scheme expressions. For example, the expression:

```
(if (< x 0) (define x 1) (define x -1))
```

is illegal, but the expression:

```
(if (< x 0) (set! x 1) (set! x -1))
```

is legal.

7.7.   Imperative Programming

> Different observers will not perceive the same physical evidence in the same way unless their linguistic backgrounds are quite similar.
>
> —Benjamin Lee Whorf, *Language, Thought, and Reality*

> Some accepted examples of actual scientific practice ... provide models from which spring particular coherent traditions of scientific research.
>
> —Thomas S. Khun, *The Structure of Scientific Revolutions*

A programming language is a toolbox filled with tools for building programs. Languages like C, Pascal, and FORTRAN provide similar program building tools: commands for updating variables; control structures for sequencing, iterating, and selecting commands; and constructors for grouping variables into arrays and structures. Functional Scheme— i.e., Scheme without commands—provides a very different set of program building tools: application for building nested expressions and lambda for turning expressions into procedures.

We shape tools to solve problems, but how we go about solving problems is often shaped by the available tools. This happens because tools are products of problem-solving models called **paradigms**, which are themselves products of cultural evolution.

Languages that do not provide commands and variables—like Miranda, Haskell, Gofer, and functional Scheme—impose on their users an expression-oriented problem solving paradigm called **functional programming**, while languages that do provide commands and variables—like C, C++, FORTRAN, Pascal, Ada, and imperative Scheme —impose a command-oriented problem-solving paradigm called **imperative programming**.

Imperative programming is based on the concept of a **mutable object**. An object is mutable if some of its properties can be changed without changing its identity. The dynamical systems studied in Chapter 4 are mutable objects because the state of a system can change without changing the identity of the system. For example, we don't think of a computer as a different computer just because its memory content has changed. People are mutable objects. Our weight, age, and height are all examples of mutable properties. Our name, social security number, and parents are all examples of nonmutable properties. By contrast, most mathematical objects are **nonmutable** or **stateless**. For example, neither the numerator nor the denominator of a rational number are mutable. If we change the denominator of $r = 1/2$ to 4, r becomes 1/4, a completely different rational number.

Variables are also mutable objects because the values they contain can change without changing the identity (i.e., location) of the variable. Variables are useful for modeling all types of mutable objects.

7.8. The Bank Account Example

A standard example of a mutable object is a bank account. The mutable property of a bank account is its balance because this can change without changing the identity of the account. One approach is to model bank accounts using simple variables:

```
(define account 0)    ; account initially contains $0

(define (withdraw! amt)
   (if (<= amt account)
       (set! account (- account amt))
       (writeln "sorry, insufficient funds"))
   'done)

(define (deposit! amt)
   (set! account (+ account amt))
   'done)
```

Here's a sample session:

```
> account
0
> (deposit! 50)
done
> (withdraw! 20)
done
> (withdraw! 40)
sorry, insufficient funds
done
> account
30
```

To indicate deposit! and withdraw! are commands—they modify the account variable—we end their names with exclamation marks. Also, because commands work by updating variables rather than returning values, we adopt the convention of having commands return the simple affirmation, "done," rather than risk confusing users with whatever value their particular implementation of Scheme returns.

7.8.1. Pass-by-Value

Unfortunately, our withdraw! and deposit! commands are not very useful. They can only be used to update a single bank account. Each time we introduce a new account variable, we will have to introduce commands for making deposits and withdrawals from that account.

Our withdraw! and deposit! commands are linked to the account variable because they contain nonlocal references to it, but if we try to make account a parameter, things go wrong. Assume two accounts are defined:

```
; two new accounts:
(define account1 0)
(define account2 0)
```

Next we define a version of the deposit! command with an account parameter:

```
; account is a parameter
(define (deposit! account amt)
   (set! account (+ account amt))
   done)
```

Here's a sample session:

```
> account1
0
> (deposit! account1 50)
done
> account1
0
```

What happened to the $50 we deposited in account1? Recall the environment model of eager evaluation described in Chapter 4:

1. Evaluate the operator.
2. Produce arguments by evaluating the operands.
3. Resolve all local definitions.
4. Extend the current environment by adding declared and parameter bindings.
5. Evaluate the parameterized body of the procedure relative to the extended environment.
6. Restore the original current environment.

When the account1 parameter was fully evaluated in step 2, its value, 0, was computed. In step 4 a new variable containing 0 was allocated, and a reference to it was bound to the account parameter. In step 5 the value of the new account variable was updated to 50. The environment-store context at this stage is shown in Figure 7.12. Because this was not the same variable as account1, account1 still contained 0 when the procedure terminated. This style of parameter passing is called **pass-by-value** because the *R*-values of variables are passed rather than their *L*-values.

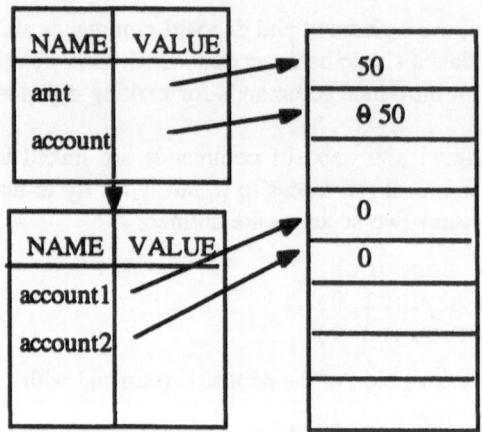

Figure 7.12

7.8.2. Pass-by-Reference

We can only update simple global variables from within a procedure if these variables are nonlocal. The same isn't true for composite variables. Composite variables can be nested to create larger variables; therefore, fearing a composite variable argument may be large, the Scheme evaluator does not allocate a new variable in step 4. Instead, the *L*-value of the operand is bound to the corresponding parameter. In effect, the parameter becomes an alias of the argument. This style of parameter passing is called **pass-by-reference**.

For example, assume the following definitions are made:

```
(define a (cons 2 3))
(define b 0)
(define (test! x y) (set! x 4) (set-cdr! y x))
```

and assume the following call is made:

```
> (test! b a)
unspecified
```

Figure 7.13 shows the environment-store context just after the evaluation of test!'s body.

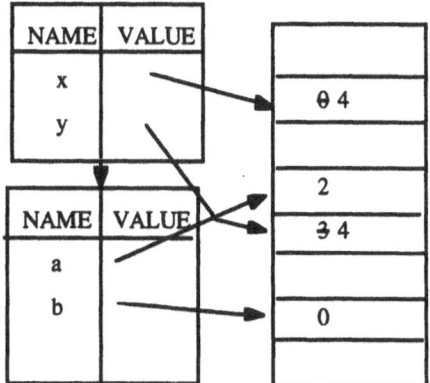

Figure 7.13

Notice that x and b are bound to references to distinct simple variables, while y and a are bound to references to the same composite variable. After the call we notice that a has been modified but b remains the same:

```
> a
(2 . 4)
> b
0
```

7.8.3. Bank Accounts Revisited

We exploit pass-by-reference in the following reimplementation of bank accounts. Our implementations of the withdraw! and deposit! commands aren't very secure. Some un-scrupulous person could easily use them to remove money from the accounts of others. Let's correct this problem by representing bank accounts as variable pairs. The cdr of the variable will contain the balance of the account, while the car will contain a password known only to the owner of the account.

Initially, unassigned accounts have the same password, 'pswrd, and balance, $0. When an account is first assigned, the new owner will customize the password using the set-password! command. Thereafter, the owner will modify the balance using the de-posit! and withdraw! commands:

```
; some unassigned accounts:
(define account1 (cons 'pswrd 0))
(define account2 (cons 'pswrd 0))
(define account3 (cons 'pswrd 0))

; selector:
(define (balance pswrd account)
    (if (eq? pswrd (car account))
        (cdr account)
        (writeln "access denied")))
```

The commands for setting a password, withdrawing money, or depositing money all have an account parameter:

```
(define (set-password! new-password
                       old-password
                       account)
   (if (eq? old-password (car account))
       (set-car! account new-password)
       (writeln "access denied"))
   'done)

(define (withdraw! pswrd amt account)
   (cond
       ((not (eq? pswrd (car acct)))
         (writeln "access denied"))
       ((>= (balance account) amt)
         (set-cdr! account (- (balance account) amt))
       (else (writeln "sorry, insufficient funds")))
   'done)

(define (deposit! pswrd amt account)
   (if (eq? pswrd (car account))
       (set-cdr! account (- (balance account) amt))
       (writeln "access denied"))
   'done)
```

Here's a sample session:
```
> (set-password! 'pswrd 'aaa acct1)
done
> (set-password! 'pswrd 'bbb acct2)
done
(deposit! 'aaa 50 acct1)
done
> (deposit! 'aaa 50 acct2)
access denied
done
> (deposit! 'bbb 50 acct2)
done
> (withdraw! 'bbb 100 acct2)
sorry, insufficient funds
done
> (withdraw! 'aaa 40 acct1)
done
> (balance acct2)
50
> (balance acct1)
10
```

Appendices

Appendix 7.1. Implementing Heaps

The following implementation of heaps will be used in Chapter 8.

LOCATION and REFERENCE ADTs

A location is a natural number equipped with a type tag, loc. A reference is a location, a location pair, or a location vector:

```
LOCATION ::= (loc . NATURAL)

REFERENCE ::=
   LOCATION | (LOCATION . LOCATION) | #(LOCATION ...)
```

For convenience, we define a location constructor, a predicate that recognizes locations, and a selector that extracts the integer value of a location:

```
(define (loc n)
   (if (natural? n)
       (cons 'loc n)
       (error "bad input" loc n)))

(define (location? val)
   (and (pair? val) (eqv? (car val) 'loc)))

(define index cdr) ; extracts int from loc
```

Our reference? predicate uses the all? predicate defined in Chapter 2:

```
(define (reference? val)
   (or (location? val)
       (and (pair? val)
            (reference? (car val))
            (reference? (cdr val)))
       (and (vector? val)
            (all? reference? (vector->list val)))))
```

Stores

A store is a vector of storable values:

```
STORE ::= #(STORABLE ...)
```

A store constructor expects as input the store capacity and uses the make-vector constructor to initialize all cells to the free token:

```
(define (make-store capacity)
   (if (natural? capacity)
       (make-vector capacity free)
       (error "bad input" make-store capacity)))
```

The capacity procedure is just a pseudonym for vector-length:

```
(define capacity vector-length)
```

Newly allocated cells will be initialized with the symbol alloc. Before a cell is allocated it contains the free token:

```
(define free 'free)
(define alloc 'alloc)
```

We will also need predicates for recognizing stores and storable values:

```
(define store? vector?)

(define (storable? val)
   (or (null? val)
       (number? val)
       (char? val)
       (boolean? val)
       (symbol? val)
       (procedure? val)
       (reference? val)))
```

It is an error to read or write to a free cell. To enforce this, we need to be able to recognize free cells and valid locations:

```
(define (free? store loc)
  (eqv? free (vector-ref store (cdr loc))))

(define (accessible? store loc)
   (and (store? store)
        (location? loc)
        (<= (index loc) (capacity store))
        (not (free? store loc))))
```

Reading, Writing, and Allocating Locations

The core procedures read, write, and allocate individual cells:

```
(define (read-loc store loc)
   (if (accessible? store loc)
       (vector-ref store (cdr loc))
       (error "bad location" read-loc loc)))

(define (write-loc! store loc val)
    (if (and (accessible? store loc) (storable? val))
        (vector-set! store (cdr loc) val)
        (error "bad input(s)" write-loc! loc val)))
```

Allocating a cell is more involved. First, a local search procedure traverses the store looking for a cell containing the free token. If and when one is found, its content is changed to the alloc token, its position is turned into a location, and the location together with the store is returned as a pair. The store is returned with the location in anticipation of situations where multiple stores may be in use or functional implementations where the old store will be replaced by the store returned by alloc-loc!.

```
; = a location-store pair
(define (alloc-loc! store env)
   (define (search next store)...)
   (define i (search 0 store))
   (vector-set! store i alloc)
   (cons (loc i) store))
```

The internal search procedure tail-recursively inspects each index, *next*, of its store vector input. If a free location is found, the corresponding index is returned and the search terminates. If no free cells are located, i.e., capacity ≤ next, then the garbage collector, gc, is called to free unused memory, and the search starts anew. Note: The garbage collector needs the environment passed to it as a parameter; hence it is necessary to pass the environment to alloc-loc! as a parameter. The environment is a nonlocal available to the search procedure.

```
(define (search next store)
   (define cap (capacity store))
   (cond
      ((>= next cap) (search 0 (gc store env)))
      ((free? store (loc next)) next)
      (else (search (+ next 1) store)))))
```

Reading and Writing References

Next we define versions of read and write that operate on references rather than locations. We can learn a lot from a reference. Not only does it tell us which locations hold components of a particular value, it also tells us how the locations are grouped together and thus how the components should be grouped together. The read-ref procedure uses this information to call the appropriate reader: read-pair, read-vector, or read-loc.

We must remember that the value stored in a cell might be a reference; hence we must recursively pass the value returned by read-loc to read-ref. If this value isn't a reference, then it will be returned as a value in the else clause.

```
(define (read-ref store ref)
   (cond
      ((location? ref)
         (read-ref store (read-loc store ref)))
      ((and (reference? ref) (pair? ref))
         (read-pair store ref))
```

```
((and (reference? ref) (vector? ref))
 (read-vector store ref))
(else ref)))
```

Read-pair knows its parameter is a pair of locations and therefore its return value must be a pair:

```
(define (read-pair store ref)
  (cons (read-ref store (car ref))
        (read-ref store (cdr ref))))
```

The parameter passed to read-vector is a vector of locations. This is coerced into a list, which is passed to an internal procedure called read-list. Read-list gathers all the stored values into a list, which is then coerced back into a vector.

```
(define (read-vector store ref)
  (define (read-list refs vals) ...)
  (list->vector (read-list (vector->list ref) '())))
```

Read-list is a tail recursion that builds a list of values in its second parameter and then returns this parameter when the end of the location list is reached.

```
(define (read-list refs vals)
  (if (null? refs)
      vals
      (let ((val (read-ref store (car refs))))
        (read-list (cdr refs)
                   (cons-last val vals)))))
```

Like read-ref, write-ref calls upon special supporting procedures to write pairs and vectors to the store. Like alloc-loc!, write-ref! updates its store parameter as a side effect and returns the modified store as a value.

```
(define (write-ref! store ref val)
  (cond
    ((location? ref) (write-loc! store ref val))
    ((and (pair? ref) (pair? val))
     (write-pair! store ref val))
    ((and (vector? ref) (vector? val))
     (write-vector! store ref val))
    (else
     (error "bad input(s)" write-ref! ref val))))
```

Write-pair! creates a new store by writing (car pair) to (car ref) in the input store. The new store then becomes the store parameter in the second call to write-ref!.

```
(define (write-pair! store ref pair)
  (define new-store
    (write-ref! store (car ref) (car pair)))
  (write-ref! new-store (cdr ref) (cdr pair)))
```

Like read-vector, write-vector finds it more convenient to coerce its vector arguments to lists and then call an internal write-list procedure:

```
(define (write-vector! store ref vec)
   (define (write-list! store refs vals) ...)
   (write-list!
      store (vector->list ref) (vector->list vec)))
```

Write-list first creates a new store by writing (car vals) to (car refs) in its input store and then tail-recursively applies itself to (cdr refs) and (cdr vals) using the newly created store:

```
(define (write-list! store refs vals)
   (if (null? vals)
       store
       (let
         ((new-store
             (write-ref! store (car refs) (car vals))))
          (write-list!
             new-store (cdr refs) (cdr vals)))))
```

Allocating References

Depending on its value parameter, alloc-ref! calls alloc-loc!, alloc-vector!, or alloc-pair! In any case, alloc-ref! returns a location-store pair.

```
(define (alloc-ref! store env val)
   (cond ((pair? val) (alloc-pair! val store env))
         ((vector? val) (alloc-vector! val store env))
         (else (alloc-loc! store env))))
```

Alloc-pair! first allocates memory for (car pair). The result of this allocation is the location-store pair (loc1 . store1). Next, memory from store1 is allocated for (cdr pair). This produces the pair (loc2 . store2). Finally, the pair ((loc1 . loc2) . store2) is returned.

```
(define (alloc-pair! pair store env)
   (define loc1.store1
      (alloc-ref! store (car pair) env))
   (define loc1 (car loc1.store1))
   (define store1 (cdr loc1.store1))
   (define loc2.store2
      (alloc-ref! store1 (cdr pair) env))
   (define loc2 (car loc2.store2))
   (define store2 (cdr loc2.store2))
   (cons (cons loc1 loc2) store2))
```

Alloc-vec! calls an iterative internal procedure to do the hard work:

```
(define (alloc-vector! vec store env)
   (define (iter-alloc i locs store) ...)
   (iter-alloc 0 '() store))
```

Iter-alloc tail-recursively traverses its vector input allocating memory for each entry. Each iteration creates a pair of the form (loc1 . store1); loc1 is saved in the location list parameter, locs, and store1 is passed to the next recursive call.

```
(define (iter-alloc i locs store)
   (define len (vector-length vec))
   (if (>= i len)
       (cons (list->vector locs) store)
       (let*
             ((loc1.store1
               (alloc-ref! store env (vector-ref vec i)))
              (loc1 (car loc1.store1))
              (store1 (cdr loc1.store1)))
          (iter-alloc
             (+ i 1) (cons-last loc1 locs) store1))))
```

Garbage Collection

Recall that the garbage collector (gc) is called by alloc-loc! when memory runs low. The garbage collector attempts to free all unused cells. A cell is determined to be unused if it contains the free token or if there is no chain of references leading from the current environment to the cell. Garbage collection is divided into two phases. The mark phase marks all cells currently in use. The sweep phase unmarks all marked cells and deallocates all unmarked cells.

The garbage collector begins by forming a list of all locations appearing in the current environment. Because an environment is a list of frames, it is first converted into one big frame with (apply append env). A frame is a list of bindings (pairs), so we can form a list of the bound values by mapping cdr across the frame. We filter out any values that aren't references, and get-locs turns the resulting list of references into a list of locations.

```
(define (gc store env)
   (define locs
      (get-locs
         (filter not-ref?
            (map cdr (apply append env)))))
   (writeln "garbage collection commencing ...")
   (writeln tab "mark phase commencing ...")
   (mark! store locs)
   (writeln tab "sweep phase commencing ...")
   (sweep! store))
```

where

```
(define (not-ref? val) (not (reference? val)))
```

Get-locs turns a list of references into a list of location lists by mapping ref->locs along refs. Finally, the list of location lists is turned into a list of locations by applying append

```
(define (get-locs refs)
   (apply append (map ref->locs refs)))
```

where

```
(define (ref->locs ref)
   (cond
      ((location? ref) (list loc))
      ((pair? ref) (list (car ref) (cdr ref)))
      ((vector? ref) (vector->list ref))))
```

Given a list of locations that appear in the current environment, the mark phase recursively traverses the list, reads the corresponding value from the store, pairs the value with a marked tag, and then writes the marked value back to the store. If the value is itself a reference, then it is also coerced to a list of locations and appended to the end of the location list

```
(define (mark! store locs)
   (if (null? locs)
       store
       (let* ((i (cdar locs))
              (val (vector-ref store i)))
         (vector-set! store i (mark val))
         (if (reference? val)
            (mark! store
                    (append (cdr locs)
                            (reference->locs val)))
            (mark! store (cdr locs)))))))
```

where

```
(define (mark val)
   (if (marked? val)
       val
       (cons 'marked val)))
```

The sweep phase uses an internal iterative procedure to traverse the store unmarking and deallocating cells.

```
(define (sweep! store)
   (define cap (capacity store))
   (define (iter-sweep i store success)...)
   (iter-sweep 0 store #f))
```

Iter-sweep traverses the store. Marked values are unmarked. If an unmarked value is found, then it is set to the free token and success is set to true. When the end of the store is reached, either the store with newly deallocated memory is returned or an out-of-memory error is thrown

```
(define (iter-sweep i store success)
   (if (<= cap i)
       (if success store (error "out of memory" gc))
       (let* ((val (vector-ref store i))
              (new-val
               (if (marked? val) (unmark val) free))
              (suc (or success (eqv? new-val free)))
          (vector-set! store i new-val)
          (iter-sweep (+ i 1) store suc)))))
```

where

```
(define (marked? val)
   (and (pair? val) (eqv? (car val) 'marked)))
```

and

```
(define (unmark val)
   (if (marked? val)
       (cdr val)
       val))
```

Appendix 7.2. Sequential Access Stores

A **sequential access store** can be represented by a pair of lists of storable values:

```
SSTORE ::= (SEEN . UNSEEN)
SEEN, UNSEEN ::= (STORABLE ...)
```

Initially, the seen elements of a sequential store are empty:

```
(define (make-sstore storables)
   (cons '() storables))
```

We have reached the end of a sequential store when there are no more unseen elements:

```
(define (end? sstore)
   (null? (cdr sstore)))
```

When this happens, we must reset the store using init-next!:

```
(define (init-sstore! sstore)
   (define seen (car sstore))
   (define unseen (cdr sstore))
   (set-cdr! sstore (append seen unseen))
   (set-car! sstore '())
   'done)
```

Reading from a sequential store returns (car unseen). As a side effect, this element is removed form the unseen list and placed at the end of the seen list:

```
(define (read-next! sstore)
   (define seen (car sstore))
   (define unseen (cdr sstore))
   (define val (car unseen))
   (set-cdr! sstore (cdr unseen))
   (set-car! sstore (append seen (list val)))
   val)
```

Writing a value into a sequential store merely adds the new element to the end of the seen elements:

```
(define (write-next! sstore storable)
   (set-car! sstore
             (append (car sstore) (list storable)))
   'done)
```

The advantage of sequential stores is that we don't need a special apparatus such as keys or locations to access members. The disadvantage of a sequential store is the need to completely traverse the store to access its members.

Appendix 7.3. Files and Ports

Psychologists distinguish between two classes of human memory systems. Most of our procedural and declarative memories are stored in long-term memory (LTM) systems, while short-term memory (STM) systems serve as staging areas for perception and problem solving.

In a computer system we often distinguish between **volatile** and **continuous** stores. Items in volatile stores are represented as voltage levels. When the power is turned off, the data is lost. Items in continuous stores are represented magnetically or optically; hence power is not necessary to maintain the data. A computer's register set, cache memory, and main memory are volatile stores, while the secondary memories—optical and magnetic disks, tapes, etc.—are continuous stores. In many ways, these secondary memory systems serve as long term memory systems for a computer, while the main memory is analogous to a short term memory system.

Often readable data on a disk is organized into **text files**. A text file is a sequential store in which the only storable values are characters or a special end-of-file token:

```
STORABLE ::= CHAR | eof
```

For example, the following file consists of five characters (not including the end-of-file token). All of the characters are as yet unseen:

```
(() . (#\4 #\2 #\space #\1 #\9 eof))
```

Creating Ports

Text files can be attached to ports using the open-input-file and open-output-file procedures. Assume file$_1$ and file$_2$ are strings containing the path names of two text files:

```
(open-input-file file₁) =
```
an input port connected to file$_1$. As a side effect all members of file$_1$ become unseen.

```
(open-output-file file₂)=
```
an output port connected to file$_2$. As a side effect all members of file$_2$ are erased.

Note: If file$_2$ doesn't exist, then open-output-file creates it. It is an error to apply open-input-file to a file that does not exist.

Reading from Ports

Assume port$_1$ is the port returned by (open-input-file file$_1$). The following procedures return printable values and characters from port$_1$:

```
(read port₁)   =
```
the next unseen value in file$_1$. As a side effect this value is moved from the front of the unseen values to the rear of the seen values.

```
(read-char port₁) =
```
the next unseen character in file$_1$. As a side effect this character is moved from the front of the unseen values to the rear of the seen values.

After each call to read or read-char, the characters composing the item read are automatically moved from the front of the unseen items to the rear of the seen items. For example, if file$_1$ is the file:

```
(() . (#\4 #\2 #\space #\1 #\9 eof))
```

then (read port$_1$) returns the number 42 and moves the characters #4 and #2 to the rear of the seen items:

```
((#\4 #\2)   (#\space #\1 #\9 eof))
```

The next read operation returns 19 and moves the next three characters to the rear of the seen values:

```
((#\4 #\2 #\space #\1 #\9) . (eof))
```

The next read returns the eof token. The unseen values list is now empty:

```
((#\4 #\2 #\space #\1 #\9 eof) . ())
```

Scheme provides a polymorphic predicate for testing if an arbitrary value is the eof token:

```
(eof-object? val)
   = #t, if val is eof
   = #f, otherwise.
```

Writing into Ports

Assume $port_2$ is the port returned by (open-output-file $file_2$). Also assume val is a printable value and char is a character. Then:

```
(write val port₂) =
   an unspecified value. As a side effect val is added to
   the rear of the seen elements of file₂.
```

```
(display val port₂)  =
   an unspecified value. As a side effect val is added to
   the rear of the seen elements of file₂.
```

```
(write-char char port₂) =
   an unspecified value. As a side effect val is added to
   the rear of the seen elements of file₂.
```

```
(newline port₂)=
   an unspecified value. As a side effect #\newline is added
   to the rear of the seen elements of file₂.
```

Note: The write procedure writes the backslash control character, delimiting quotations, and the #\ prefix into $file_2$, while display does not.

Deallocating Ports

There is a limit to the number of ports that can be allocated at any time.[1] For this reason, it is sometimes necessary to deallocate old ports before new ones can be allocated. Scheme provides procedures for deallocating ports. Assume $port_1$ is an input port and $port_2$ is an output port:

```
(close-input-port port₁)=
   an unspecified value. Deallocates port₁.
```

```
(close-output-port port₂)  =
   an unspecified value. Deallocates port₂.
```

---

[1] In DOS this is determined by the command FILES=n in the config.sys file, where $8 \leq n \leq 20$.

Peeking into the Future

The read procedure reads the next printable value from a file or device. If the next item in the file is not a proper Scheme value, an error message results. This commonly happens if the next item is a comma that does not appear in the context of a quasi-quote. (See the exercise in Chapter 1 concerning quasi-quote and unquote.) We can deal with this problem using peek. Assume port is an input port:

```
(peek-char [port])   =
    the next unseen char (or eof) in port. Does not add this
    character to the rear of the seen values.
```

Thus peek-char allows us to view the head of the unseen characters without moving this character to the rear of the seen characters. We can use peek-char to implement a "safe" version of read that won't complain when commas are encountered outside the scope of a quasi-quote operator:

```
(define (safe-read port)
   (if (equal? (peek-char port) #\,)
       (read-char port)
       (read port)))
```

Example: Files to Lists

Recursion and iteration are useful for file-processing applications because the length of the file is not usually known in advance.

The following procedure "coerces" a file into a list. The input is a file name. The procedure begins by creating an input port connected to the file. The do-loop iteratively reads values from the file and conses the values into a list called vals. When the eof-object is read, the port is closed and the reversed list is returned:

```
(define (file->list file)
   (define port (open-input-file file))
   (do ((next (safe-read port) (safe-read port))
        (vals '() (cons next vals)))
       ((eof-object? next)
            (close-input-port port)
            (reverse vals))))
```

We can use make-sstore to turn a file into the sequential store model:

```
(define (file->sstore file)
   (make-sstore (file->list file)))
```

If an input port has already been created, then the following procedure turns it into a file:

```
(define (port->stream port)
   (cons-stream (safe-read port) (port->stream port)))
```

Example: Changing Case

The next example copies a source file to a destination file changing every lowercase letter into an uppercase letter in the process. The inputs are the names of the source and destination files. The procedure begins by creating an input port connected to the source file and an output port connected to the destination file. A do-loop iteratively reads from the input port using read-char. Each char is written to the output port in the body of the do-loop using write-char. When the eof-object is detected, both ports are closed and the procedure terminates:

```
(define (file-upcase source-file dest-file)
    (define sport (open-input-file source-file))
    (define dport (open-output-file dest-file))
    (do ((next (read-char sport) (read-char sport)))
        ((eof-object? next)
            (close-input-port sport)
            (close-output-port dport)
            'done))
        (write-char (char-upcase next) dport)))
```

Problems

Solutions to the following problems may be given in imperative Scheme.

Problem 7.1.

Imperative programs are more memory-efficient than functional programs. To demonstrate this, write a procedure that expects a string variable, *str*, as input, returns a token value, and as a side effect, reverses the characters in *str*. For example, assume the variable *x* has been defined:

```
(define x "Hello World")
```

The effect of applying string-reverse to *x* can be seen by inspecting *x* after the call:

```
> (string-reverse! x)
done
> x
"dlroW olleH"
```

It might be helpful to first define a supporting procedure that exchanges two characters within a string:

```
; swaps chars in str at positions m & n
(define (swap-chars! str m n) ???)
```

Warning: If the input to string-reverse! isn't a string variable, then the result is unspecified.

Problem 7.2.

In an imperative model of a dynamical system the state is maintained in a variable. The state variable can be encapsulated inside the control-loop, which is identified with the system itself:

```
(define (control-loop init update final?)
    (define state init)
    (do ((cycle 0 (+ cycle 1)))
        ((final? state) 'done)
        (set! state (update state))
        (writeln "cycle = " cycle " state = " state)))
```

Build an imperative implementation of the digital clock simulation done in Chapter 5.

Problem 7.3. Associative Stores

An associative store allows users to store data along with a key that can be used to retrieve the data. The basic operations on an associative store are:

```
(read-assv astore key)  =
    the value associated with key in astore. If no
    association is found, 'fail is returned.

(write-assv! astore key val)  =
    an unspecified value. As a side effect val is associated
    with key and stored in astore.

(erase-assv! astore key)   =
    an unspecified value. As a side effect the value
    associated with key in astore is deleted.
```

Earlier, we said that a mutable object was an object with properties that could be changed without changing the overall identity of the object itself. We called these properties **mutable properties**. Curiously, what makes an object mutable is not having mutable properties, but having at least one nonmutable property we can identify with the object itself. This nonmutable property is the object's **essence**. Other properties may change, but as long as the object's essence remains the same, we continue to regard its identity as unchanged.

The essence of a person has been a hot philosophical topic through the ages. A person can go through major changes: plastic surgery, sex change, name change, etc. but it's hard to imagine a change so dramatic that we would regard the person as an entirely new individual.

In the case of associative stores we don't need to get that philosophical. If we represent associative stores as type-tagged alists:

```
ASTORE ::= ('astore ASSOCIATION ...)
```

then the type tag functions as the essence of the accompanying association list. Even after all of the associations have been erased from an associative store, its type tag remains. We can express this as a Scheme predicate:

```
(define (empty-astore? astore) (null? (cdr astore)))
```

Implement the read, write, and erase procedures described earlier.

Problem 7.4. Hashing

Our implementation of associative stores is terribly inefficient. Each operation traverses the list of associations comparing keys. If an associative store contains n elements, then all three operations require $O(n)$ steps to perform.

A more efficient strategy is to represent an associative store as a **hash table**. A hash table is a vector of associative stores called **buckets**.

```
HASH ::= #(BUCKET ...)
BUCKET ::= (bucket ASSOCIATION ...)
```

Accessing buckets in a hash table depends on a **hash procedure** capable of decoding keys into hash table indices:

```
(define (hash key) ...) ; returns index of a bucket
```

The basic idea is that the ith bucket will be relatively short, containing only associations of the form (key . storable), where (hash key) equals i. If the hash procedure evenly distributes its outputs, all of the buckets will have approximately the same length. Thus, if there are c buckets, then each bucket will have length approximately n/c where n is the total number of associations stored.

Define read, write, and erase procedures for buckets. These procedures are identical to the procedures defined in the previous problem; only the names have been changed:

```
(define (read-bucket bucket key) ???)
(define (erase-bucket! bucket key) ???)
(define (write-bucket! bucket key storable) ???)
```

Next, fix a size for our hash table:

```
(define capacity 64) ; = # of buckets
```

Use make-vector to construct an associative store represented as a hash table:

```
(define (make-astore)
   (make-vector capacity (make-bucket)))
```

To read an entry from a hash table we first use the hash procedure to compute the appropriate bucket; then we call the read-bucket procedure to search the bucket:

```
(define (read-assv astore key)
   (define bucket (vector-ref astore (hash key)))
   (read-bucket bucket key))
```

Following this style, implement the following procedures so that their behavior matches the specifications given in the previous problem:

a. `(define (erase-assv! astore key) ???)`
b. `(define (write-assv! astore key storable) ???)`

To finish, implement a hash procedure that converts symbols to integers below capacity.

```
(define (hash symbol) ???) ; = int < capacity
```

Your procedure should do a good job of evenly distributing its outputs. (Hint: Try coercing the symbol to a string to a list of characters, then change this list of characters into a list of ASCII codes. Now combine the ASCII codes in some creative way.)

Problem 7.5. LIFO Stores

A LIFO store (Last In First Out) is called a **stack**. Only the last item stored in a stack can be read or erased from the stack. The basic stack operations are:

```
(push! stack val) =
   an unspecified value. As a side effect, val is added to
   stack.
```

```
(top stack) =
   the last item added to the stack. The item is not
   removed.
```

```
(pop! stack)   =
   an unspecified value. As a side effect, the last item
   added to the stack is removed.
```

```
(empty-stack? stack)
   = #t if stack is empty,
   = #f, otherwise
```

```
(make-stack)   = a new empty stack.
```

Implement a stack ADT with these operations.

Problem 7.6. FIFO Stores

FIFO stores (First In First Out) are called **queues**. Only the item that has been in the store longest can be read or erased. The basic queue operations are:

```
(enqueue! queue val) =
    an unspecified value. As a side effect, val is stored in
    queue.

(dequeue! queue)  =
    an unspecified value. As a side effect the item stored
    longest in queue is removed.

(front queue)  =
    the item stored longest in queue. The item is not
    removed.

(empty-queue? queue)
    = #t if queue is empty,
    = #f, otherwise

(make-queue)   = a new empty queue.
```

Implement a queue ADT with these operations.

Hint: A queue can be represented as a list of storable values together with a pair of the form (FRONT . REAR). The car of the pair contains a pointer to the first item in the list, and the cdr contains a pointer to the last item in the list.

Problem 7.7.

Develop an object-oriented implementation of bank accounts.

Problem 7.8. Improved Cell Allocation

Every time a Scheme constructor (cons, list, vector, string, make-string, make-vector) is called, the procedure alloc-locs! must be called to allocate the cells needed to hold the constructed sequence. For this reason it is important that alloc-locs! be as efficient as possible. Unfortunately, our implementation of alloc-locs! is not efficient. Each time cells are needed, the entire store is searched for a sufficiently large block. This may not seem too inefficient when the store consists of eight cells, as in our example, but a more realistic store might consist of thousands of cells.

We can improve our implementation of alloc-locs! by maintaining a list of **block descriptors**. A block descriptor is a pair consisting of the starting location and size of a free block in the store. We call this the **free list**. A free list must be part of every store:

```
STORE ::= (FREE-LIST . #(STORABLE ...))
FREE-LIST ::= (BLOCK-DESCRIPTOR ...)
BLOCK-DESCRIPTOR ::= (SIZE . LOCATION)
SIZE ::= NATURAL
```

Assuming this definition of STORE, reimplement the following basic store operations so they operate on (cdr store) instead of directly on store:

`display-store, access-loc and update-loc!`

Reimplement make-store. The initial free list should consist of a single block descriptor: (capacity . (loc . 0)).

Now reimplement alloc-locs!. Instead of searching the entire store, alloc-locs! searches the free list (i.e., (car store)) until it finds a sufficiently large block. After allocating the number of cells needed from the free block, alloc-locs! modifies the block descriptor so that it describes the block of remaining free cells (if there are any). For example, assume (alloc-locs! 50) is called, and assume (75 . (loc . 42)) is the first block descriptor on the free list with size ≥ 50. Then this block descriptor must be modified to: (25 . (loc . 92)).

Finally, modify gc!. The main complication is that sweep! must form a new free list.

Test your code on a store of 64 cells.

P   lem 7.9. Best Fit versus First Fit

There are several variations on the alloc-locs! algorithm in the last exercise. The variation presented is called the **first fit algorithm** because alloc-locs! searches the free list until it finds the first block of cells large enough to accommodate the requested number of cells. Unfortunately, this algorithm quickly leads to **fragmentation**, a situation in which the free blocks become so small that subsequent requests for multiple cells fail. (Why?)

The **best fit algorithm** searches the free list for the *smallest* block of cells large enough to accommodate the requested number of cells. This algorithm can be implemented by always insuring that the free list is sorted from small to large blocks. This means that each time a new block descriptor is created (for example, by sweep! or alloc-locs!), it must be carefully inserted into the free list to maintain the ordering property. Of course, this means these procedures will be less efficient than their first fit counterparts. (Why?) Reimplement sweep! and alloc-locs! to implement the best fit algorithm.

Problem 7.10. Fragmentation

We can correct fragmentation by **compacting**. Compacting involves moving all free blocks to the top of the store, where they form one giant free block. Of course, the variables they displace must be relocated to the bottom of the store. This is difficult because the locations of these blocks are bound to symbols in the active environments. One way around this difficulty is to introduce a secondary store that holds references to the primary store. Symbols in active environments are bound to locations in the reference store, where the actual references reside. Each time a variable is moved, we only need to change the reference store to reflect its new location.

Reimplement the definition of store and all store operations to accommodate the compactification algorithm. Implement compactification. Compactification should be called each time alloc-locs! fails immediately after a garbage collection.

Problem 7.11. Stores in Functional Scheme

Our implementation of stores is given in imperative Scheme because update-loc!, alloc-loc!, dealloc-loc!, etc. use Scheme's vector-set! command to modify the store. Pedagogically this is both good and bad. It is good because it gives us plenty of practice using commands (vector-set!) to model stores and commands. It is bad because if a person (or computer) truly didn't understand how stores and commands work, our model would be useless because it assumes an understanding of how the vector-set! command works.

Reimplement all of the store procedures here in functional Scheme. In this implementation there won't be a single global store; instead there will be many stores. In fact, a new store is created each time a store is modified by a command. This being the case, it will be inefficient to represent stores as vectors. Instead, represent stores as alists:

```
STORE ::= (CELL ... )
CELL ::= (LOCATION . STORABLE)
```

Problem 7.12.

Assume file is a string naming a file. Implement:

```
(list->file vals file)  = 'done. Writes each value in vals
     on a line in file
```

Problem 7.13.

Assume file is a string naming a file. Implement:

```
(vowel-count file)   =
     a list of pairs of the form (a . n) where n = the number
     of upper or lower case #\a characters in file.
```

Problem 7.14. Depth First Search

A labeled tree allows each node (parent or leaf) to be labeled by a nonlist. We can represent labeled trees as nested list if we agree that the car of the list is the label of the root.

For example, the labeled tree in Figure 7.14 can be represented by the list $(a\ (b\ (e\ f))$ $(c\ (g\ h))\ (d\ (i\ j)))$.

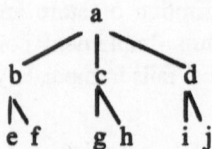

Figure 7.14

Often, we need to search a labeled tree for a particular label. The **depth first search** algorithm searches each branch from left to right. It works by maintaining a stack of nodes. When a node is visited for the first time, it is pushed on the stack. When a node is visited for the last time it is popped off the stack. Implement depth first search using the stack operations implemented earlier.

Problem 7.15. Breadth-First Search

Breadth first search of a labeled tree visits each level of the tree from top to bottom. It works by maintaining a queue of visited nodes. It begins by adding the root node to an empty queue. Thereafter, it removes the front item from the queue, checks it to see if its label is the one being searched for, then enqueues the children. Implement breadth first search.

8
Expressions as Values

Sick of philosophical debates deteriorating into shouting matches, the philosopher-mathematician Gottfried Leibniz (1646-1716) wondered why philosophy couldn't be more objective, like science and mathematics. He then hit upon an idea that would inspire thinkers for centuries to follow: What if philosophical propositions could be proved or refuted by procedures that manipulated them as pure symbolic data:

> If we had it we should be able to reason in metaphysics and morals in much the same way as geometry and analysis. If controversies were to arise, there would be no more need of disputation between two philosophers than between two accountants. For it would suffice to take their pencils in their hands, to sit down to their slates, and to say to each other (with a friend as witness, if they liked): Let us calculate.

This was an early articulation of the expressions-as-data idea. It eventually led to mathematical logic, stored program computers, artificial intelligence, and meta-programming.

8.1. Macros

We begin with a simple but useful example of meta-programming: macro expanders. A **macro expander** expects an expression as input and returns a new "expanded" expression as output. The Scheme macro facility allows programmers to associate macro expanders with certain types of expressions. When the interpreter encounters these expressions, it automatically expands them using the associated expander, then evaluates the expanded expression instead (see Figure 8.1).

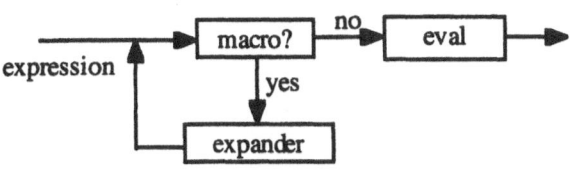

Figure 8.1

8.1.1. While Structures

As a simple example, let's add a while structure to Scheme. The syntax of a while structure is:

```
WHILE ::= (while EXPRESSION EXPRESSION ...)
```

The first expression is called the while-condition; the remaining expressions are the while-body. While structures are iterative expressions, like the do-loops encountered in Chapter 5. The while-condition is evaluated. If it isn't false, then the while-body is evaluated from left to right, and the process repeats. If the while-condition is false, then #f is returned. Presumably, the expressions appearing in the while body produce cumulative side effects.

How does a while structure stop repeating? It may not. However, if the while-body contains a command that updates a variable the while-condition depends on, then eventually the while-condition may be false.

Here's an imperative-style procedure that uses a while structure to compute n factorial:

```
; = (* n ... 1), C-style!
(define (fact n)
   (define result 1)
   (while (< 0 n)
      (set! result (* n result))
      (set! n (- n 1)))
   result)
```

The macro expander for while structures uses the quasi quote (backquote) operator introduced in the problem section of Chapter 1. Recall that like the quote operator, the expression behind a backquote is unevaluated unless unquoted by a comma. For example, assume the following definitions have been made:

```
(define a 100)
(define b 200)
(define c 300)
```

Study the following transcript:

```
> `(a b c)
(a b c)
> `(a b ,c)
(a b 300)
> `(,a ,b c)
(100 200 c)
```

Notice that in the second and third expressions unquoted components of the list were evaluated.

We use the comma operator to insert the while-condition into a do-loop:

```
; while-exp = (while condition body)
(define (while-expander while-exp)
   (define condition (cadr while-exp))
   (define body (cddr while-exp))
   (append `(do () ((not ,condition) #f)) body))
```

Here's a simple test of while-expander:

```
> (while-expander '(while (< 0 n) (set! n (- n 1))))
(do () ((not (< 0 n)) #f) (set! n (- n 1)))
```

How do we associate while-expander with while structures? Scheme's **define-syntax** procedure (PC Scheme calls it **macro**) installs a binding between while and while-expander in a structure table that's consulted by the interpreter each time it reads an expression:

```
(define-syntax while while-expander)
```

8.1.2. Lazy Procedures

Lazy procedures were introduced in Appendix 6.1 as a way to avoid eagerly evaluating operands unless they are needed. The basic idea is to assume that all operands are promises that must be explicitly forced if, when, and where they are needed. For example, the lazy-switch procedure only forces one of its case parameters:

```
(define (lazy-switch key case1 case2 case3)
   (define key-val (force key))
   (cond ((< key-val 0) (force case1))
         ((even? key-val) (force case2))
         (else (force case2))))
```

The problem with lazy procedures is that poor users must explicitly delay all operands each time they call them:

```
(lazy-switch
   (delay x)
   (delay (exp 500))
   (delay (fact 40))
   (delay 100))
```

Using macros, we can hide this complexity from users. First, we define an expander that automatically delays the operands:

```
; exp = (switch key case1 case2 case3)
(define (switch-expander exp)
   (define key (cadr exp))
   (define case1 (caddr exp))
   (define case2 (cadddr exp))
```

```
(define case3 (caddddr exp))
 (lazy-switch (delay ,key)
              (delay , case1)
              (delay ,case2)
              (delay ,case3)))
```

Next, we install switch-expander as a macro expander associated with the name switch:

```
(define-syntax switch switch-expander)
```

Now, when the user calls

```
(switch x (exp 500) (fact 40) 100)
```

this expression automatically expands into the expression:

```
(lazy-switch
   (delay x)
   (delay (exp 500))
   (delay (fact 40))
   (delay 100))
```

3. Implementing Streams

As a final example, recall the definition of stream presented in Chapter 6.

```
STREAM ::= $() | (VALUE . {STREAM})
```

where {STREAM} represents a promise to compute the tail of the stream if and when it's needed. Not all implementations of Scheme provide streams, but we can easily implement our own. If we interpret the empty stream as the empty list, then we can make the following identifications:

```
(define the-empty-stream '())
(define empty-stream? null?)
(define head car)
```

Unlike lists, the cdr of a stream is a promise that must be forced when the tail of the stream is needed:

```
(define (tail stream) (force (cdr stream)))
```

The only problem left is cons-stream. We could try to delay the second input and then use cons:

```
(define (cons-stream head tail)
   (cons head (delay tail)))
```

Unfortunately, this doesn't work. Because cons-stream is an ordinary programmer-defined procedure, eager evaluation will completely evaluate the second input before we have a chance to turn it into a promise. Instead, the application:

```
(cons-stream head tail)
```

needs to be expanded into the expression:

```
(cons head (delay tail))
```

before eager evaluation begins. This is a perfect application for macros. The macro expander performs the necessary conversion:

```
; exp = (cons-stream head tail)
(define (cons-stream-expander exp)
   (define head (cadr exp))
   (define tail (caddr exp))
   `(cons ,head (delay ,tail)))
```

Finally, the "expander = cons-stream" binding is installed using define-syntax:

```
(define-syntax cons-stream cons-stream-expander)
```

8.2.   Semantic Prototyping

We can use EBNF rules to formally specify the syntax of a programming language —i.e., the domain of all legal programs —but how do we specify the semantics of a programming language? How do we specify the behavior of a legal program?

Until now, we have been relying on informal descriptions of evaluation algorithms, environments, and stores. This is fine for beginners, but as experience with a language is gained, subtle ambiguities arise that are unresolved by informal descriptions. For this reason, a formal specification of semantics is required. Often this specification takes the form of a machine-independent interpreter for the language.

Philosophers, linguists, and mathematicians use the term **meta-language** to refer to any language used to describe another language. In this context, the language being described is referred to as the **object language**. So far, the meta-language used in this text has been English (with a little EBNF notation thrown in), and the object languages have been the various fragments of Scheme we have studied. If we are to give a formal specification of Scheme, we will need a formal meta-language.

This can lead to a sticky philosophical problem: Will we be required to give a formal specification of our meta-language? If so, will this entail the need for a meta-meta-language and a formal specification of it? If we aren't careful, we will be led into an infinite regress of formal specifications!

Our way out of this problem is to choose a meta-language that is simple enough that an intuitive understanding of its semantics will be sufficient. Because we already have such an understanding of functional Scheme, we choose it as our meta-language. Our plan is to build interpreters for two object languages that resemble the fragments of Scheme we have been studying. We call these languages Alpha and Beta. Informally, we can characterize these languages as follows:

> Alpha = functional Scheme – some redundant features
> Beta = imperative Scheme – some redundant features

Although our interpreters will run, they won't be particularly efficient. That's okay; their purpose is to specify semantics, not to efficiently execute programs. Still, the ability to execute programs has an advantage. If we are considering a commercial interpreter for either of these languages, we can use our inefficient interpreters as prototypes. For this reason the technique of building interpreters to specify semantics is called **semantic prototyping**.

8.3. Alpha

The Alpha language is similar to functional Scheme without some redundant features.

8.3.1. Alpha Values and Phrases

The values produced by Alpha expressions are numbers, Booleans, procedures, the empty list, and pairs:

```
VALUE ::=
    NUMBER | BOOLE | PROCEDURE | () | (VALUE . VALUE)
```

There are two types of phrases Alpha users can enter: definitions and expressions:

```
PHRASE ::= DEFINITION | EXPRESSION
```

An Alpha definition has exactly the same format as a Scheme definition:

```
DEFINITION ::= (define NAME EXPRESSION)
```

We will need a predicate to determine if a phrase (or any value) is a definition:

```
(define (definition? phrase)
    (and (pair? phrase) (eqv? (car phrase) 'define)))
```

After a definition has been made, we will need to extract the name and expression. For efficiency, we dispense with input validation and introduce these selectors as synonyms for Scheme's cadr and caddr:

```
(define def-name cadr)
(define def-exp caddr)
```

As in Scheme, value-producing algorithms are described in Alpha by one of four types of expressions—literals, names, applications, or structures:

```
EXPRESSION ::=
    LITERAL | NAME | STRUCTURE | APPLICATION
```

As in the case of definitions, we will need a predicate to determine if an arbitrary phrase is an expression:

```
(define (expression? phrase)
   (or (literal? phrase)
       (name? phrase)
       (structure? phrase)
       (application? phrase)))
```

It makes sense to think of the domain of legal Alpha expressions as a Scheme abstract data type. Toward this end we introduce predicates for distinguishing the different types of expressions and selectors for dissecting out the components of an expression. We could also introduce Alpha expression constructors, but this isn't necessary because users will type Alpha expressions directly into the Alpha interpreter.

Recognizers and Selectors for Names and Literals

Any Scheme symbol is an Alpha name:

```
(define name? symbol?) ; NAME ::= SYMBOL
```

Alpha literals include numbers, Booleans, or any printable Alpha value preceded by a single quote.

```
LITERAL ::= NUMBER | BOOLE | 'VALUE
```

```
(define (literal? exp)
   (or (number? exp)
       (boolean? exp)
       (quoted? exp)))
```

When a user enters an expression like '5, the Scheme read procedure produces the expression (quote 5). We can use this fact to recognize quoted literals:

```
(define (quoted? exp)
   (and (pair? exp) (eqv? (car exp) 'quote)))
```

We can use Scheme's cadr to extract the value from a quote:

```
(define rem-quote cadr)
```

Recognizers and Selectors for Structures and Applications

We begin with a modest collection of structures:

```
STRUCTURE ::= IF | LAMBDA | DELAY | AND | OR
```

All structures are lists beginning with characteristic reserved words; hence we can test if an arbitrary expression is a structure merely by testing if it's a pair, and then determining if the first entry in the list belongs to a list of reserved words:

```
define (structure? exp)
   (and (pair? exp) (memv (car exp) structures)))))
```

where

```
(define structures '(lambda if and or))
```

Like its Scheme counterpart, an Alpha if-structure consists of a condition, a consequent, and an optional alternative expression:

```
IF ::= (if EXPRESSION EXPRESSION [EXPRESSION])
```

Without input validation, we can identify the condition and consequent selectors with Scheme's cadr and caddr:

```
(define condition cadr)
(define consequent caddr)
```

Because the alternative of an if-structure is optional, we need to first check to make sure it is present before applying Scheme's cadddr to extract it. If it's not present, our selector merely returns #f:

```
(define (alternative if-exp)
   (if (null? (cdddr if-exp))
       #f
       (cadddr if-exp)))
```

Alpha's lambda-structure is similar to Scheme's, except that only single expressions can appear in the body:

```
LAMBDA ::= (lambda (NAME ...) EXPRESSION)
```

The parameters selector returns the list of parameters. The body selector returns the expression part of the lambda-structure. Without input validation these, too, can be identified with Scheme's cadr and caddr:

```
(define parameters cadr)
(define body caddr)
```

Applications, and-structures, and or-structures are identical to their Scheme counterparts:

```
APPLICATION ::= (EXPRESSION EXPRESSION ...)
AND ::= (and EXPRESSION ...)
OR ::= (or EXPRESSION ...)
```

The operator of an application or structure is the car of the expression. The operands is the list formed by dropping the operator. In other words, the cdr of the expression:

```
(define operator car)
(define operands cdr)
```

For now we will recognize any list as an application. This is very dangerous because structures are lists but are not considered applications. Our plan is to call the application? predicate only after the structure? predicate has failed:

```
(define application? list?) ; dangerous
```

Reserved Words

As a first step to prevent users from redefining reserved words, we introduce a predicate that determines if a name is reserved:

```
(define (reserved? name)
   (memv name reserved-words)))
```

where

```
(define reserved-words
   (append structures
           imported-names
           '(q quit quote promise define)))
```

8.3.2. The Alpha Control Loop

The Alpha control loop perpetually prompts the user for an input phrase, then reads the next phrase typed. If the phrase is a quit command, the control loop terminates; if the phrase is a definition, the resolve procedure creates a binding and adds it to the global environment; if the phrase is an expression, its value is computed by the evaluate procedure, then displayed; otherwise an unrecognized-phrase error is displayed:

```
(define (control-loop env)
   (call-with-current-continuation receiver)
   (let ((phrase (get-phrase)))
      (cond ((quit? phrase) 'bye)
            ((definition? phrase) ...)
            ((expression? phrase) ...)
            (else ...))))
```

The control loop's parameter is the current global environment, env. In each case the ellipsis "..." involves displaying a value, token, or error message using writeln, then a tail-recursive call to control-loop. In the definition clause, the recursive call is passed the environment with the newly created binding added.

Notice the current continuation is captured at the top of the control loop and passed to receiver. Recall from Chapter 3 that receiver assigns its input to the return procedure:

```
(define (return val) val) ; for now

; reassign return to be the current continuation:
(define (receiver cont) (set! return cont))
```

Recall that the error procedure defined in Chapter 3 prints an error message, then calls the return procedure:

```
(define (error gripe source . irritants)
   ... ; display error message
   (return error-token))
```

If the return procedure has been redefined as a continuation, it abandons its caller, error, and resumes the computation represented by this continuation. The continuation given eralier, captured at the top of the control loop, represents the start of the last cycle through the control loop. Thus, if errors are discovered deep inside a complicated expression, we can call error and return control to the point in time just before the troublesome expression was entered.

The get-phrase procedure merely displays a prompt, and returns the next phrase typed on the keyboard:

```
(define (get-phrase)
   (display alpha-prompt)
   (read))
```

where

```
(define alpha-prompt "Alpha> ")
```

Here's the complete code for the Alpha control loop:

```
(define (control-loop env)

   ; return errors here
   (call-with-current-continuation receiver)

   (let ((phrase (get-phrase)))
      (cond ((quit? phrase) 'bye)

            ((definition? phrase)
               (let ((new-env (resolve phrase env)))
                  (writeln 'done)
                  (control-loop new-env)))

            ((expression? phrase)
               (let ((val (evaluate phrase env)))
                  (writeln val))
                  control-loop env)))

           (else
            (writeln "Unrecognized phrase: " phrase)
            (control-loop env)))))
```

The Global Environment

To start the control loop we pass it the initial global environment:

```
(define (start-alpha)
    (writeln "Type q to quit")
    (control-loop global-env))
```

An environment can be represented as a list of frames:

```
ENVIRONMENT ::= (FRAME ...)
```

A frame is merely an association list. In this context we call the associations **bindings**:

```
FRAME ::= (BINDING ...)
```

A binding is a pair consisting of a name (i.e., a symbol) and an Alpha value:

```
BINDING ::= (NAME . VALUE)
```

The global environment is a list containing a single frame, which initially holds bindings of names to imported Scheme procedures. We can use the map procedure to form this initial frame:

```
(define global-env
    (list
        (map cons imported-names imported-procs)))
```

Imported procedures (also called **native procedures**) are those defined in Scheme, which can be called as primitive procedures in Alpha. These typically include primitive Scheme procedures for manipulating numbers, pairs, and Booleans, but in theory they could also include user-defined Scheme procedures:

```
(define imported-names
    '(+ * - / < <= > >= = not null?
       car cdr cons pair? eq? equal?))

(define imported-procs
    (list + * - / < <= > >= = not null?
        car cdr cons pair? eq? equal?))
```

8.3.3. The Alpha Declaration Resolver

Recall that the format of an Alpha definition is:

```
DEFINITION ::= (define NAME EXPRESSION)
```

After determining the name inside its definition input (def) isn't a reserved word, the Alpha definition resolver calls evaluate (defined soon) to compute the value produced by the expression inside def, binds this value to its new name, and then returns the environment gotten by adding this new binding to the first frame in the current environment:

```
(define (resolve def env)
   (define name (def-name def))
   (if (reserved? name)
       (error "can't redefine a reserved word"
              resolve
              name)
       (let* ((exp (def-exp def))
              (val (evaluate exp env name)))
          (install-binding name val env))))
```

If there is one, install-binding extracts the first frame in its environment input, env, calls the put procedure defined in Chapter 6 to actually create the binding and place it into this frame, and then uses cons to replace the new frame in front of the tail of env:

```
(define (install-binding symbol val env)
   (if (null? env)
       (error "empty environment" install-binding)
       (let ((frame (car env)))
          (cons (put symbol val frame) (cdr env)))))
```

8.3.4. The Alpha Expression Evaluator

The Alpha evaluator determines the type of its expression input, then calls the appropriate specialized evaluator. The evaluator requires an environment input to determine the values of names occurring in its expression input. The optional parameter is only used by the definition resolver to pass the name together with the body of a definition to evaluate. More on this later.

```
(define (evaluate exp env . options)

   ; extract the optional parameter
   (define name
      (if (null? options)
          'anonymous
          (car options)))

   (cond ((literal? exp) (eval-lit exp env))
         ((name? exp) (eval-name exp env))
         ((structure? exp)
            (eval-structure exp env name))
         ((application? exp) (eval-apply exp env))
         (else (error "unrecognized expression"
                      evaluate
                      exp))))
```

Evaluating Literals and Names

The value of a simple literal is itself. The value of a quoted literal is gotten by simply removing the quote:

```
(define (eval-lit exp env)
   (if (quoted? exp)
       (rem-quote exp)
       exp)
```

We search the environment to determine the values of names:

```
(define (eval-name exp env)
   (search-env exp env))
```

Using the get procedure defined in Chapter 6, the search-env procedure searches each frame until either a value is found or until there are no more frames. In the first case the value is returned; in the second case an undefined-symbol error is raised.

```
(define (search-env symbol env)
   (if (null? env)
       (error "undefined symbol" search-env symbol)
       (let* ((frame (car env))
              (val (get symbol frame)))
         (if (eqv? val fail)
             (search-env symbol (cdr env))
             val)))))
```

Evaluating Structures

Structures are evaluated by still more specialized evaluators called from eval-structure:

```
(define (eval-structure exp env name)

   (define proc (operator exp))

   (case proc
     ((lambda) (eval-lambda exp env name))
     ((if) (eval-if exp env))
     ((and) (eval-and exp env))
     ((or) (eval-or exp env))
     (else (error   "unrecognized structure"
                    eval-structure
                    proc)))))
```

Short Circuit Evaluation

Recall the definition of short circuit evaluation from Chapter 3:

Evaluate operands from left to right until a return value is determined.

Two variants of short circuit evaluation are implemented by tail-recursive procedures inside eval-and and eval-or. Inside eval-and we assume the value is true until we either run out of operands or find an operand that evaluates to #f:

```
(define (eval-and exp env)

   (define (tail-eval result exps)
      (if (or (not result) (null? exps))
          result
          (tail-eval (evaluate (car exps) env)
                     (cdr exps))))

   (tail-eval #t (operands exp)))
```

Inside eval-or we assume the value is false until we either run out of operands, or encounter an operand that evaluates to anything but #f:

```
(define (eval-or exp env)

   (define (tail-eval result exps)
      (if (or result (null? exps))
          result
          (tail-eval (evaluate (car exps) env)
                     (cdr exps))))

   (tail-eval #f (operands exp)))
```

Conditional Evaluation

Conditional evaluation in Alpha simply reduces to conditional evaluation in Scheme:

```
(define (eval-if exp env)
   (if (evaluate (condition exp) env)
       (evaluate (consequent exp) env)
       (evaluate (alternative exp) env)))
```

Evaluating Lambda

Evaluating a lambda expression produces a representation of an Alpha procedure. We choose to represent this Alpha procedure by a related Scheme procedure. This procedure is created inside eval-lambda, where it is called meta-proc, and is returned as the value of eval-lambda:

```
(define (eval-lambda ...)
   (define (meta-proc ...) ...)
   meta-proc)
```

The meta-proc procedure expects a list of actual values as input (these will be provided by eval-apply, defined soon). It forms a temporary frame consisting of the parameters (these can be found inside the lambda expression) and the arguments. This temporary frame is placed at the head of the evaluating environment to form a temporary environment, then the body of the lambda expression is evaluated relative to this temporary environment:

```
(define (eval-lambda lambda-exp env name)

   ; extract components
   (define params (parameters lambda-exp))
   (define exp (body lambda-exp))

   (define (meta-proc . args)
      (define temp-frame (map cons params args))
      (define eval-env ???) ; see below
      (define temp-env (cons temp-frame eval-env))
      (evaluate exp temp-env))

   meta-proc)
```

Implementing the Static and Dynamic Scope Rules

Our strategy has two problems. The first is how to define the evaluating environment, eval-env. The best idea is simply to use env, the environment parameter passed to eval-lambda:

```
(define eval-env env)
```

Because lambda is used to define procedures, env represents the define-time environment, hence this approach implements the static scope rule discussed in Chapter 4.

The dynamic scope rule requires us to evaluate exp, the body of the lambda expression, relative to the calling environment. Because we don't know the calling environment at define time, like the argument list, args, it will have to be passed to meta-proc by eval-apply:

```
(define (meta-proc call-env . args)
      (define temp-frame (map cons params args))
      (define eval-env call-env)
      (define temp-env (cons temp-frame eval-env))
      (evaluate exp temp-env))
```

We can implement both the static and dynamic scope rules and let users decide which rule to use by toggling a global flag:

```
(define static-enabled #t) ; #t = static scope rule
                           ; #f = dynamic scope rule
```

Here's the newest version of meta-proc:

```
(define (meta-proc call-env . args)
   (define temp-frame (map cons params args))
   (define eval-env
```

```
        (if static-enabled env call-env))
   (define temp-env (cons temp-frame eval-env))
   (evaluate exp temp-env))
```

The Environment Obsolescence Problem

The second problem is that when the static scope rule is used, the define-time environment, env, is hard-wired into meta-proc, but because environments are nonmutable objects in functional Scheme (all values are), subsequent changes to the global environment don't show up in env. This is called the environment obsolescence problem, and it can't be completely solved in functional Scheme.

For example, suppose we make the following definitions in Alpha:

```
Alpha> (define x 100)
done
Alpha> (define add-x (lambda (y) (+ x y)))
done
Alpha> (add-x 42)
142
Alpha> (define x 200)
done
Alpha> (add-x 42)
142
```

Notice the second call to add-x produced the same result as the first call, 142. Apparently, add-x didn't pick up the change made to x in the global environment.

The usual approach when faced with an anomaly like this is to claim it as a feature. We could almost get away with this, except the worst consequence of the Environment Obsolescence Problem occurs when we attempt to define recursive procedures. For example, consider what happens when we try to define the recursive factorial procedure in Alpha:

```
(define fact
   (lambda (n)
      (if (= n 0)
          1
          (* n (fact (- n 1)))))))
```

The definition resolver calls evaluate to determine the value of the lambda expression. Evaluate calls eval-lambda, which returns meta-proc with env hard-wired inside. Subsequently the binding (fact . meta-proc) is created and installed in the global environment. Because this addition occurs after the creation of meta-proc, the new binding for fact is not present in the now-obsolete env. Consequently, when (fact 3) is called, meta-proc attempts to evaluate (fact 2) relative to env. But because fact is not bound inside env, an undefined-name error occurs.

We can overcome this problem if eval-lambda knows the name of the procedure it is creating. Because only the resolve procedure knows this name, it is up to resolve to pass the name to evaluate, which passes the name along to eval-lambda. Meta-proc can now install a binding of itself to its name in the evaluating environment:

```
(define (meta-proc call-env . args)
   (define temp-frame (map cons params args))
   (define eval-env
      (if static
           (install-binding name meta-proc env)
           call-env))
   (define temp-env (cons temp-frame eval-env))
   (evaluate exp temp-env))
```

In a weird way this makes meta-proc a recursive procedure. Here's the final definition of eval-lambda:

```
(define (eval-lambda lambda-exp env name)

   ; extract components
   (define params (parameters lambda-exp))
   (define exp (body lambda-exp))

   (define (meta-proc call-env . args)

      (define temp-frame (map cons params args))
      (define eval-env
         (if static-enabled
              (install-binding name meta-proc env)
              call-env))
      (define temp-env (cons temp-frame eval-env))

      (evaluate exp temp-env))

   meta-proc)
```

Evaluating Applications

Unlike the Scheme interpreter, the Alpha interpreter supports both eager and delayed evaluation of procedure applications. The method used is controlled by a global flag, which can be toggled before the Alpha interpreter is started:

```
(define eager-enabled #t) ; #t = eager evaluation
                          ; #f = lazy evaluation
```

The application evaluator recursively evaluates the operator of app, its application input:

```
(define proc (evaluate (operator app) env))
```

There are two possibilities: either proc is an imported procedure or proc is a user-defined procedure. If proc is user-defined, then it has the form of a meta-proc created inside a call to eval-lambda.

If eager evaluation is enabled or if proc is an imported procedure, eval-apply eagerly evaluates the list of the application's operands by mapping evaluate, with its environment input fixed, across the operands list:

```
(define inputs (operands app))
(define (eval-in-env e) (evaluate e env))
(define args (map eval-in-env inputs))
```

In case eager evaluation is disabled and proc is not imported, eval-apply lazily converts its operands into promises that will be forced by proc on an as-needed basis:

```
(define inputs (operands app))
(define (delay-in-env e) (make-promise e env))
(define args (map delay-in-env inputs))
```

The make-promise procedure merely encapsulates the unevaluated expression, e, together with its delaying environment, env, into a type-tagged list[1]:

```
(define (make-promise exp env)
  (list 'promise exp env))
```

If proc is imported, it is applied to args using apply:

```
(apply proc args)
```

If proc is user-defined, we use almost the same strategy, but we attach the calling environment, env, to the front of the argument list in case it's needed inside proc:

```
(apply proc (cons env args))
```

Here's the complete code for eval-apply:

```
(define (eval-apply app env)

    ; extract components
    (define proc (evaluate (operator app) env))
    (define inputs (operands app))

    ; amplifiers for map
    (define (eval-in-env e) (evaluate e env))
    (define (delay-in-env e) (make-promise e env))

    (define args (if (or eager-enabled (imported? proc))
                     (map eval-in-env inputs)
                     (map delay-in-env inputs)))
```

---

[1] *Warning*: Alpha promises aren't memoized.

```
(if (imported? proc)
    (apply proc args)
    (apply proc (cons env args)))))
```

Forcing Promises

To make lazy evaluation work, we need to automatically force Alpha promises as they are encountered. This can be done by modifying eval-name to automatically call eval-promise when it encounters promises bound to parameters:

```
(define (eval-name exp env)
   (define val (search-env exp env))
   (if (promise? val)
       (eval-promise val env)
       val))
```

Recall that a promise has the form:

```
PROMISE ::= (promise EXPRESSION ENVIRONMENT)
```

Let's create a few selectors to hide this representation:

```
(define promise-exp cadr)
(define promise-env caddr)
```

We can use the type tag to identify promises:

```
(define (promise? val)
   (and (pair? val) (eqv? 'promise (car val))))
```

To evaluate a promise, we use promise-exp to extract its expression, and then evaluate this expression relative to some environment, but which environment? The environment parameter passed to eval-promise is the forcing environment. This is different from the delaying environment encapsulated inside the promise. This is the same problem we faced defining the evaluating environment inside meta-proc when we had to choose between the static and dynamic scope rules.

In fact, there are two flavors of lazy evaluation: **call-by-name** requires promises to be forced relative to their delaying environments, while **call-by-text** (very rare) uses the forcing environment. Again, we can give users a choice by creating a global flag:

```
(define call-by-name #t)    ; #t = call-by-name
                            ; #f = call-by-text
```

Here's the definition of eval-promise:

```
(define (eval-promise promise env)
   (if call-by-name
       (evaluate (promise-exp promise)
                 (promise-env promise))
       (evaluate (promise-exp promise) env)
```

8.4.   Beta

The Beta language is similar to imperative Scheme without a few redundant features. More accurately, Beta is Alpha with variables and commands.

8.4.1. Beta Commands

Beta expressions are the same as Alpha expressions, but with four new structures, the set!, set-car!, and set-cdr! commands, and begin expressions used for sequential evaluation:

```
CMMD ::= (SET NAME EXPRESSION)
SET ::= set! | set-car! | set-cdr!
BEGIN ::= (begin EXPRESSION ...)

(define structures
   '(lambda if and or begin set! set-car! set-cdr!))
```

8.4.2. The Beta Control Loop

The differences between Alpha and Beta can be summarized by comparing their control loops. First, the Beta control loop has an extra parameter representing the current store. Second, the resolve procedure returns an environment-store pair rather than a simple environment. Finally, the evaluate procedure returns a value-store pair rather than a simple value.

Environment-store pairs are needed because resolving a declaration produces a new environment and, in the case of a variable declaration, a new store.

Value-store pairs are needed because evaluating an expression produces a value and, in the case of a command, a new store.

```
(define (control-loop env store)

   ; return errors here
   (call-with-current-continuation receiver)

   (let ((phrase (get-phrase)))
      (cond
         ((quit? phrase) 'bye)

         ((definition? phrase)
            (let* ((env1.store1
                     (resolve phrase env store))
                   (env1 (car env1.store1))
```

```
               (store1 (cdr env1.store1)))
          (writeln 'done)
          (control-loop env1 store1)))

   ((expression? phrase)
    (let*  ((val.store1
             (evaluate phrase env store))
            (val (car val.store1))
            (store1 (cdr val.store1)))
        (writeln val)
        (control-loop env store1)))

   (else
      (writeln "unrecognized phrase: " phrase)
      (control-loop env store)))))
```

Starting the control loop requires an initial environment and an initial store:

```
(define mem-cap 1024) ; 1 Kb memory, for now

(define (start-beta)
   (writeln "type q to quit")
   (control-loop global-env (make-store mem-cap)))
```

Of course, Beta needs its own prompt:

```
(define prompt "Beta> ")
```

8.4.3. The Beta Resolver

Like Alpha and Scheme, the format of a Beta definition is:

```
DEFINITION ::= (define NAME EXPRESSION)
```

After determining the name inside its definition input (def) isn't a reserved word, the Beta definition resolver calls evaluate (defined soon) to compute the value-store pair produced by exp, the expression inside def:

```
(let*
    ((val.store1 (evaluate exp env store name)) ...)
```

If val is a procedure (i.e., if exp was a lambda expression), no further modification of store1 is needed. A constant binding between name and val is installed in env to produce a new environment, which is paired with store1 and returned as the result of resolve:

```
(let ((new-env (install-binding name val env)))
   (cons new-env store1))
```

If val isn't a procedure, then we may conclude that def is a variable declaration. In this case memory in store1 will have to be allocated to store val. We assume the implementation of stores given at the end of the last chapter:

```
(let*
    ((ref.store2 (alloc-ref! store1 env val)) ...)
```

Allocating memory returns a reference-store pair. We use ref to write val to memory (this produces a new store), then bind name to ref in a new environment. The new environment is paired with the new store and returned as the result of resolve:

```
(let* ...
        (new-store (write-ref! store2 ref val))
        (new-env (install-binding name ref env)))
    (cons new-env new-store))))))
```

Here's the complete definition of resolve:

```
(define (resolve def env store)

    (define name (def-name def))
    (define exp (def-exp def))

    (if (reserved? name)
        (error "can't redefine a reserved word"
                resolve
                name)
        (let*
            ((val.store1 (evaluate exp env store name))
             (val (car val.store1))
             (store1 (cdr val.store1)))
            (if (procedure? val)
                (let
                    ((new-env
                        (install-binding name val env)))
                    (cons new-env store1))
                (let*
                    ((ref.store2
                        (alloc-ref! store1 env val))
                     (ref (car ref.store2))
                     (store2 (cdr ref.store2))
                     (new-store
                        (write-ref! store2 ref val))
                     (new-env
                        (install-binding name ref env)))
                    (cons new-env new-store))))))
```

8.4.4. The Beta Evaluator

The only change in the Beta evaluator is that each specialized evaluator is passed an extra parameter representing the current store:

```
(define (evaluate exp env store . options)

   (define name
      (if (null? options) 'anonymous (car options)))

   (cond ((literal? exp) (eval-lit exp env store))
         ((name? exp) (eval-name exp env store))
         ((structure? exp)
            (eval-structure exp env store name))
         ((application? exp)
            (eval-apply exp env store))
         (else (error "unrecognized expression"
                      evaluate
                      exp))))
```

Evaluating Literals and Names

Evaluating literals requires one adjustment to its Alpha counterpart; we must remember to return value-store pairs instead of values.

```
(define (eval-lit lit env store)
   (if (quoted? lit)
       (cons (rem-quote lit) store)
       (cons lit store)))
```

Evaluating names also requires the return of a value-store pair. Also, references are automatically dereferenced. This means that when a reference is encountered, eval-name returns the *R*-value (i.e., the stored value) rather than the *L*-value (i.e., the reference bound to name):

```
(define (eval-name name env store)
   (define val (search-env name env))
   (cond ((promise? val) (eval-promise val env store))
         ((reference? val)
            (cons (read-ref store val) store))
         (else (cons val store))))
```

Evaluating Structures

Aside from four extra cases representing the four new structures, and aside from the additional store parameters, Beta's version of eval-structure is not significantly different from Alpha's version:

```
(define (eval-structure exp env store name)
   (let ((proc (operator exp)))
      (case proc
         ((lambda) (eval-lambda exp env store name))
         ((if) (eval-if exp env store))
         ((and) (eval-and exp env store))
         ((or) (eval-or exp env store))
         ((begin) (eval-begin exp env store))
         ((set! set-car! set-cdr!)
            (execute exp env store))
         (else (error "unrecognized structure"
                      eval-structure
                      proc)))))
```

Executing Commands

Like all Beta expressions, Beta commands (set!, set-car!, and set-cdr!) return value-store pairs. The difference is that for commands, the value component of this pair is uninteresting:

```
(define command-return-value #f) ; for now
```

but the store component contains an updated variable. For pure expressions (i.e., expressions that aren't commands), the opposite is true. The value component is new and interesting, but the store component is unchanged.

Recall the format of a Beta command is:

```
CMMD ::= (SET NAME EXPRESSION)
SET ::= set! | set-car! | set-cdr!
```

Execute first extracts the name and expression (exp) from its command input, then recursively applies evaluate to exp, producing a value-store pair:

```
(define val.store1 (evaluate exp env store))
```

Next, the current environment is searched for the reference bound to name:

```
(define ref (search-env name env))
```

If ref isn't a reference (e.g. if it's a procedure), an error is thrown; otherwise val is written to store at either ref, (car ref), or (cdr ref) depending on if the operator of the input command is set!, set-car!, or set-cdr!. The write produces a new store. The new store is paired with the uninteresting command-return-value and returned as the value of execute:

```
(define (execute cmmd env store)

   (define name (cadr cmmd))
   (define exp (caddr cmmd))
```

```
(define val.store1 (evaluate exp env store))
(define val (car val.store1))
(define store1 (cdr val.store1))

(define ref (search-env name env))

(if (reference? ref)
    (let ((ref1 (case (operator cmmd)
                  ((set-car!) (car ref))
                  ((set-cdr!) (cdr ref))
                  (else ref))) ; = set!
          (store2
            (write-ref! store1 ref1 val)))
      (cons command-return-value store2))
    (error "L-value must be a reference"
           execute
           name)))
```

Conditional Evaluation

We only need to add value-store pairs to Alpha's conditional evaluation algorithm to produce the Beta version:

```
(define (eval-if exp env store)

  (define val.store1
    (evaluate (condition exp) env store))
  (define val (car val.store1))
  (define store1 (cdr val.store1))

  (if val
      (evaluate (consequent exp) env store1)
      (evaluate (alternative exp) env store1)))
```

Short Circuit Evaluation

Short circuit evaluation in Beta is nearly the same as short circuit evaluation in Alpha. The only adjustment is coping with and returning value-store pairs.

```
(define (eval-and exp env store)

  (define (tail-eval result.store exps)
    (let ((store (cdr result.store))
          (result (car result.store)))
      (if (or (not result) (null? exps))
          result.store
```

```
                    (tail-eval
                     (evaluate (car exps) env store)
                     (cdr exps)))))

   (tail-eval (cons #t store) (operands exp)))

(define (eval-or exp env store)

   (define (tail-eval result.store exps)
      (let ((store (cdr result.store))
            (result (car result.store)))
         (if (or result (null? exps))
             result.store
             (tail-eval
                (evaluate (car exps) env store)
                (cdr exps)))))

   (tail-eval (cons #f store) (operands exp)))
```

Notice that the internal tail-eval procedures tail-recursively call themselves with the value-store pair produced by evaluating the next operand in the operands list of the and-expression or or-expression. Thus, any changes to the store made by command operands will be propagated to future operands.

Sequential Evaluation

Evaluating a sequence of expressions contains an idea similar to the one just mentioned. We must propagate any modifications in the store to subsequent expressions. Also, only the last value-store pair in the sequence is returned:

```
(define (eval-begin begin-exp env store)
   (define vals.store1
      (eval-seq (cdr begin-exp) env store))
   (define vals (car vals.store1)) ; vals is a list
   (define store1 (cdr vals.store1))
   (cons (last vals) store1))
```

All of the real work is done by eval-seq. We could have defined it as an internal procedure, but it turns out to have applications in other parts of the Beta evaluator. Unlike other Beta evaluators, eval-seq returns a list-store pair rather than a value-store pair. The list represents the list of values of each expression in the sequence, while the store represents the last store computed:

```
(define (eval-seq exps env store)

   (define (tail-eval vals exps store)
      (if (null? exps)
          (cons vals store)
```

```
      (let* ((val.store1
                (evaluate (car exps) env store))
             (val (car val.store1))
             (store1 (cdr val.store1)))
        (tail-eval
           (cons-last val vals)
           (cdr exps)
           store1)))))

   (tail-eval '() exps store))
```

Evaluating Lambda

Like Alpha procedures, Beta procedures are represented by special Scheme procedures (meta-proc). These procedures are nearly identical to their Alpha counterparts except for the additional parameter representing the calling store. This will be provided when the procedure is called.

```
(define (eval-lambda lambda-exp env store name)
   (define params (parameters lambda-exp))
   (define exp (body lambda-exp))
   ; for dynamic scoping also pass call-env
   (define (meta-proc call-env call-store . args)
      (define temp-frame (make-frame params args))
      (define base-env
         (if static-scope-enabled env call-env))
      (define temp-env
         (cons
            temp-frame
            (install-binding name meta-proc base-env)))
      (evaluate exp temp-env call-store))
   (cons meta-proc store))
```

Evaluating Applications

The operands of a Beta application could involve commands that update the store. Naturally, as each operand is evaluated, the updated store must be propagated to the next operand. This is done using the eval-seq procedure defined earlier. To implement lazy evaluation, delay-seq is applied to the operands:

```
(define (eval-apply app env store)
   (define proc.store1
      (evaluate (operator app) env store))
   (define proc (car proc.store1))
   (define store1 (cdr proc.store1))
   (define args (operands app))
   (if (or (imported? proc) eager-enabled)
```

```
(let*
  ((inputs.store2 (eval-seq args env store1))
   (inputs (car inputs.store2))
   (store2 (cdr inputs.store2)))
  (if (imported? proc)
      (cons (apply proc inputs) store2)
      (apply proc
             (cons env (cons store2 inputs)))))
(let* ((inputs (delay-seq args env store1)))
  (apply proc
         (cons env (cons store1 inputs))))))))
```

Delay Sequence

Like eval-seq, delay-seq uses a tail-recursive internal procedure, tail-delay, to traverse its list of inputs, delaying each entry:

```
(define (delay-seq exps env store)
  (define (tail-delay promises exps store) ...)
  (tail-delay '() exps store))
```

The tail-delay procedure builds a list of promises from a list of expressions. When the expression list is emptied, the corresponding list of promises is returned.

```
(define (tail-delay promises exps store)
  (if (null? exps)
      promises
      (let*
        ((promise (make-promise (car exps) env)))
        (tail-delay
        (cons-last promise promises)
        (cdr exps)
        store))))
```

where cons-last was defined in Chapter 2:

```
(define (cons-last val vals) (append vals (list val)))
```

Forcing Promises

Evaluating a Beta promise is the same as evaluating an Alpha promise except we must remember to pass the additional store argument to evaluate:

```
(define (eval-promise promise env store)
  (if call-by-text
      (evaluate (promise-exp promise) env store)
      (evaluate (promise-exp promise)
                (promise-env promise)
                store)))
```

Appendices

Appendix 8.1. Lambda

We have worked in several fragments of Scheme:

IS = imperative Scheme   = IEEE/ANSI Scheme
FS = functional Scheme   = IS - commands
AS = applicative Scheme   = FS - structures

The surprising expressiveness of these fragments leads us to wonder about the nature of Scheme without any redundant features:

NS = necessary Scheme   = IS - all redundant features

In some of the problems at the ends of Chapters 2 through 6 we saw that many structures, primitive procedures, and primitive data types could be implemented in terms of a few basic elements: apply, lambda, #t, #f, if, cons, car, cdr, null?, pair?, and ().

In this appendix we formalize necessary Scheme as a language called Lambda:

NS = Lambda

Lambda is based on a language called Lambda calculus developed by Alonzo Church, Haskell Curry, and others in the 1930s, before electronic computers were invented. Years later, Lambda calculus served as a model for John McCarthy when he created LISP.

The remarkable thing about Lambda is the absence of any sort of data other than procedures:

```
VALUE ::= PROCEDURE
```

(This shouldn't be too surprising because at some level, the only sort of data manipulated by modern computers are bits.)

Although it can be shown that definitions are redundant, we will allow them in Lambda along with expressions:

```
PHRASE ::= EXPRESSION | DEFINITION
DEFINITION ::= (define NAME EXPRESSION)
```

Names, too, are redundant, but we will allow them along with the only two essential features of Lambda, applications and lambda expressions:

```
EXPRESSION ::= NAME | APPLICATION | LAMBDA
```

We could restrict ourselves exclusively to unary procedures, but we will allow procedures with multiple parameters:

```
LAMBDA ::= (lambda (PARAMETER ...) EXPRESSION)
APPLICATION ::= (EXPRESSION EXPRESSION ...)
```

Adjustments to the Alpha Interpreter

With a few adjustments, we can turn the Alpha interpreter into a Lambda interpreter. Obviously, there will be no imported procedures, so the control loop will be started with an empty environment:

```
(define (start-lambda)
   (writeln "Type q to quit")
   (control-loop '())) ; empty environment!
```

Of course, the prompt needs to be changed:

```
(define prompt "Lambda> ")
```

Lambda is the only structure recognized:

```
(define structures '(lambda))
```

Because we only get to keep one evaluation algorithm, it must be lazy evaluation:

```
(define eager-enabled #f)
```

Lambda has no literals:

```
(define (literal? exp) #f)
```

Because Lambda values are always procedures and because procedures are unprintable in Scheme, it's convenient to modify the control loop so that when possible, it displays the names of procedures rather than the procedure objects themselves:

```
(define (control-loop env)
   ...
   (let (...)
      (cond
         ...
         ((expression? phrase)
          (let ((val (evaluate phrase env)))
             (writeln (val->name val env))
             (control-loop env)))
         ...)))
```

Given a procedure value returned by evaluate, the val->name procedure inverts each frame in the current environment and then searches it for the name bound to this value.

```
(define (val->name val env)
   (if (null? env)
       val ; give up and return the original value
       (let* ((frame (car env))
              (iframe (invert frame))
              (name (get val iframe)))
          (if (eqv? name undefined-symbol)
```

```
          (val->name val (cdr env))
          name))))
```

The definition of invert is left as an exercise.

Lambda Calculus Definitions

What can be accomplished in Lambda? Obviously, we need to represent data using procedures, but unlike object-oriented programming introduced in Chapter 4, which also represented data as procedures, the data we need to represent are basic items such as numbers, Booleans, and pairs.

Booleans

Our choice of representations for true and false may at first seem odd, but they are crucial to all else that follows. True is the procedure that merely returns the first of its two inputs, while false is the procedure that returns the second of its two inputs:

```
(define true (lambda (x y) x))
(define false (lambda (x y) y))
```

Assuming the condition of an if-expression will be either true or false, we can simply apply it to the consequent and alternative. If the condition is false, it returns its second input, the alternative; if it's true, it returns its first input, the consequent:

```
(define if
   (lambda (x y z) (x y z)))
```

Remember, because we are using lazy evaluation, we don't have to worry about eager evaluation needlessly evaluating the alternative or consequent. Lazy evaluation also makes short circuit evaluation unnecessary:

```
(define and
   (lambda (x y)
      (if x y false)))

(define or
   (lambda (x y)
      (if x true y)))

(define not
   (lambda (x)
      (if x false true)))
```

Pairs

We can represent the pair $(x . y)$ as a procedure that given an input z, applies it to x and y:

```
(lambda (z) (z x y))  ; = (x . y)
```

By inputting true or false to this procedure we can extract *x* and *y*.

```
(define cons
    (lambda (x y)
        (lambda (z) (z x y))))
```

```
(define car
    (lambda (pair) (pair true)))
```

```
(define cdr
    (lambda (pair) (pair false)))
```

Natural Numbers

We can use pairs to represent natural numbers. The car of a natural is interpreted as a flag indicating if the number is zero or not. If not, the cdr represents the number's predecessor:

```
NATURAL ::= (true . true) | (false . NATURAL)
```

The pair (true . true) represents zero:

```
(define n0 (cons true true))
```

We use car to test for zero:

```
(define zero?
    (lambda (z) (car z)))
```

Adding one to a number just involves consing false onto it:

```
(define add1
    (lambda (num)
        (cons false num)))
```

Thus,

```
    one   = (false . zero) = (false . (true . true))
    two   = (false . one)
          = (false . (false . (true . true)))
    three = (false . two)
          = (false . (false . (false . (true . true))))
    etc.
```

In essence, the cardinality of a number is the number of nested false flags. Here are definitions of the first ten nonzero naturals:

```
(define n1 (add1 n0))
(define n2 (add1 n1))
(define n3 (add1 n2))
(define n4 (add1 n3))
```

```
(define n5 (add1 n4))
(define n6 (add1 n5))
(define n7 (add1 n6))
(define n8 (add1 n7))
(define n9 (add1 n8))
(define n10 (add1 n9))
```

Subtracting one from a number merely involves using cdr to extract its predecessor. Our convention is that the predecessor of zero is itself. (There are no negative natural numbers.)

```
(define sub1
   (lambda (num)
      (if (zero? num) num (cdr num))))
```

Using add1, sub1, and recursion, we can begin to define addition, multiplication, less-than, equality, and all the other basic arithmetic procedures. Here are two examples:

```
(define +
   (lambda (x y)
      (if (zero? x) y (+ (sub1 x) (add1 y)))))
```

```
(define =
   (lambda (x y)
      (if (and (zero? x) (zero? y))
          true
          (if (or (zero? x) (zero? y))
              false
              (= (sub1 x) (sub1 y))))))
```

After loading these definitions into the Lambda interpreter's prompt, we can conduct some simple tests:

```
Lambda> (sub1 n8)
n7
Lambda> (cdr (cons n9 n3))
n3
Lambda> (+ n3 n2)
#[procedure #x171C8E]
```

Although the result of (+ $n3$ $n2$) is an unprintable procedure physically distinct from $n5$, it is mathematically equivalent to $n5$:

```
Lambda> (= n5 (+ n3 n2))
true
```

Hints for representing integers, rationals, reals, complex numbers, lists, characters, and strings are given in the problem section.

Problems

Problem 8.1.

The while-structure introduced in this chapter is an example of a test-at-top iteration because it evaluates its condition before it evaluates its body. Thus, if the condition is initially false, the body will never be evaluated.

Languages like C and Pascal also provide test-at-bottom structures that first evaluate their bodies, and then their conditions. In Pascal the iteration terminates when the condition becomes true (i.e., unfalse).

Add a test-at-bottom structure to Scheme. The syntax is:

```
UNTIL ::= (until EXPRESSION EXPRESSION ...)
```

The first expression is the condition; the remaining expressions are the body. The expressions in the body are evaluated sequentially. Next, the condition is evaluated. If the condition is false, then the process repeats, otherwise #t is returned.

Use your until-structure to define an imperative version of the triangle procedure specified in Chapter 3.

Problem 8.2.

Recall the definitions of lazy-cube and lazy-small? given in Appendix 6.1. Copying the technique used earlier to define switch, define macro expanders that expand calls to small? and cube into calls to lazy-small? and lazy-cube, respectively. Of course your macro expander should automatically delay operands.

Problem 8.3.

The definitions of cube-expander and small?-expander given earlier were quite similar. It should be possible to write a single procedure called lazy-expander that expands expressions of the form (proc A B C ...) into expressions of the form (lazy-proc (delay A) (delay B) (delay C) ...). Thus, when a programmer wants to create a lazy procedure, foo, he defines the corresponding procedure lazy-foo, and then types:

```
(define-syntax foo lazy-expander)
```

(It doesn't matter if the same expander is bound to multiple macro names.) Implement lazy expander and test it.

Problem 8.4.

Implement lazy procedures that prove:

1. Operands aren't evaluated if they aren't needed.
2. Operands are only evaluated once, even if they are needed several times.

Problem 8.5.

Assume your implementation of Scheme didn't provide force and delay. Implement your own versions, but call them thaw and freeze so they won't conflict with force and delay. Hint: (freeze exp) should expand into a let-expression similar to the one involving (exp 1000) shown earlier.

Problem 8.6.

Add a load-defs command to the Lambda control loop. When a user types (load-defs FILE), the Lambda definitions in File are automatically resolved.

Problem 8.7.

A Lambda integer is a pair consisting of a sign and a natural number:

```
INTEGER ::= (SIGN . NATURAL)
```

We use true to represent positive and false to represent negative.
   Find Lambda implementations of int+ and int=.

Problem 8.8.

A Lambda real is a pair consisting of an integer base and a natural number exponent:

```
REAL ::= (INTEGER . NATURAL)
```

The interpretation of $(a . b)$ is a * 10^{-b}.
   Find Lambda implementations of real+ and real*.

Problem 8.9.

Add let and let* structures to Beta.

Problem 8.10.

Beta lets users choose between using the defining environment or the calling environment when evaluating applications (static-scope-enabled). What arguments would you raise against the idea of giving users the same choice for stores?

Problem 8.11.

Implement a macro facility for Alpha. In addition to the environment, the control loop will need a parameter representing a table of macro expanders and their names.

Problem 8.12.

Add a while structure to Beta similar to the one implemented using macros earlier in the chapter. Of course, Beta doesn't have macros, so it will have to be a new Beta structure. Do not use a do-loop to implement eval-while. Instead, use tail recursion.

Problem 8.13.

Add a cond-structure to Beta.

Problem 8.14.

A file system is an association list of the form:

```
((FILE . SSTORE) ...)
```

where FILE is the string name of a file and SSTORE is a sequential store (see Chapter 7). Add a file system parameter to the Beta control loop. The file system should allow users to open, close, read, and write files.

Problem 8.15.   Static Type Checking

Enhance Alpha's resolve procedure so that it performs static type checking:

```
(define (resolve def env)
   ...
      (let* ((exp (def-exp def))
             (type (get-type exp env)))
         (if (eqv? type 'error-type)
             (error "type error" resolve exp)
             (let ((val (evaluate exp env name)))
               (install-binding
                 name val type env))))))
```

The get-type procedure expects an Alpha expression, exp, and an environment, env, as input and returns a value in the TYPE domain, where

```
TYPE ::= SIMPLE-TYPE | COMPOSITE-TYPE
SIMPLE-TYPE ::= error-type | number | boole | nil-type
COMPOSITE-TYPE ::=
   (pair TYPE TYPE) | (proc TYPE ... TYPE)
```

The error-type is a token that's returned if the type of exp is inconsistent, for example, (+ "42" 3). The nil-type is returned if exp is the literal, '( ). If A and B are types, the type (pair A B) is returned if exp produces a pair of the form $(x . y)$ where x is of type A and y is of type B. The type (proc A B C) is returned if exp produces a procedure that expects two inputs of types A and B, respectively, and returns a value of type C.

You must also modify the environment and environment operations so that frames are lists of triples of the form: (SYMBOL VALUE TYPE). The types of imported procedures must be hand-computed and installed in the global environment at start-up time.

Your implementation of get-type may not call evaluate. Instead, you must infer the type of exp by recursively computing the types of all subexpressions and then combining them based on exp's operator.

Problem 8.16.

Unfortunately, the preceeding type system only types monomorphic procedures. What happens when you try to define a polymorphic procedure?

Problem 8.17.

Suppose you didn't know if static scoping was enabled in Beta. How could you find out without looking at the flag that controls it?

Problem 8.18.

Suppose you didn't know if pass-by-text was enabled or disabled in Alpha. Without looking at the flag that controls it, how could you tell?

Problem 8.19. Gamma

Beta lacked one crucial feature of imperative Scheme: continuations. Gamma is similar to Beta with continuations, but unlike Beta, Gamma only allows unary procedures. (This is no problem because multiparameter procedures can be simulated by unary procedures by Currying.)

A Gamma continuation expects a value-store pair as an input and returns a Gamma value.

The current continuation, cont, is an additional parameter of the Gamma evaluator:

```
(define (evaluate exp env store cont . name) ...)
```

The initial continuation supplied to evaluate by the control loop is the identity procedure:

```
(define (init-cont x) x)
```

If exp is a literal, evaluate returns (cont (cons exp store)). If exp is a symbol, then evaluate returns (cont (cons value store)), where value is the value gotten by searching the environment. Evaluating an application of the form (proc arg) causes a recursive call to evaluate:

```
(evaluate arg env store new-cont)
```

where new-cont is a new continuation formed from the current continuation, cont:

```
(define (new-cont exp.store)
    (define exp (car exp.store))
    (define store (cdr exp.store))
    (cont (cons (proc exp) store))
```

Finally, Gamma features call-with-current-continuation. Like its Scheme counterpart, when evaluate encounters expressions of the form:

```
(call-with-current-continuation receiver)
```

it returns (receiver cont).
    Implement Gamma.

References

Abelson, Harold, and Gerald J. Sussman, with Julie Sussman. 1985. *Structure and Interpretation of Computer Programs*. Cambridge, MA: MIT Press and New York, NY: McGraw-Hill Book Co.

Adams, Douglas. 1979. *The Hitch Hiker's Guide to the Galaxy*. London, UK: Pan Books.

Alexander, Christopher. 1979. *The Timeless Way of Building*. London, UK: Oxford University Press.

Boole, George. 1854. *The Laws of Thought*. New York, NY: Dover Publications, Inc.

Capra, Fritjof. 1982. *The Turning Point: Science, Society, and the Rising Culture*. New York, NY: Bantam Books, Inc.

Friedman, Daniel P., Mitchell Wand, and Christopher T. Haynes. 1992. *Essentials of Programming Languages*. Cambridge, MA: MIT Press and New York, NY: McGraw-Hill Book Co.

Gibson, William. 1986. *Neuromancer*. New York, NY: Ace Books.

Hume, David. 1748. *An Inquiry Concerning Human Understanding*. New York, NY: The Bobbs-Merrill Co.

Kuhn, Thomas S. 1962. *The Structure of Scientific Revolutions*. Chicago, IL: The University of Chicago Press.

Nietzsche, Friedrich. 1967. *The Will to Power*. New York, NY: Vintage Books.

Rucker, Rudy. 1995. *The Hacker and the Ants*. New Yory, NY: Avon Books.

Schmidt, David A. 1986. *Denotational Semantics, A Methodology for Language Development*. Dubuque, IA: Wm. C. Brown Publishers.

Springer, George, and Daniel P. Friedman. 1989. *Scheme and the Art of Programming*. Cambridge, MA: MIT Press and New York, NY: McGraw-Hill Book Co.

Watt, David A. 1990. *Programming Language Concepts and Paradigms*. London, UK: Prentice-Hall.

Watt, David A. 1991. *Programming Language Syntax and Semantics*. London, UK: Prentice-Hall.

Index